# CHAUCER'S EARLY POETRY

*by the same author*

THE DEVELOPMENT OF SHAKESPEARE'S IMAGERY

ENGLISH TRAGEDY BEFORE SHAKESPEARE

# Chaucer's Early Poetry

WOLFGANG CLEMEN

Translated by C. A. M. Sym

LONDON

METHUEN & CO LTD

11 NEW FETTER LANE, LONDON EC4

*First published in Great Britain in 1963*
*Reprinted 1968*
*S.B.N. 416 26740 6*
*1.2*

*First published as a University Paperback*
*in 1968*
*S.B.N. 416 29740 4*
*1.1*

© *Wolfgang Clemen, 1963*
*Printed in Great Britain by*
*Latimer Trend & Co. Ltd. Whitstable*

*Distributed in the U.S.A. by Barnes & Noble Inc.*

# Contents

# Prefatory Note

The material of the present book is partly based on my former study *Der junge Chaucer* which was published in 1938 but soon went out of print. During the last ten years I had often been asked to prepare an English version of this book. Re-reading Chaucer's early poems, however, I realized that a mere translation would not do and that the former text would have to be expanded, altered and revised in order to take into account recent developments of Chaucerian studies as well as my own somewhat changed approach. Most chapters have therefore been re-written. In supplementing the notes, however, no effort was made to include all articles referring to these early poems, as such a procedure would have unduly encumbered the pages.

I wish to express my sincere thanks to Dr D. S. Brewer and Dr J. E. Stevens who read my manuscript and offered many valuable suggestions of which I availed myself. For further advice and information I feel obliged to Dr Eric Stanley, Mrs Ursula Dronke, Professor Dorothy Bethurum and Professor B. Bischoff. A considerable debt of thanks for help in the preparation of this book is due to my students who in the course of a Chaucer seminar helped me to clear up certain points and to investigate single aspects. For permission to make use of these valuable contributions I should like to thank H. Castrop, W. Füger, W. Maurer, M. Musiol, W. Riehle, G. Sievers, B. Thaler, H. Weber, W. Weiss. For the checking of notes and quotations, I owe many thanks to Gudrun Mattauch and to Gertrud Walter. Finally I should like to express my appreciation of the understanding and circumspection with which Dr C. A. M. Sym has undertaken the English translation. The German version of this book will be published simultaneously.

WOLFGANG CLEMEN

# Abbreviations

*Arch. f. Relig. Wissensch.*  Archiv für Religionswissenschaft
BD  The Book of the Duchess
EC  Essays in Criticism
ELH  English Literary History
ES  English Studies
ESt  Englische Studien
HF  The House of Fame
*Hist. Jbch.*  Historisches Jahrbuch
JEGP  Journal of English and Germanic Philology
MLN  Modern Language Notes
MLR  Modern Language Review
MP  Modern Philology
NED  New English Dictionary
PF  The Parliament of Fowls
PMLA  Publications of the Modern Language Association
PQ  Philological Quarterly
RES  Review of English Studies
RR  Roman de la Rose
SATF  Société des anciens textes français
SP  Studies in Philology
*Spec.*  Speculum
ZfFSL  Zeitschrift für französische Sprache und Literatur

The following books, which are repeatedly referred to in the notes, are mostly quoted merely with the author's name.

Bennett  Bennett, J. A. W., *The Parlement of Foules*, 1957
Besser  Besser, Ingeborg, *Chaucer's Hous of Fame* (Britannica 20), 1941
Brewer  Brewer, D. S., *Chaucer*, 1953

| Brewer PF | Brewer, D. S. ed., *The Parlement of Foulys*, 1960 |
| Bronson | Bronson, Bertrand H., *In Search of Chaucer*, 1960 |
| Brusendorff | Brusendorff, A., *The Chaucer Tradition*, 1925 |
| Chesterton | Chesterton, G. K., *Chaucer*,[2] 1948, repr. 1959 |
| Coghill | Coghill, Nevill, *The Poet Chaucer*, 1949, repr. 1960 |
| Curry | Curry, Walter C., *Chaucer and the Mediaeval Sciences*,[2] 1960 rev. enl. ed. |
| Curtius | Curtius, Ernst R., *European Literature and the Latin Middle Ages*, 1953 |
| Everett | Everett, Dorothy, *Essays on Middle English Literature*, 1955 |
| Huizinga | Huizinga, J., *Waning of the Middle Ages* (Penguin), 1955 |
| Kittredge | Kittredge, George L., *Chaucer and his Poetry*, 1915, repr. 1956 |
| Lewis | Lewis, C. S., *The Allegory of Love*, 1936 |
| Lowes | Lowes, John L., *Geoffrey Chaucer*, 1934 |
| Malone | Malone, Kemp, *Chapters on Chaucer*, 1951 |
| Muscatine | Muscatine, Charles, *Chaucer and the French Tradition*, 1957 |
| Patch | Patch, Howard R., *On Re-reading Chaucer*, 1939, repr. 1948 |
| Shannon | Shannon, E. F., *Chaucer and the Roman Poets*, 1929 |
| Shelly | Shelly, Percy V. D., *The Living Chaucer*, 1940 |
| Speirs | Speirs, John, *Chaucer the Maker*, 1951 |
| Sypherd | Sypherd, W. O., *Studies in Chaucer's Hous of Fame*, 1908 |
| Tatlock | Tatlock, J. S. P., *The Mind and Art of Chaucer*, 1950 |
| Ten Brink | Ten Brink, B., *Chaucers Sprache and Verskunst*, [3]1920 |

Chaucer's poems are quoted after the text of Robinson (*The Works of Geoffrey Chaucer*, ed. F. N. Robinson, 2nd edition, 1957). This edition is referred to in the notes as Robinson.

# Introduction

Until a short while ago Chaucer's work was viewed and judged from the perspective of the *Canterbury Tales*. These have appealed most to the modern reader; with their humour and realism they seemed almost to be speaking 'our own language', and they could be understood and relished even by readers not versed in literary history. Indeed, the *Canterbury Tales* stand out from among the rest of English medieval literature as a remarkably modern work. A good deal of what is considered 'modern' in the *Canterbury Tales* is, to be sure, based upon faulty interpretation; yet the past three centuries have produced much evidence[1] that this quality of 'modernity' is precisely what has determined the value and the place which the *Canterbury Tales* hold in English literature. Furthermore, this same criterion has affected our judgment of Chaucer's early poetry;[2] for even up till quite recently his early poems have been thought of not so much as possessing a value and a discipline of their own, but rather as representing a transitional stage, a preliminary step towards the *Canterbury Tales*. Such a point of view, however, was bound to overlook much; for it involves succumbing to the bias of noticing and praising in the first place whatever seems to foreshadow the *Canterbury Tales*.

It led former critics to stress the humour and realism in Chaucer's early poetry.[3] Yet even qualities of this sort do not appear without foundation; and we shall only come to appreciate their uniqueness once we have grasped the characteristic changes in style and manner of composition which these early poems exemplify. We shall then realize that what is of importance are these structural alterations; the humour and the realism are

[1] Cf. C. Spurgeon, *Five Hundred Years of Chaucer Criticism and Allusion*, 1925.

[2] On this term, as used in the present book, see p. 21 f.

[3] Although, as Miss Spurgeon shows, it was not until during the nineteenth century that Chaucer's humour came to be truly appreciated. Cf. the critical account in H. R. Patch, *On Re-reading Chaucer*, 1948 Ch. 1.

merely resultant phenomena, appearing at surface-level and denoting profounder fundamental changes.

Another prejudice which has hindered our approach to the early poems has been the idea that in writing his first poems in the French style and the idiom of allegory, Chaucer had as it were made a false start. It was thought that he only gradually discovered his true and individual manner after having tried out literary forms unsuited to his own temper and to the age he lived in. Any such opinion – surely untenable as so expressed – was bound to lead to an underestimation of the early poems; for it overlooked the task Chaucer had set himself from the beginning. This was to take the French mode of composition – which was then at a more advanced stage in regard to techniques and design – and by transposing it into English, to give the language of English poetry as it were the 'entrée' to the court.

Finally, overemphasis on French and Italian influences has adversely affected our assessment of Chaucer's early poetry. The now discredited division of Chaucer's work into a French, an Italian, and an English period, is based upon the delusion that he copied first French, then Italian, and finally English models. In reality he was always making use of sources in other languages, even in his 'English period'; even in his 'French period', too, he was continually altering and reshaping such sources until the expression and the manner became his very own. His 'English period' begins with his first poem – it is hoped in the chapters that follow to demonstrate the truth of this statement.

Chaucer's early poems can tell us much about the relation between outside influence and a poet's own manner of composition, between tradition and originality, between convention and its application in a new way; some of what we shall learn applies to medieval poetry in general, some in particular to Chaucer. The medieval poet was not primarily concerned with originality, with his own inventiveness, but with giving due consideration to prescribed forms and genres, rules of composition and stylistic conventions. These accepted forms and rules carried far more weight then than they did in later times. A precise knowledge of literary traditions, 'topoi', stylistic models and rhetorical devices, was among the most important conditions which the poet was obliged to satisfy if he was to do justice to his task. For they outlined the well-defined framework within which the poet had to keep. His merit did not consist in stepping outside these transmitted forms, in contributing something completely 'new'; it lay in keeping – as tradition demanded – within this framework and yet at the same time moving freely within these given limits and displaying his individuality through his own particular use of the traditional formal and stylistic elements. The medieval reader or hearer, meeting with new poems or a new poet, had no wish to 'break new ground'. What he wanted was to be reminded of what he knew already, to meet once again with what was familiar, and at the same time to take pleasure in the variations and occasional differences in the shaping and treatment of these well-known phrases and expressions. This tension between adjustment to tradition and deviation from it should be kept in mind; for that is what must have determined both the poet's process of creation and his reader's attitude. In the case of each poem, we must not fail to recognize this mutual relationship between on the one hand the limitations diversely imposed by these models, poetic conventions and genres, and on the other, the poet's individual idiom revealed both despite and within these restraints.

Chaucer's case is a particularly strongly contrasted and unusual one. Not only was he conversant with the complex development of his own native literary tradition; he also knew the French and Italian writers – better, indeed, than his English contemporaries did – and he was widely read in medieval Latin literature. This enabled him to link up with the most diverse developments and to draw upon the most varied sources. Chaucer had an extensive knowledge of literary tradition together with a feeling for the formal and stylistic merits of what had been handed down; and both these faculties were united in a remarkable way with a superb ability to deal in a new and often quite revolutionary manner with all these differing elements rooted in tradition. He sets free much of what he borrows from the past by turning it to new uses. He disregards what had previously been the function of certain themes, and gives them a new connotation which often produces an ironic contrast between their former overtones and what they now imply and signify. With light-hearted dexterity he simply reverses the plus and minus signs in front of these

3

traditionally conditioned themes, and fits them into a context which is the very opposite of their previous one.

But Chaucer's early poetry displays the phenomenon of literary influence, too, in a new and unusual light. The very numerous instances in the early poems of either literal borrowing, similarity, or conscious imitation, at first seem to give colour to the view formerly held that French and Italian poetry must have 'very strongly influenced' Chaucer. But in this case we must carefully define and delimit what is meant by 'influence'. We shall have to consider what affinity or specific poetic aim may lie behind Chaucer's response to certain influences in a given case. We shall further have to distinguish between those elements in another writer which most strongly influenced Chaucer and other essential features in the same writer to which he was consistently resistant or unresponsive. We must recognize what fruitful impulses in Chaucer were released by these stylistic models, and what elements enriched his diction. By concentrating not merely on the authentication of parallels and similarities, but making a more general view which would include the function, connotation, context and aim of what he took over, we shall arrive at an appreciation of Chaucer's artistry in transforming what largely belonged to others until it became all his own. Often minute changes, inversion, trifling additions, or fresh arrangement suffice for Chaucer to bring the considerable material he borrows by almost imperceptible stages into line with the new basic aim and style of his own poems. Over and over again Chaucer takes two similar elements, and without necessarily altering much, makes them entirely different from one another. Even the poets of today who are particularly adept in the art of quoting, borrowing and alluding, can admire Chaucer's virtuosity in this field, a skill which he hides beneath a cloak of artlessness and improvisation.

As Chaucer's contemporaries read these early poems, it must have been an added delight to them to meet again with familiar turns of phrase in a new connotation, and they must have responded to Chaucer's skill in waking an 'echo' of other poets' work. But if we readers of today are also to appreciate this art we shall be obliged to undertake a comparison at different levels. The method used in former studies, that of comparing Chaucer's earlier poetry with its sources, models and literary tradition, should be applied to a new purpose. For our aim will not be to establish Chaucer's 'debt' to this or that source or to detect isolated parallels in the texts, but to use comparison and contrast to recognize Chaucer's own achievement, the manner of composition which characterizes his writings even from an early stage. We shall also hope to assemble criteria for estimating his poetic intention and use the method of comparison in order to gain some insight into the development of literature during the later Middle Ages. Comparison and contrast can serve as 'heuristic principles' leading us to recognize what is characteristic and what is 'different'.

A study of Chaucer's early poems in particular brings out the truth now recognized that a historical method of analysis must be accompanied by intensive textual interpretation. If we merely ask what aspects of Chaucer's early poetry we feel to be 'alive' and aesthetically attractive today, we shall overlook much that is essential and the result will be a picture which is not only incomplete but even distorted. It would, however, be equally misguided to try to make Chaucer and medieval poetry in general fit into the modern conception of poetry whereby everything is 'symbolic' and to be interpreted as an extended metaphor. This, too, would give a false picture. The 'historical approach' cannot of course claim to be the only gateway to an artistic appreciation of the individual poems. For what determines the artistic impact of a poem and of its individual themes is not their earlier development, provenance and historical limitations, but the entire verbal shaping and composition, the way in which each part is linked to the whole, how one item follows on from another and how certain images and impressions are awakened thereby. The aim of the three chapters devoted to the major poems (*The Book of the Duchess*, *The House of Fame*, and *The Parliament of Fowls*) will be to lay bare this essential structure, the cumulative effect of the poem and to show by what stages this is brought about. Every poem has, to be sure, two aspects; it does not exist purely in isolation as an individual work of art; it also represents a stage in its creator's development as an artist and in the course of literature. Every work of art is thus permeated with tendencies and trends that lead backwards and forwards beyond its own individual limits. The pursuit of literary history involves a recognition of these overlapping processes of growth, these lines of development, and these relationships. Yet, we must also avoid misinterpreting or even disrupting the unity of the individual work of art which offers us once and for all its own imprint and shaping of the diverse material.

A consideration of the basic tendencies and lines of development in the course of late medieval literature will help us to recognize the foundations of Chaucer's early poetry. We must know something of this basis, too, if we are to appreciate Chaucer's own achievement in developing and recasting existing elements of form and style and in infusing them with new life. In the case of any poet we must know what he started with if we are to understand his subsequent artistic development. In Chaucer we have a striking example of how the earlier stages of artistic growth can throw special light on the establishment of certain characteristic features.

With Chaucer, however, 'artistic development' is by no means the same thing as the evolution of the poet's own personality. In his case, as in that of almost every medieval poet, it would be quite inappropriate to regard the development of the artist as reflecting certain individual experiences, to try to reach the person – even the 'inner life' of the poet, perhaps – by way of the poem. All we can do is to come to some idea of how he writes and of how at times he envisages the world about him. As a 'person', despite the many apparently personal touches in certain of his poems, Chaucer escapes us. More than other poets, he remains hidden behind a part he has assumed in his poems, in which he plays the dreamer, the narrator, the innocent and artless spectator. And even here there is a paradox; for while Chaucer himself more than once appears in his poems, with characteristic touches that portray both himself and his attitude, yet he always gives us a blend of what we can believe and what we can not; and we are never quite sure where we stand. Chaucer applies his own typical evasion and disguise, his quizzical manner, in his own case as well. He draws an ironical picture of himself; and what his poems offer is a composite and refracted image of the poet.

For this reason the present study makes no attempt to recapitulate the various theories concerning certain historical personages or contemporary events which might fit in with the 'allegory' of the poems. None of these hypotheses can be proved to satisfaction; and even if it could be established, the fact that some event at court, in politics or within the country was alluded to in the poems, would after all do little to further our appreciation of their individual artistic quality.

But there is an important aspect of the connection between these early poems and a courtly audience. From the beginning it was Chaucer's intention to give the idiom of English poetry the entrée to the court,[1] to ennoble it after the French pattern. His contemporaries and successors held that by so doing Chaucer had done great service to English poetry; he was extolled as the master of refined eloquence, of rhetoric, as the man

> That made firste to distille and reyne
> The golde dewe droppis of speche and eloquence
> In-to oure tounge thourg his excellence
> And founde the flourys first of rethoryk
> Oure rude speche oonly to enlumyne.
>
> John Lydgate, *The Life of our Lady*[2]

– to quote the well-known passage from Lydgate. But Lydgate is not alone in his high opinion: Occleve, Shirley, Caxton, Dunbar, Hawes and many other fifteenth-century poets praise Chaucer in particular as the first to beautify and refine the English language, ridding it of 'roughness' and stiffness; like 'Tullius', he was a master of rhetoric. These views, then, all stress something less obvious to the reader of today who looks in the main for the more 'modern' elements in Chaucer's art.

The course of English literature since the Norman Conquest offers repeated instances of English poets seeking to transplant French poetry, with its greater refinement and elaboration of stylistic forms, into their own tongue. There were of course other tendencies besides, which aimed at banning French elegance and fostering a style of poetry based on the tradition of the country. Chaucer combines both tendencies. In fact he was

[1] This was the period, too, when English was ousting French as the language of the courts and parliament and then of instruction as well. In 1362 Parliament ordered that court cases were to be tried in English; and in 1363 Parliament was opened for the first time with an address in English, etc.

[2] Spurgeon, *Five Hundred Years of Chaucer Criticism* I, p. 19.

the first to succeed in implanting within the English idiom the skilled discipline, the polished speech, the elegance and the flexibility of Romance metres. He thus realized an old ambition of English poetry;[1] and his example shows how fruitful foreign influences can be to the literature of the country that receives them. Yet despite this close familiarity with French and Italian thought and expression, how very English Chaucer in essence remains![2] So English, indeed, that many passages from his work can still be quoted today for their typically English quality; and this quality is quite unmistakable even in the poems of his youth. Chaucer combines two things in a most fortunate way; he is exceedingly responsive to influences from other poets, and he possesses the most vigorous poetic individuality imaginable.

The following chapters will give concrete examples from individual poems which illustrate Chaucer's attitude towards French and Italian literature. His responsiveness to the qualities of Romance verse led to a greater stressing of artistic considerations in the composition and structure of poems; more attention was now paid to achieving polished expression and a clear, well-turned narrative style. Other examples of poetry of high artistic standard in the fourteenth century, about the time of Chaucer and Gower, *Sir Gawain and the Green Knight* and a few other alliterative works, belong to quite a different literary tradition. It is not certain whether Chaucer knew these poems; at least he did not draw upon them. The rhymed romances, on the other hand, with few exceptions have no artistic pretensions and often try to give no more than an artless rendering of the story. These works do occasionally contain a lively and forceful account, but there is little sign of any subtlety in tone or mood, or of artistry in expression. If we look at the works of doctrinal instruction, the political and religious satires, the didactic allegories, then the general absence of artistic or aesthetic principles is still more striking. It is true that the writers of these works had other aims.

[1] Cf. W. P. Ker, *Essays on Medieval Literature*, 1905 p. 137.

[2] This must be stressed in view of interpretations which see Chaucer as essentially a French poet at heart. In Legouis and Cazamian we can still read: 'C'est son esprit même qui est français comme son nom . . . Il descend en droite ligne de nos trouvères et il a tout d'eux sauf la langue' (*Hist. de la Littérature Anglaise*, 1925, p. 131).

## Introduction

They intended to impart instruction and salutary doctrine in a form which the laity could understand; their poetry served – in so far as it is religious – to popularize the spread of doctrinal teaching during the thirteenth and fourteenth centuries.

Chaucer's early poems contrast with most of these works; for they are the creation of a conscious artist; in those works in particular, where he used models and had before him formal patterns – largely lacking in artistic principles – and applied them to the traditional forms he employs. We can now do justice at more than one level to Chaucer's 'art' in these early poems; we can, indeed, appreciate his skill in expression and portrayal, in combination and transition, in veiled reference and subtle allusion. It is just this subtlety, however, which often conceals Chaucer's art that may present itself in an artless guise. Especially in the early poems he frequently expresses something 'by implication', making the sense he intended reveal itself without the need of words, and keeping silent where others would have spoken out plainly. Today we see all this as an indication of a great degree of artistic skill; and it is by precisely these features (which are not found in this form in any of his contemporaries or immediate successors) that Chaucer anticipates developments not carried through in English poetry until very much later.

In general, new traits can only come to the fore when other and opposing tendencies recede. In Chaucer's case a strongly didactic basic tendency had to make way before any new qualities could emerge. Didacticism had been very largely dominant in the literature of the thirteenth and fourteenth centuries. Even those middle-English rhymed romances (now toned down to middle-class proportions) which seem at first glance to aim purely at 'entertainment', seek to edify and bring home some practical moral by means of a tale skilfully told. Their endeavour to make the story easier to follow and thereby to point the moral more clearly may be the reason for the lack of vivid description of milieu and for the very simplified action in these works.

Later generations praised Chaucer as a 'moral poet', and his work certainly contains didactic elements; but these are introduced in a subtle, unobtrusive fashion which exactly matches the form in which they are presented. He has achieved a new way of uniting entertainment with instruction. But the blending of the two is not always the same; for at times the didactic element is entirely absorbed in the delight at telling a story, while at other times it may emerge more clearly. We may note this in the range of the *Canterbury Tales* from 'moral' tales to rollicking farces – although in the *moral tales*, delicate irony and skill in delineating characters and types not only balances the didactic element but often exposes it in a different light. What characterized didactic poetry at that time was that everything was expressly stated and made plain. The reader was very seldom indeed left in any doubt, he always knew what this or that 'meant' and he was always told what precisely was the point in question. This same endeavour to 'make things plain' is also present in allegorical poetry, for in spite of all the disguise allegory uses we find the significance of what is portrayed yet more strongly emphasized and expounded. Yet though he interposes as narrator, commenting and taking sides, we do not find Chaucer expressly stating the essential point in his early poems. Not that we get anything in Chaucer comparable to the obscurity of modern poetry. On the contrary, Chaucer almost invariably speaks clearly and plainly. But in regard to the significance of whole sections or poems, he developed a new art of silence, of reserve, of cautious suggestion, unique in his own age. His silence even amounts at times to what might be called mystifying the reader; and there are endless puzzles especially in the *House of Fame* and the *Parliament*. The individual themes and vivid scenes seem for the most part understandable, and yet it is a hard matter to discover what Chaucer means to convey by their sequence and by the essential relationship in which the individual parts of a poem are placed. Chaucer has clearly evolved a novel process to impart the significance of his poems – a process indeed that strikes us as almost modern. By putting different elements together without comment, simply by the sequence or juxtaposition of his episodes or symbols, he can convey a definite way of interpretation, a train of possibilities, a line of choice. The reader is always left to draw his own conclusions. The 'significance' however lies in the realm of imaginative, poetic logic, in the 'logic of imagination' rather than on the plane of mere logical deduction. And this makes things more difficult for any literary critic intent upon discovering some conclusive formula and significance. Chaucer cannot be tied down like this; and in the early poems there are many juxtapositions and sequences which still leave scope for new interpretations in the future. We ought to admit these ambiguities and open questions and we should not feel limited to one meaning alone where Chaucer had so clearly avoided this. Chaucer did not want to present his reader with a complete answer and dismiss him, accurately primed, at the end of the poem; what he was seeking to do was rather to induce in him a state of questioning disquiet, of 'wonderment', to awaken his faculty of imagination and in this way to set him thinking. When we read Chaucer's early poems we feel the author's awareness of how complex and involved the events and circumstances of life are, of how they defy any single interpretation.

We have noted Chaucer's unobtrusive ease in dealing with didactic moralizing elements; and the same is obvious in his way of imparting knowledge and information in his poems. He is continuing the process of popularizing knowledge, a process particularly noticeable from the thirteenth century onwards; and his method is to lessen the gap between learning and entertainment. We find his 'Dame Pertelote' of the *Nun's Priest's Tale* in an entertaining and charming way discussing with 'Chaunteclere' the complex problem of the medieval doctrine of dreams; and in the course of her inimitable speeches on the burdens of the married state his 'Wife of Bath' considers certain doctrines held by the Fathers of the Church and by the ancient philosophers, as well as ideas from Dante and from Boethius. No other English poet of the Middle Ages has managed to incorporate so much philosophical and scientific material into his poems in so unobtrusive and natural a way, seeming indeed as he does so to increase rather than diminish the entertainment that his poems afford. The reader, however, is scarcely aware how much there is of book-learning and of things remembered behind these brisk, vigorous lines which often appear so spontaneously to reflect their author's own observation. The intimate connection between literary background and actual observation in Chaucer adds a particular charm to his poetry.

This remarkable ease in taking over and incorporating material reflects Chaucer's general receptiveness. Compared to his contemporaries, who usually followed only one direction,

Chaucer's response has a far more comprehensive range. He was helped here by the great improvement in the possibilities for exchange of ideas among the countries of Europe, which had taken place by the fourteenth century; the cultural links between England and the Continent had become closer and more varied. Chaucer's work is a particularly striking instance of this late medieval intercourse of cultures and literatures. In this case it was only made possible, however, by the intellectual mobility which distinguishes Chaucer from his contemporaries Gower and Langland.

This careless ease with which details of structure and of style, and themes from French, Italian and classical literature are mingled in Chaucer's poetry, as well as his technique of combining the most heterogeneous elements, are characteristic features of the style of any outgoing period, one already in process of breaking up. Chaucer's early poems in particular show that much of what he took over was of a light, decorative kind. It is typical of a transitional period that its writers make play with what had formerly been firmly-established and traditional forms. Often periods of fresh development make use of clear and simple forms, their style and essence can more easily be reduced to a common denominator, their characteristics are not so numerous but are more distinct and prevalent. It is harder for the literary historian to find some formula to cover the fourteenth-century variety of such diverse and often contradictory tendencies, the medley of genres and styles. Earlier forms are still utilized, but their underlying principles have undergone a change. Thus, inconsistency and the emergence of hybrid forms are favoured. Lack of harmony between expression and subject-matter, style and content, leads to exaggeration, to a purely decorative use of borrowed forms, to a trivial handling of themes and incidents. Chaucer's early poetry partakes to some degree of this development; it is therefore appropriate to ask to what extent he here made a virtue of necessity, displaying a new ease and confidence in this play with forms and themes to enrich his poetic and artistic resources.

For a poet of Chaucer's range this condition – typical of an outgoing literary period – offered an opportunity that was both tempting and beneficial. What proved fatal to other poets who wrote on mechanically, confining their work within what had now become empty forms, seems to have acted as a most fruitful influence on Chaucer's art; particularly his early poems display a characteristic blending of greatly differing forms and genres. In a single work we find him combining not only material from contradictory sources but also the most varied literary forms. A new artistic unity serves to bridge the inevitable and irreconcilable contrasts.

Chaucer's poetry draws upon a century of development in forms, themes and ideas. It unites and combines much that had been typical of its various stages; Boethius, Martianus Capella, Alanus de Insulis, the *Roman de la Rose*, Virgil, Statius, Ovid, Seneca and Cicero (as seen through Macrobius) are but a few. But these authors' ideas and themes which Chaucer often recalls, touching on them in passing, had forfeited a good deal of their depth and authority in the course of the centuries. Their essence had become diluted as they were handed on from one writer to another. But the manner in which they are now brought in as passing references and simplified abridgements, reflects not merely the popularizing tendency already noted, but may perhaps also be taken as revealing a new desire for education on the part of Chaucer's audience. The audience was now a wider one, comprising courtiers, the landed gentry, the upper middle-class. The standard of intellectual and literary education reached was far from negligible; Chaucer's readers must have been able to recognize the many remote allusions in his works, and to follow the explanations in the *Astrolabe* or the many references in *Troilus* to 'Free Will'. Such readers will not have looked to Chaucer for any specific exhaustive or systematic instruction. He does, however, meet a rather different need felt by his readers; this was the unscholarly yet expert recognition and enjoyment of the store of learning gleaned from past centuries. Confined within a well-turned, attractive poem, this educational material was bound to forfeit some of its gravity. The allegorical poem, too, no longer served as a methodical analysis and a full exposition of whatever lesson was to be imparted; it was now used in a new way, as we shall see, exploiting the aesthetic possibilities of fanciful invention and imaginative description. In interpreting Chaucer's early poems, we have to take into account this different function of philosophical subject matter and doctrine. Alanus as he appears in Chaucer's poems is not the Alanus of the twelfth century.

The fact that Chaucer is writing for a much larger circle of readers draws our attention to the most significant sociological change that took place during the fourteenth century – the rise of the middle classes. It is therefore of importance to note how this development is mirrored in Chaucer's poetry. Although he came of a middle-class family, Chaucer was living near the court when he began writing; his literary models belonged to the sphere of court and he wrote at first for a mainly courtly public. In what way, then, do the 'middle-class' elements in him make themselves apparent within this stylistic atmosphere with its artificiality and its exaggeration? What can be described as 'middle-class' about Chaucer's poetry? Is it the sound common-sense, the compelling vigour in his manner of portrayal, his way of making 'concrete' what had been 'abstract', the straight-forward forcefulness of the form in which certain basic truths are put before us, the preference for plain and practical workaday wisdom? Asking and studying such questions, one soon realizes how hard it is to single out individual essential traits in Chaucer and to fit them into any supra-personal development. Even although one finds numerous examples belonging to the above categories, no single feature is present in isolation; its import-ance and artistic function depend upon how it combines and works in with the other elements. Side by side we find vigour matched with subtlety, the jargon of every day with an elaborate and refined poetic diction, the ingenuous openness that 'blurts things out' with an exceedingly cautious, suggestive 'disin-genuous' mode of expression, simplicity with complexity. This gives some indication of the wide range of Chaucer's means of portrayal and the highly individual blend of diverse charac-teristics within his own nature.

It is more difficult with Chaucer than with Langland to assess the relation between his work and the troubled events of the fourteenth century. This connection however exists; and we ought always to try to see where the two meet, even although much evidence is still lacking and much individual research has still to be made in this field.[1] Chaucer's period is usually described as one of the darkest and most calamitous in English history. Chronicles tell of the evil effects of the French wars pursued at a gigantic cost in men and money, of crippling taxation, of corruption in the administration, of the cliques which split the great nobles into separate factions, and of many other misfortunes. The outbreaks of the plague must surely have ranked high among the current distresses and constant threats; for by 1380 this scourge had swept away between a third and a half of the entire population. The Peasants' Revolt of 1381 was a clear indication of wide social unrest which the ensuing years did nothing to allay.

Even while we admit, then, late nineteenth-century historians have probably exaggerated these aspects, Chaucer's age appears to us as a time of ferment, social unrest and above all of profound agitation. At times our own era bids fair to equal it – at least in regard to the 'unrest' and 'agitation'; indeed, there is much in our present-day experience which may enable us to understand Chaucer's period better. In his century, as in ours, a new social order was coming into being while the old one was still in existence but had ceased to be really effective. To some extent there was a similar disharmony in the sphere of literature, where obsolete forms contrasted with a new spirit.

It was above all in the field of domestic affairs that new powers were most in evidence, presenting a challenge to the King. Local administration was expanding, parliament extending its influence and functions, representation on the basis of the 'estates' was becoming established. England was earlier than France or Germany in experiencing the decay of medieval feudalism as well as the development of new forms of government which led to the early establishment of the nation-state in England. The hitherto accepted authority was called in question in several spheres of government and administration; and the unchallenged theories which had supported this authority were now meeting with opposition. Chaucer's age is a period of preparation, of re-orientation, leading up to this development that was to foreshadow modern times. No balance had as yet been

[1] The recently published Alexander Lectures by B. H. Bronson (*In Search of Chaucer*, 1960, p. 11) recommend this task as a subject for future research.

struck; politics were characterized during the period by constant fluctuation, shifting and compromise, sharply punctuated by the sudden rise of isolated groups; clearly, the age lacked the dynamic central force that could have given a definite shaping to political life.

This absence of any prevailing direction, this failure to reach security and clarity, is also obvious in the field of literature, which displays a great variety of styles and forms. The established categories of the genres are no longer heeded; numerous works of this period do not conform to them, and authors blend or indeed mingle styles and forms in the strangest fashion. There is not one sphere in which this period achieves an enduring and typical style.

The process of dissolution which in later medieval times was causing the former obligations and powers to be called in question, was nowhere so obvious as in the case of the highest authority of the Middle Ages, the Church. Particularly in England the clergy's authority was called in question and the sharpest criticism was levelled against the church. The efforts of Wiclif, Chaucer's important contemporary, represent an extraordinary movement which foreshadows the Reformation; the two are alike in combining a spirit of criticism with an awakening of new national feeling and a claim to an independent attitude.

In the sphere of philosophy this critical spirit seems to have found its most marked expression in England. The fourteenth century has been accurately summed up in the statement that 'after the century that raised the lofty pile of scholasticism came the century of its critical self-disintegration'[1]; and it was above all William of Ockham who helped forward this criticism and 'self-disintegration'. Not only did he strengthen the sceptical direction that thought was then taking; by reviving nominalism he also led to a stressing of individualism, indeed of empiricism. Both these lines of thought were to prove of importance as the century progressed.

A certain sceptical and critical trait is characteristic of later scholasticism; and we find this recurring in literature and not least in Chaucer's poetry, though it would be a grave mistake

[1] Karl Joël, *Wandlungen der Weltanschauung* I, 1928, p. 215.

to equate the philosophical scepticism of the period with his subtle irony and critical outlook. The basic critical tendency of the age does however constitute the common ground which produced such very different growths as the Wiclif movement and Chaucer's critical attitude of mind. His contemporaries Langland and Gower express more direct criticism of social conditions and of Institutions in their age. For Langland, the social misery of his day is something closely bound up with moral decay; his poems speak warnings and prophecies. Gower's severe criticism of the social orders, though it relates to the past[1], is directed against his own times; the politico-social wisdom in the *Vox Clamantis* also bears witness to the poet's profound sympathy in face of the evils in state and society. Furthermore, the century's political verse and satire[2] is full of accusation, dissatisfaction and criticism of prevailing conditions.

By contrast, Chaucer's poetry seems almost unmoved by these storms. The situation in his day did not make a moralizer, an admonitory reformer of him; it led him to a serenely humane contemplation of the contradictions and diversity in life and mankind. Every reader familiar with his complete work knows that he was aware of the distresses and conflicts and unresolved problems of his own day. But he looks at them as it were from some distance, his poetic view and artistic sense unshaken by what his contemporaries saw first and foremost. At the same time however his art is very far from shunning reality and this world. In the *Canterbury Tales* he gives us a clearer and more vividly comprehensive picture of society and its condition in his day than either Gower or Langland does. Instead however of *criticizing* the social orders by the methods of admonition and attack, Chaucer chooses to *portray* them. With matchless intensity, 'sine ira et studio', he traces the distinctive features of each individual type, depicting their failings and their strong points with the same humane tolerance and humour. The gay, ironical way the *Tales* are told have blinded us to their essentially serious character. But in his early poetry, too, as well as in the *Canterbury Tales*, serious criticism wears a delightful and entertaining mask. There we have the same blend of fun and earnest;

[1] Cf. Ruth Mohl, *The Three Estates in Medieval and Renaissance Literature*, 1933.
[2] Cf. John Peter, *Complaint and Satire in Early English Literature*, 1956.

and there, too, Chaucer's subtlety, his frequently reserved and quizzical tone, have often obscured his fundamentally serious intent. Yet it is just these elements, the subtly-shaded, elegant portrayal blended with humour, cautious reserve, and evasive ambiguity, that lend such charm to his poetry and make it appeal to us more strongly than the work of Gower or of Langland.

At the same time however, the highly individual complexity of these same traits make the poems more difficult of interpretation. Even a writer like G. K. Chesterton, who in his own writing made conscious use of ironical ambiguity, had to confess that when it comes to Chaucer we often do not know what he means.[1] The 'hide and seek' that Chaucer plays with his readers is not met with to this extent in any medieval writer before him; and it is only in later centuries that we encounter it more frequently. Chaucer's irony and roguishness, his obviously intentional ambiguity, express something of the man himself, something that pushes its way through the very structure of his design and lets us sense the actual presence of the poet himself.

In an unusual way, the pattern of Chaucer's life[2] throws light on the real nature of his poetry. Middle-class and aristocratic elements meet in his art; sound realism, common sense, and a practical zest for living, united with elegance, beauty of form and refinement in expression, combine to mirror the union exemplified in the course of Chaucer's own life. The wide range and manifold variety of his poetry, embracing widely-distant poles, is matched in his life by the width of his horizon.

Chaucer's father and grandfather were well-to-do vintners who probably owned some land as well. His father had connections with the court and is mentioned as a member of Edward III's retinue on his journey to Cologne. Both his father and his grandfather had already acted as collectors of customs dues. Chaucer thus belonged to the rising middle-class, whose influence and social importance were particularly on the increase throughout the fourteenth century. The son was therefore able to receive an expensive education at the 'Inner Temple', otherwise reserved

---

[1] G. K. Chesterton, *Chaucer* 1959, Ch. I.
[2] The latest short life is that by E. T. Donaldson in his *Anthology of Chaucer's Poetry* (1958).

## Introduction

for the sons of noble families.[1] The training given at the Inner Temple went far beyond the specific study of the law. The young men received instruction in all the arts and faculties proper to the training of a 'gentleman'. They learned singing, music, dancing, 'and such other accomplishments and diversions (which are called revels) as are suitable to their quality, and such as are usually practised at Court', as John Fortescue tells us in his description of the course of training. Chaucer is believed to have been a page in the household of Elisabeth de Burgh, Countess of Ulster, and here he would have learned at a very early age how to move in courtly circles. Refined behaviour, French etiquette, the art of entertainment, were all aspects of Chaucer's upbringing in which he was perfectly at ease. But his life took its most decisively aristocratic turn when he married Philippa Root, daughter of a Flemish nobleman and possibly the sister of the Katharine Swynfort who later became the third wife of the influential John of Gaunt.[2] This marriage gave Chaucer access to a higher social level and so to special opportunities in regard to his profession. No doubt he obtained his post as chief Controller of Customs at the Port of London because his personal ability and excellent education made him seem eminently suited for it, and not because he had distinguished himself as a writer. And similar reasons surely lie behind his appointment as Justice of the Peace for Kent, the important office of 'Clerk of the King's Works', and later that of Forester in the Royal Forest-park of North Petherton. Most significant of all, the King would hardly have sent him no fewer than six times between 1370 and 1378 on diplomatic missions to France, Flanders and Italy, had his personal gifts – his knowledge of languages and his skill in negotiation – not been a special recommendation for such particular commissions.

These responsible and varied activities brought Chaucer into contact with much that is echoed in his poetry and that underlies it in the form of practical sense, penetration and alertness of mind. It is quite obvious that even his early poems must have

[1] This biographical item is based on conjecture. For support of this theory cf. Manly, *Some New Light on Chaucer*, 1926, and Edith Rickert, 'Was Chaucer a Student at the Inner Temple?' *Manly Anniversary Studies*, 1923.

[2] On the probability of this relationship, see Manly, *Some New Light on Chaucer*, 1926.

been written by a man familiar with the most diverse spheres of life, who knew how to handle people and could not be limited to any specific degree in the social scale. His subtlety, the sensitive artistry with which he gives us an exploratory conversation or a balanced sequence of suggested views, as well as the impartial objectivity with which (in the *Parliament of Fowls*, for instance) he does justice to all the relevant attitudes and shades of opinion – all this surely bears witness to a ripe experience of life and a humane outlook which could then be transposed by him into the artistic medium of poetry.

Furthermore, it helps us towards an appreciation of such poems as the *Book of the Duchess* and the *Parliament*, if we remember Chaucer's close connection with the court and bear in mind how, for all his familiarity with the forms and expressions of court life, the poet viewed them with the critical understanding of one who sprang from a different social stratum. This particular situation of his gave Chaucer a keener eye for what the typical features of the court were than anyone could have who belonged entirely to that sphere of society. The same is true of the middle-class types which Chaucer drew and whose characteristics he saw more vividly and clearly, just because he knew the 'other social level' so well. By reason of his intermediate position between the middle-class and the aristocracy, Chaucer seems ideally fitted to portray different types and to offer a criticism of the social order.

This unique combination of middle-class and aristocratic aspects in Chaucer's poetry was made possible by the close connection which had sprung up between the court and the City and which was expressed in other careers and in many inter-marriages. The literature of the fifteenth century, however, contains no more striking instance of the linking up of these two levels. The influence of the *Canterbury Tales*, where this synthesis can best be seen, is slighter than might have been expected.[1] The poets imitated Chaucer's skilled use of language, his melli-fluous lines, but without their substance or their fidelity to real life. And when – as happened more seldom – they imitated Chaucer's realism, in their hands it grew coarse and rough, and Chaucer's subtlety of presentation was lost. No later writer has

[1] Cf. E. E. Kellett, 'Chaucer and His Influence', *Reconsiderations*, 1928.

shown his consummate artistry in combining such abundance of life and such fidelity to it.

Although Chaucer's early poetry contains stylistic features proper to his own day, in some respects it represents a healthy reaction from certain contemporary trends. Above all it maintains a balance between the centrifugal, over-subtilized tendencies of the later medieval period. One striking characteristic of this late-Gothic concluding period is the exaggerated, conventionalized, over-contrived quality of the forms employed. In Gothic architecture this appears in the guise of exaggerated lines and over-elaborate ornament; we have a disintegration and subdivision of masses and surfaces which is carried to excess, and a well-nigh rigid system of complex ramifications that affects the whole building. In poetry we have a corresponding formalism; the themes of some subtilized case of love-casuistry are treated in a hundred different ways, spun out without reference to the original impulse or the occasion. And there are parallels, too, in the over-emphasis that characterizes the brilliant and complicated techniques of rhyme and metre, in the bizarre artificiality of the allegories and furthermore in feeling, gesture and expression not merely stylized but analysed and parcelled out piecemeal. Late Gothic style indeed seemed in the end to fall a victim to its own exuberance. Chaucer's work with its freedom and release from the stiffness of conventions represents a healthy reaction from all this; poetry, which had been in danger of setting fast in a mould of formalism, is guided back by him to the natural sources of personal experience. However markedly Chaucer's early poetry bears the stamp of this late Gothic period, he has escaped its real danger, namely exaggeration and over-subtlety. He avoids both the frequently absurd tricks and devices found in French poetry of the fourteenth and fifteenth centuries, and also the crudeness and want of proportion which we find in this period as well. Seen before the background of French courtly poetry Chaucer certainly displays less art; compared, however, with the preceding English literature he possesses far more art and artistry. His poetry indeed constitutes a fine balance and strikes a happy mean between the extremist tendencies observable in almost every field.

For the present we shall take 'Chaucer's Early Poetry' as

meaning those poems written before the approximate date of 1380, i.e. during the first 10–12 years of Chaucer's literary career. *Parliament of Fowls*, assigned by most modern critics to a year near 1380, therefore marks the end of our study, while the *Book of the Duchess* (1369–70) and *An ABC* (probably *before* 1369) will be our point of departure. The chronology of Chaucer's works is with few exceptions (e.g. *Book of the Duchess*) rather uncertain; it has to be based on stylistic criteria, interdependence of individual works, questions of technique, and the use of sources, and it has to establish a probable sequence for the remaining works between the fixed points deduced from those works which can be dated with some certainty.[1] A more precise dating of certain writings (e.g. *House of Fame* and the *Parliament*) by means of allegorical interpretations of assumed personal allusions will be expressly avoided here.

[1] Cf. Robinson's Chapter on 'Canon and Chronology of Chaucer's Writings' p. xxviii f. His chronology will be followed here.

# 1

# *The Book of the Duchess*

Chaucer's early work does not spring from some particular inner experience discernible to us in his poems, but rather from an awareness that the poetic equipment at his command fell short of the forms and techniques displayed by French poetry of the period. For Chaucer's early work is addressed to a courtly audience, one to whom so far French rather than English poetry offered an appropriate stock of forms and expressions. If Chaucer was to succeed with his poetry, which in part recalled real occurrences among this courtly society and in part was no doubt commissioned by the court circle, he had to make the style and form of French poetry come alive within the English idiom. The 'influence' which contemporary French poetry, in particular that of Machaut, exerted upon Chaucer is therefore naturally very marked. But, as we have recently been reminded,[1] there was a more extensive influence behind this contemporary one, namely that of the great French poetry of the twelfth century, culminating in Chretien de Troyes. For Chaucer's verbal resources, the variety and range in the methods of presentation he chooses, and the rich expressiveness of his style, are evidences that his reading had been extended beyond such restricted and uniform models as Machaut or Froissart. But although we can assume this influence as a 'formative element', it is virtually impossible to particularize it, to point to specific borrowings and exact parallels. Yet Machaut's influence and that of his contemporaries as far back as the *Roman de la Rose* is tangible and can be exemplified.

Chaucer's early work was designed for a public obviously familiar with the framework, the conventions and the idiom of this courtly love-poetry. It is one of the essential features of his art during this earlier period that he retains the framework and many of its conventions and yet within that same framework

[1] Cf. Charles Muscatine, *Chaucer and the French Tradition*, 1957.

strikes out on a different path and offers something quite new. He arouses and satisfies expectations, only to disappoint them at a later stage; after linking up with what is familiar, he proceeds to the unknown.

## THE POEM AND ITS FRENCH SOURCES

The fact, then, that numerous lines and expressions in the *Book of the Duchess* are derived from various poems by Machaut is obviously not evidence of 'slavish imitation' – an earlier point of view[1]; it denotes a conscious process of selection, an early instance of Chaucer's 'art of borrowing'.[2]

The *Book of the Duchess* clearly illustrates the fact that even a large number of literal borrowings and close parallels is no proof that a poem lacks originality. Kittredge's examination of correlated passages from Machaut and Chaucer shows the latter slightly modifying Machaut's wording and so at times revealing his own more humoristic attitude as well as his more concrete treatment.[3] But the collation of parallel passages is not an adequate basis for estimating degrees of originality or the extent of a given influence. What a poet has *not* taken over, how far his basic plan and his aim deviate from those of his models, is often more revealing than what he has in fact borrowed. Let us now compare the *Book of the Duchess* with its models from this point of view.

It was becoming progressively rarer for French dream-poetry of the fourteenth century, which carried on the tradition of the *Roman de la Rose*, to be consistently allegorical. Real persons were now being introduced as well as personified abstractions. Machaut's poems can no longer be classed as 'allegorical', for only here and there do they make use of allegory as one of their means of presentation. Where personified abstractions make their appearance, they are no longer linked together within the

[1] See for example Sandras, *Etude sur Chaucer*, 1859.

[2] Cf. the chapters 'On Chaucer's Borrowings' in Shelly (p. 94) and 'Old Forms and New Content' in Lowes (p. 92). Cf. the references in Robinson's Notes.

[3] Kittredge, *Englische Studien*, 26 (1899), pp. 321 ff.; *MP*, 7 (1910), pp. 456 ff.; *PMLA*, 30 (1915), pp. 1 ff. Cf. also A. T. Kitchel, 'Chaucer and Machaut's *Dit de la Fontaine Amoureuse*', *Vassar Medieval Studies*, 1923.

allegory, as they are for instance in the *Roman de la Rose*, by being used to express some consistent psychological action. Nevertheless in almost every longer narrative poem Machaut, and Froissart also, still employ personified abstractions chiefly borrowed from the *Roman de la Rose*, who utter lengthy didactic speeches. In the *Book of the Duchess* to be sure the dream begins with these same properties found in all allegorical dream-poems since the *Roman de la Rose*: the May morning, the heavenly bird-song, the balmy air. But we do not go on, as we might expect, to encounter the love-god or the customary personified abstractions; the dream has dropped the allegory altogether, and what we have is a meeting between real people. This turning away from the artificial world of personified abstractions engaged in didactic disputation to a dialogue between real people is a significant feature of Chaucer's novel aim.

For the aim of French love-visions was predominantly didactic. Either the poet himself was instructed in a dream by the god of love or some personified abstraction, or else a debatable case of love-casuistry led to an exposition of the rules of courtly love. The dream as the setting of these poems was intended to invest this instruction with some authority, to provide a suitable background for the appearance of these strange, unreal, personified abstractions. But Chaucer in his dream gives us neither definite instruction nor supernatural abstractions; instead we have an actual meeting between real people. The function of the dream, in other words, is altered; and the content of Chaucer's dream bears a resemblance to the dreams of real life.

## THE POETIC USE OF THE DREAM

Chaucer's own particular poetic use of the dream, a characteristic of his early poetry, prompts the question, why the medieval poets made use of the dream as a framework for their works; and what did they think about dreams?

The use of the dream as a convention originated in the medieval poet's need to present his poem as possessing objective truth and not as his own invention. For the medieval Christian mind saw certain dreams as sent by God and thus as revealing objective truth.[1] Besides this, the allegorical poem introduced strange, fantastic figures and images, possible against a dream-background but hardly credible as actual experience. Moreover, the language of the dream and that of the allegory are closely akin; the images and events in them have an inner significance, they always 'mean' something, and therefore require some explanation if they are to be rightly understood. Macrobius's commentary to the *Somnium Scipionis* is a good illustration of this medieval conception of the relations which for the medieval mind existed between the dream and the allegory.

Theoretical discussion of dreams[2] during the Middle Ages was concerned in the main with two points: What causes dreams? Where do they come from? Are dreams true or false? Here Macrobius distinguished between 'true' dreams, which derive from divine inspiration, and those which originate in a man's mood or temperament. These latter he described as useless and 'cura interpretationis indigna'. Yet later medieval poets, in particular Chaucer's French predecessors, relate dreams which according to Macrobius are in reality *insomnia*, that is to say of purely human origin and devoid of any deeper significance. Machaut even tries to show how dreams grow out of a man's preceding thoughts and frame of mind. And this technique of transition from everyday reality to the dream (seen in Machaut for instance in the *Fonteinne Amoureuse*) had its influence upon Chaucer also. There was furthermore the tendency (in contrast to the *Roman de la Rose*) to absorb more and more topical and autobiographical material into the dream – a trait also present in Chaucer.

But many poets clearly no longer made this original distinction between 'true' and 'false' dreams. Not a few court poets of the French school – following the precedent of the *Roman de la Rose*

[1] In speaking of dreams the Middle Ages distinguished between apocalyptic dreams which are sent by God, and those dreams which are mere fantasies and delusions. Early medieval poets favour the 'apocalyptic dream'; but from the thirteenth century onwards more stress is laid on the dream as a 'psychological illusion'. Cf. Wilh. Schmitz, *Traum und Vision in der erzählenden Dichtung des deutschen Mittelalters*, 1934.

[2] Cf. W. C. Curry, *Chaucer and the Medieval Sciences*, 2nd ed. 1960. A compilation of various dream theories in the works of Vincent of Beauvais, *Speculum Naturale*, Liber xxvii, and Bartholomeus Anglicus, *De Proprietatibus Rerum*, Liber vi, c. 27: De Somno.

– made use of the dream purely as a *device* without asking why and whence it came. Not so Chaucer, however, with his 'sense of the dream'. Yet it is not of first importance to ask whether he was himself genuinely interested in the theoretical discussions on the nature of dreams (treated in the poem of the *House of Fame*) or whether he adopts any definite attitude here. The essential point is that Chaucer saw new poetic and artistic possibilities in the use of the dream. He links it with reality and with the preceding action, he deliberately uses the illusion inherent in the dream and he portrays his own second self within this dream world. Artistic problems of specific nature thus arose which Chaucer solved in his own way: the transition into the dream-state, the relation between the dream and reality, the rendering of 'dream psychology'. In the *Book of the Duchess* the dream is furthermore used to achieve a particular kind of distance and detachment.[1]

## THE OPENING OF THE POEM

The opening of Chaucer's *Book of the Duchess* invites some comparison with existing theories of the causes of dreams. The *somnium animale* had its origin in 'great anguish and perturbation of spirits'[2] – just the state of mind that Chaucer here describes: Both Machaut and Froissart had in fact used this as an introduction to a following dream; so it is not in the matter itself but in its treatment that we must look for something new.

Reading the forty-three lines with which Chaucer opens his *Book of the Duchess* one feels baffled and wonders what lies behind them. Froissart clearly states the reason for his melancholy (and the author of the *Songe Vert* describes both his low spirits before the dream and the reason for them); Chaucer however says nothing about such causes. Already, then, we meet with the avoidance of explicit statement which later recurs in another form in the conversation between the knight and the poet. But this strange opening to the poem has also other aspects. The mood of wondering, of indecision, of not-knowing, which pervades the whole opening passage, infects the reader; filled

[1] For Chaucer's use of the device of the 'daswed dreamer', see E. Birney, 'The Beginnings of Chaucer's Irony', *PMLA* 54 (1939), p. 645.

[2] According to Petrus Albanus; see Curry, pp. 207 ff.

with curiosity, almost with bewilderment, he asks himself what the poet's intention can be. Chaucer himself voices such questionings on his reader's part (30), only to dismiss them again (32–5). This reserved, evasive utterance would seem to be typically Chaucerian. In the same way at the beginning of the *Parliament of Fowls* (17) he hints and suggests, taking back what he had only half expressed; and we find too the same technique of smooth transition. His style seems less precise, subtler, and so more individual than any definite pronouncement devoid of uncertainty and vagueness. Not a few passages in Chaucer's introduction (e.g. 30 ff.) sound like a man talking to himself, touching as if in passing now on this thought, now on that. Some topics already mentioned recur later (3–22, 44), others are intentionally shelved and dropped (40–1). The frequent interpolations and asides, the natural way the lines run on, make Chaucer's writing sound like a man thinking aloud to himself, while the French poets' smoother but less supple diction bears the hallmark of 'bookish' style.

Chaucer, unlike Froissart, describes his sleeplessness and melancholy as a state of utter lassitude and perplexity (6, 9 ff., 26). The tenor of the whole introductory passage could be summed up in his 'So I not what is best to doo' (29). This state of uncertainty, indeed of vague emptiness, unconsciously evokes a mood of expectancy; we feel that something must be about to happen and expect what follows to impart some direction to this sensation of vagueness and possibly to indicate some way out of the dilemma. These are our feelings, then, as we listen to the story of Ceyx and Halcyone; and what this story does, after all, is to help the poet out of his state of dejected perplexity towards a clearly-pictured conception; it guides his aimless thoughts (so many an ydel thought) in a definite direction and it also acts as a bridge leading from sleeplessness to the sleep he craves. In this way Chaucer has refined the stereotyped theme of sleeplessness and melancholy and related it to the subject-matter of the rest of the poem. What ushers in the poem is not a tendentious exposition but a man's own personal mood; in the place of a narrative theme proceeding by logical stages we are offered somewhat indeterminate musings, hints and evasions.

And yet these first forty-three lines, vague and unusual as they may appear, have considerable value as an introduction and a preparation. We see this more clearly as soon as we consider some details in line with the main theme of the whole poem. Just as the poem as a whole was to console the Duke, John of Gaunt, in particular lines 16–21 of the introductory passage can be taken as a covert exhortation to the bereaved.[1] For they state that obstinate persistence 'in sorwe' is both unnatural and unendurable. At the same time, however, the poet's 'sorwful ymagynacioun', as he decribes his mood (14), prepares us for what is to follow. He is filled with sorrow at this point, as is the knight in the later dream-encounter: and when we come to this later conversation we find that a deeper understanding on the poet's part for the knight's situation has thus been prepared and ensured. It has often been conjectured[2] that the poet's grief sprang from an eight years' 'sickness' (36–7), taken to signify unrequited love. Though no proof of this is possible, it would constitute another example of the poet's veiled and subtle manner.

CEYX AND HALCYONE

It is through the story of Ceyx and Halcyone that Chaucer gradually approaches his theme. It sets the tone and indirectly prepares us for what is not expressed until much later on; it also contains parallels with the dream that follows. From the point of view of expository technique it represents a further postponement of the real theme, the choice of a roundabout way. This love of the roundabout approach, the ornamental portal to the actual house, is noticeable in all Chaucer's early poetry. It is as though he constructed a long spiral staircase by which he gradually reaches his theme. This method of composition which results among other things in what we now consider a 'much too

[1] Cf. John Lawlor, 'The Pattern of Consolation in the *Book of the Duchess*', *Speculum* 31 (1956), p. 635.

[2] Marshall W. Stearns's interpretation ('A Note on Chaucer's Attitude towards Love', *Speculum* 17, 1942) that Chaucer here meant Blanche herself ('Chaucer says that he, too, "suffred" from the charms of this lady,' p. 573) is not altogether convincing. For Lawlor (*loc. cit.*) these lines afford a starting point for a new interpretation of the meeting between the dreamer and the knight. He saw Chaucer's Dreamer as 'love's doctrinaire' who, lacking the actual experience of satisfied love, was to learn its meaning from the knight. On the 'eight years' sickness' cf. also R. S. Loomis in *MLN* 59, 1944.

lengthy' prologue, contrasts with present-day taste, and it has frequently aroused adverse criticism.[1] Yet Chaucer's contemporaries admired such long introductions. The liking for an indirect method of presentation, for shrouding the theme in exuberant ornament and disguise, corresponds to the *gout des complications* illustrated in the flamboyant style of late Gothic art.[2] Here we see the typical style of a period past its prime; the existing stock of forms is refined, expanded and elaborated, without any corresponding renewal of the substance. In the later Middle Ages, indeed, we find a profusion of forms and ornament that smothers the underlying thought. The poetry of Machaut and his contemporaries, for instance, shows us the gradual ascendancy of expression. As a poet belonging to this formal tradition Chaucer must therefore be assessed in terms of the question, how far has the poet succeeded in expressing genuine feeling in such an artificial and elaborate guise?

In almost every instance so far, French allegorizing poetry had made use of classical tales as 'exempla'.[3] They are introduced when something specific is to be demonstrated. Some 'doctrine' is expressly stated, often before the story begins. With Chaucer, however, we have no idea at the outset why he chooses the story he does; moreover, he does not 'bring it in', he reads it; that is to say he appears to come upon it by chance. The connection thus appears more personal, less purposive. The 'application' of the story is made in a subtle and disguised fashion; for its fundamentally vital relation to the dream-content is never expressly revealed; we hear only of its usefulness as a 'way of getting to sleep'; and this is set forth by Chaucer in his own characteristic manner. (Cf. p. 57.)

In Machaut this more superficial connection is the sole reason for relating the episode.[4] For Chaucer, however, this was a

[1] Cf. R. K. Root, *The Poetry of Chaucer*, 1922, p. 61.

[2] Cf. André Michel, *Histoire de l'Art depuis les premiers temps chretiens jusqu' à nos ours*, Vol. III, 1907.

[3] Cf. Ernst Hoepffner, *Oeuvres de Machaut*, 1908, Introduction, p. lxxiii.

[4] In Machaut's *Fonteinne Amoureuse*, the lover, a victim of unrequited passion, finds this episode of Ceyx and Halcyone an instance of the mediation of Morpheus, which might benefit him likewise if the same Morpheus were to tell his lady in a dream what he is suffering on her account. This same theme occurs later in Deschamps's work (Balade XXXV), and again, with a change of names, in Froissart, *Le Joli Buisson de Jonece*, 2102 ff., and cf. Kittredge, p. 56 f.

human story akin to the one he himself was to set forth in his dream. Just as Halcyone was comforted by the reappearance of her husband in a dream, the knight was comforted by recalling his dead wife to mind as he told his own story. It was to bring out this and other parallels that Chaucer made some alterations in the tale.

### CHAUCER AND OVID

When he was writing his version of the Ceyx-Halcyone story, Chaucer had both Ovid and Machaut at hand. But Ovid's influence on his style and descriptive technique is very slight here; it is only later in the *House of Fame* and the *Legend of Good Women* that Ovid's influence was to render his descriptive style more plastic, richer in concrete detail. Beside Ovid's vivid, subtle presentation of the Ceyx episode in the eleventh Book of the *Metamorphoses* Chaucer's recital seems meagre and somewhat monotonous. Little is therefore to be gained by contrasting them as to *style*. But a comparison between Ovid and Chaucer – incomparable as each version is – may help us to realize how different were Chaucer's conception of the story and the emphasis he laid on its various episodes.

Many differences in the presentation spring from the fact that the versions are sited upon different planes. One can detect in Ovid, too, a tendency to render myths less heroic, more human, yet his version moves on a higher plane than Chaucer's; for besides a heightened pathos we have a refined, polished poetic tone, the poet leading us from time to time towards what is grand, magnificent, even sublime. Chaucer's presentation on the other hand is more modest, more realistic; it almost brings the classical story right down to our level and its incidents to within the range of everyday possibility.

This effect is aided by Chaucer's repeated habit – here as elsewhere – of interposing as narrator and commentator, drawing his readers more closely into the story and incorporating their probable reactions into his own narrative (cf. 84, 96–100, 107). And the poet's keen sympathy, the *pittee* and *routhe* he avows at Halcyone's *sorwe* at the same time pave the way for the poem's central theme, the lament on the death of Blanche.

31

In contrast to both Ovid and Machaut, Chaucer places Halcyone squarely in a central position. Her loyalty, her grievous longing for her vanished husband and her desire to see him once again, if only in a dream – these were the important aspects of the story as Chaucer saw it. For they were directly related to the main theme of his own poem. And the alterations he makes in the story[1] spring from his endeavour to awaken and gradually to focus attention on the human situation which he describes in the main part of his poem.

This is why Chaucer disposes rapidly, almost cursorily, of the long preliminary account of the storm at sea in which Ceyx is drowned. He deals with this episode in fourteen lines as opposed to Ovid's one hundred and sixty-five, and here we note how he sweeps us along, almost impatiently condensing the story, sketching in the actual events in a rapid succession of verbs of action without any attributive words or explanatory phrases, in order to get on to the 'essential point'.

As soon as Chaucer comes to Halcyone, however, the proportion is altered. In ten lines Ovid had described the diverse precautions which Halcyone undertakes as she waits for Ceyx; but in his thirty lines Chaucer describes above all her *state of mind*, her keen anxiety, her fears and doubts. It is moreover a different Halcyone whom Chaucer shows us in this distress. The queen whom Ovid in his elegant portrayal represents as still retaining a regal bearing and displaying the majesty of suffering, has become in Chaucer's version a sensitive woman who awakens our sympathies and whose speech is touchingly simple, at times almost naïve. In the place of Ovid's declamatory lament, heightened by the use of hexameters, we have an ingenuous 'Alas!' quoth shee, 'that I was wrought!' (90); and her naïve vow, 'Certes, I nil never ete breed' (92) takes us a long way from Ovid's world. In the portrayal of Halcyone's anguish of mind Ovid aims at bringing out the 'shock', the 'horror' (e.g. 458); but Chaucer wants to show us something different, namely how Halcyone is moved and overwhelmed by grief,[2] and so to enlist our human sympathies for her.

---

[1] Cf. Shelly's summary of these alterations (p. 64 f.).

[2] Halcyone is 'forweped and forwaked' (126), often faints (103) and weeps 'that pittee was to here' (107).

The same is true, too, of Halcyone's prayer to Juno, an addition that Chaucer gives us. In Ovid's poem Juno, unwilling to bear the sight of Halcyone's grief any longer, of her own accord sends her a dream-vision in which her dead husband appears, but Chaucer makes Halcyone herself turn to the goddess in prayer, begging for a dream in which she may see her husband once again. There are times when the eager, loving words in which Halycone in her anguish confidently begs help from the goddess, sound like a prayer to the Virgin.[1] In this way Halcyone's human distress is brought within a field of experience to medieval readers.

For the central theme in our poem, however, the last section of Chaucer's Ceyx-Halcyone episode is the most important, for it contains a direct reference to the situation of the mourning knight. Ovid (like Machaut) gives us a Ceyx filled with bitter despair and resignation, who stresses the hopelessness of Halcyone's prayer, calls her 'miserrima coniunx' (242) and is at pains to emphasize that though death has ravaged his features he is still the same. But Chaucer shuns the horror of this deathly apparition, and imparts an entirely different mood to the scene. Even when the actual fact of death is brought in, this is done as if to calm, to comfort her:

> My swete wyf,
> Awake! let be your sorwful lyf!
> For in your sorwe ther lyth no red.
> For, certes, swete, I nam but ded;
> . . .
> I praye God youre sorwe lysse.     (201)

These comforting words of Ceyx suggest the same theme as that of the later conversation between the knight and the dreamer. But the tender, trusting directness of his words (cf. his way of addressing her: swete wyf, goode swete herte, swete, my worldes blysse) also helps to awake the reader's sympathy, to bring the Ceyx episode home to him and to prepare him for the intimate tone that pervades the account of the knight.

At the same time it is characteristic of the spirit governing

[1] 'A! mercy! swete lady dere!' 'Helpe me out of thys distresse, And yeve me grace my lord to se . . .' (108 ff., cf. also 114–16).

the whole poem that with Chaucer the mournful Ceyx-Halcyone episode is brightened by a number of amusing, arresting details not mentioned by Ovid. The short scenes between Juno, the 'messager' and Morpheus may illustrate this. The 'messager' is as little like Ovid's graceful, radiant Iris as Juno is made to resemble a regal goddess. Ovid recounts Juno's command to Iris in four lines; in Chaucer there are seventeen, as his Juno is obliged to impress her commission at some length and with fussy energy on the messenger of whose intelligence she clearly has a low opinion:

> 'Go bet,' quod Juno, 'to Morpheus, –
> Thou knowest hym wel, the god of slep.
> Now understond wel, and tak kep!
> . . .
> Goo now faste, and hye the blyve!'     (136)

It is with his usual delight in what he finds strange and odd (and at the same time slightly comical) as he roams through the fields of mythology and legend  that Chaucer tells us how this 'messager' comes to the cave in the 'derk valeye' and there finds 'these goddes' – truly a strange company – asleep in the most varied attitudes. This subtle humour is still more obvious in the forthright and scarcely respectful terms in which the messenger arraigns the sleepers and tries to rouse them; and several commentators have remarked on the robustly abrupt and comic elements in this passage.[1] Machaut had admittedly already suggested one of the comic details in this awakening scene; 'This god of slep *with hys oon yë*/Cast up, axed' (184).[2] But with Machaut this can hardly have been intentionally comic and indeed is lost in the smooth description which centres round the elegant Iris and not the rugged 'messager'. In Chaucer's poem, however, it becomes a humourous effect in a scene where the other features are in keeping with it. By transplanting an isolated detail into a different context Chaucer here – as so often elsewhere – releases its latent comic effect. The messenger's opening laconic 'Hyt am I', void of any rhetorical flourish, is as characteristic of Chaucer's method of presentation as is the plain way

---

[1] Cf. J. L. Lowes, p. 96; Shelly, p. 50; Muscatine, p. 104.

[2] Ovid simply says of Somnus, 'vix oculos tollens' (619).

in which he carries out his charge: 'Juno bad thow shuldest goon' (187). Chaucer breaks off here with 'Hyt ys no nede reherse hyt more'; yet this abrupt break rounds off the forceful little scene better than any skilfully varied repetition of the message could have done.

The scene with the 'messager' and Morpheus invites us to a further comparison with Machaut, who makes the gentle, charming Iris address Morpheus in politely formal language.[1] Compared to Machaut's polished, elegant but unvaried mode of speech, Chaucer's style has an everyday, colloquial quality, at times even rough and drastic. Machaut's diction is more balanced; Chaucer's has a certain urgency, even impatience. He gives the impression that he framed his sentences *while* he was writing them down, and not *beforehand*. His style thus often seems 'colloquial', as Machaut's never does. Further, this restless, urgent phrasing which resembles the spoken word, also leads Chaucer away from the French ideal of formal courtly composition which he had chosen as his earlier model. His greater stylistic freedom makes his narration seem not only livelier, more 'true to life', but also more keenly personal; compared with Machaut, Ovid, and indeed Gower, he reveals a gift for dramatization, for recasting a story in short, vivid scenes.[2]

For the purpose he had in mind, Chaucer could make no use of the comforting outcome, the metamorphosis of the couple, with which Ovid had concluded the Ceyx-Halcyone episode. His ending, dramatic in its sharpness and brevity, seems to foreshadow the abrupt conclusion of the Black Knight's tale with which the whole poem finishes. In any case a metamorphosis-theme would hardly have suited the mental state of one bereaved and mourning his loss; it would besides have introduced a strange, supernatural element which Chaucer avoids here as elsewhere when he borrows a story from the *Metamorphoses*.[3]

[1] Machaut, *Fonteinne Amoureuse* (cf. Lowes, p. 96).

[2] In his *Confessio* (IV, 3024), Gower tells this same story; he prefers to 'recount' it, whereas Chaucer 'dramatizes' and splits it up into separate short scenes (cf. e.g. *Conf*. IV, 2964, and *BD* 108).

[3] Chaucer invariably omits the metamorphosis. What most medieval writers seek in Ovid is a tale of wonder; Chaucer utilizes him for the sake of the human interest in his material and stresses the realism in his presentation. (Cf. W. F. Schirmer, 'Chaucer, Shakespeare und die Antike', *Warburg Institute Lectures*, 1930–1).

After having told this story of Ceyx and Halcyone, Chaucer motivates it solely as a means to procure the sleep he longs for. He had particularly stressed this point by making Halcyone turn expressly to Juno to beg her for sleep and for a dream (there is no such request in Ovid). This essential connection between the tale and the chief content of the poem, the parallel in their characters' stories, remains implicit. Chaucer's subtlety thus lies in making his tale fulfil a double function while leaving the vital connecting link unexpressed.

### THE USE OF MYTHOLOGY

The device of bringing in the classical gods to cause the poet to fall asleep is typical of the manner in which allegorizing poetry of the fourteenth century made use of mythology; for it introduced the gods of antiquity when some mediating figure or some piece of magic was required. This almost mechanical use of the gods is characteristic of the second half of the fourteenth century in particular, when mythological deities begin to appear as well as personified abstractions.[1]

Machaut, Froissart and Deschamps had seemed to manipulate the mythological deities almost as if they were puppets; but now this is done intentionally, one might almost say gleefully. Chaucer is astounded and wonders if this tale be true:

> Me thoghte wonder yf hit were so;
> For I had never herd speke, or tho,
> Of noo goddes that koude make
> Men to slepe, ne for to wake;
> For I ne knew never god but oon.
> And in my game I sayde anoon –
> And yet me lyst ryght evel to pleye –     (233)

Thus doubt and irony pervade this ingenious playing with mythology. As so often before in dream-poems, the poet assumes the air of an astonished, naïve innocent[2] – a highly Chaucerian way of working upon the reader. 'In my game' – although he

---

[1] Cf. Huizinga, *Waning of the Middle Ages*, 1955, p. 331 f.
[2] Cf. E. Birney, 'The Beginnings of Chaucer's Irony', *PMLA* 54 (1939), p. 645.

feels in no such mood – the poet will try what Morpheus can do. In Machaut or Froissart there is never any sign of the ambiguous utterance, the critical appraisal of his own material and the humorous asides[1] that accompany this objective attitude. Machaut and Froissart do not believe in the existence of either Morpheus or Juno any more than Chaucer does. But he contrives to show up this kind of game *as* a game, to see himself involved in it and to smile. Even in the vow to Morpheus which follows and which Chaucer alters in one particular from the versions of Machaut and Froissart,[2] a new, half-amused tone is noticeable. In this odd world of the gods, name and rank matter little so long as one of them can bring sleep, whether 'Morpheus . . . , dame Juno, or som wight elles, I ne roghte who . . .' (242).[3]

Before beginning the dream Chaucer assures us in somewhat inflated language that no one, not even Joseph of Egypt or Macrobius, could have interpreted it. This kind of exaggerated claim belongs of course to the rhetorical conventions to be met with everywhere in medieval poetry.[4] Yet Chaucer may well have had some quite specific intention here. This dream does not contain any far-fetched inventions and incidents capable of the usual allegorical interpretation; and so one can catch his meaning directly, without the need of any 'key'; yet on the other hand the dreamer-knight relationship presents subtle problems of interpretation still debated today. Chaucer was indeed right when he said: 'Y trowe no man had the wyt to konne wel my sweven rede' (278).

### THE BEGINNING OF THE DREAM

As we have already seen, Chaucer's dream begins in conventional fashion with a May morning and bird-song. Tradition always seems strongest when it comes to the *framework*, the opening

[1] Cf. e.g. 256.

[2] 'Chaucer has decorously omitted the night-cap but retained the feather-bed' (Lowes, p. 97). Cf. also Kittredge, p. 58.

[3] Cf. Machaut, *Fonteinne Amoureuse* (ed. Hoepffner, *SATF*, III), 795 ff. Kittredge takes 'som wight elles' to refer to Oleus.

[4] In *BD* cf. 435, 568, 971, 1056. Cf. B. S. Harrison, 'Medieval Rhetoric in the *Book of the Duchesse*', *PMLA* 49 (1934), p. 430.

and transitional formulae.[1] In course of time these may grow more rigid, and their connection with the content may be lost. We must ask ourselves if this is also the case in Chaucer's poetry. In the *Roman de la Rose* we had a May morning, bird-song, and an idyllic spring scene – a suitable background for the love-allegory symbolically linked with it.[2] In the works of Machaut and his contemporaries it is possible to see how the allegorical aspect of these details gradually dwindles, though at the same time the traditionally close connection between them and the ever-present theme of love is retained. Chaucer carries this development a stage further.[3] In the *Book of the Duchess* the connection between these details and the dream-content is quite unusual. For with his dream Chaucer is giving us an elegy, but this in part takes the form of a typical tale of love in the tradition of *fine amour*. Yet the poet's awakening in the dream on a May morning has little to do with a tale of love which concerns someone other than himself – unless this conventional opening to the dream were considered as a suitable framework for what the knight has to say at a later stage. The linking of this conventional framework of the 'love vision' to what comes near to being an elegy[4] constitutes one of those novel combinations of heterogeneous elements so characteristic of Chaucer's early work in particular – though certain analogies do exist in French fourteenth-century poetry.[5]

[1] Long before the *Roman de la Rose*, this 'natural opening' with a May morning and bird-song had been common in Old French, Provençal and Middle-Latin poetry; in fact it had spread to religious and theological poetry, and even into prose tracts. Cf. Wright, *Anglo-Latin Satirical Poets*, I, p. 146, or the Prologue to the *Book of the Knight of La Tour-Landry* (*EETS – OS* 33). Cf. D. Scheludko, 'Zur Geschichte des Natureinganges bei den Trobadors', *ZfFSL* 60, 1936; E. R. Curtius, Ch. 10.

[2] In the *Roman de la Rose* the singing birds stand for the angels in the paradise of love (475, 661), a comparison which Chaucer omits though he borrows many other lines from the work. Cf. the treatment of these aspects of the *Roman de la Rose* in M. Gorce's *Le Roman de la Rose*, 1933, p. 78, pp. 81 ff.

[3] On the decline of allegory in Chaucer see C. S. Lewis, *The Allegory of Love*, 1936.

[4] In his introduction to the *Book of the Duchess* Robinson finds the 'chief originality of the work in Chaucer's idea of adapting a love-vision of the familiar kind to the uses of an elegy' (p. 266).

[5] Cf. Constance L. Rosenthal, *MLN* 48 (1933), and Haldeen Braddy, *MLN* 52 (1937), p. 487.

This being so, the question of what the natural opening and the equally conventional details that accompany it may be said to signify in this poem, is one which must be treated in a new light altogether. The mood that pervades the whole opening dream-section, where we see the poet waking and looking around him, is one of joy, of relief, of happy expectancy; yet also it is one of frank astonishment at such incomparable splendour. The birds' 'mery crafty notes' ring out, the sun shines with 'many glade gilde stremes', and 'hyt was gret joye' to view the windows and the paintings. Chaucer reaffirms the indescribable sweetness and charm of the bird-song in one hyperbole after another (303, 307, 310, 314). All this must surely be viewed in the context of the poem and not merely as a 'topos'. Before the dream, the poet seems dejected, suffering, full of care: he has lost 'al lustyhede'. When after such wretched wakefulness at last he falls asleep, this relief blossoms into happiness thanks to his strange and wonderful dream. In it the poet awakes with a feeling of joy and release, takes full pleasure in his surroundings, and eventually, after he has met with the hunting-party, comes upon the lonely knight. It is tempting to see this mood of the poet's, one of joy and release from crushing sorrow, as applicable to the case of the bereaved John of Gaunt. A man who has been freed from despair and grief and can feel joy once more, is better able to give comfort than one still sunk in sorrow. And besides, the glowing background afforded by this happy setting at the opening of the dream suitable sets off the knight's eulogy of Blanche. The recalling of past happiness which is the intention behind the knight's story is placed in a setting radiant with beauty and delight, and furthermore was linked by literary tradition with the idea of the greatest earthly happiness of all. Finally, this whole beginning to the dream is an example of the art by which, even in a poem which is in fact an elegy, Chaucer established a balance between the darker and the lighter aspects of life which even in such a grievous accident is maintained.[1]

The poet, then, not without intention, carries over this feeling of joy, of grief overcome, into the description which now follows of the wonderful country of woods and pastures to which

[1] This balance is emphasized by C. S. Lewis, p. 169. Cf. also H. R. Patch, p. 33.

he comes. He says of the earth that it 'envye **wo**lde /To be gayer than the heven' (406).

> Hyt had forgete the povertee
> That wynter, thorgh hys colde morwes,
> Had mad hyt suffre, and his sorwes,
> All was forgeten. . . . (410)

The fresh, carefree impression made by this whole opening episode is created too by Chaucer's own particular mode of description, so different from that of his French contemporaries. What they took over from the *Roman de la Rose* was above all the personifications and the doctrine of love, whereas it was Guillaume de Lorris's gift for sensuous description which influenced Chaucer. His early preference for visible reality as against the artificial world of abstractions is shown by his response to this particular aspect of the work.[1]

The *Roman de la Rose*, indeed, stimulated Chaucer's powers of description to the point of surpassing those of his model. If we compare the opening of Chaucer's dream (291–343) with a set scene from the *Roman de la Rose*, or from Machaut or Froissart, we see plainly how in less space Chaucer offers a much greater wealth of individual touches and also shows a much stronger sense of the unity behind the details that go to make up the picture. With Machaut the bird-song and the May morning are stereotyped clichés, not details integrated into a colourful general picture; but with Chaucer they are elements in a coherent situation vividly seen and accurately rendered. We can watch the poet as he wakes up in the sunny room and we take in the successive impressions as they strike him, and as they are described:

> for I was waked
> With smale foules a gret hep
> That had affrayed me out of my slep,
> Thorgh noyse and swetnesse of her song.
> And, as me mette, they sate among
> Upon my chambre roof wythoute,
> Upon the tyles, overal aboute,
> And songen, everych in hys wyse, . . . (294)

[1] On this point see the parallel passages in D. S. Fansler, *Chaucer and the Roman de la Rose*, 1914, pp. 127 ff.

Even in this early poem it is not an 'objective' description, an inventory made by some neutral party, that Chaucer gives us, but a picture of things as they strike him and as *he* observes and experiences them – in short, *impressions* and not statements.

They are impressions, too, that come into the room from out-side – sounds, noises, voices reaching the ear. As Chaucer looks across at the familiar and famous medieval and classical tales portrayed on the walls and windows of his room – his own world of books, one might say – the sound of the hunting-horn calls him out of doors to what is new, what is then happening at that moment.

### THE HUNTING SCENE

In this 'impressionistic' narrative, that tells how the poet gets caught up almost by chance in the bustle of the hunt and is then drawn further off into the wood by one of the hounds, some commentators[1] have quite rightly detected features characteristic of 'dream psychology'. The confused, indefinite voices and sounds (y not now what) which reach the poet, the sudden arbitrary departure (taking his horse and going out of his room, 357!), strange names mentioned but neither explained nor followed up (emperour Octavyen 368), the whole scene flitting past like a shadow, and the poet being lured away by an 'unmoti-vated' dog into a strange untravelled 'dream-country'[2] – these are all incidents typical of dreams. As in the first dream-section, too, we have an undertone of astonishment that makes us feel it is all taking place on a different plane.

The little hunting-scene is often cited as a proof of Chaucer's power of 'realistic' description. Hunting-scenes, however, are also among the stock themes of chivalric poetry. Expert descrip-tions of the hunt are particularly common in the poetry of the fourteenth century. What we are inclined to call 'realistic' in

---

[1] Kittredge, p. 68, Lowes, p. 94, Patch, p. 32; but Muscatine (p. 102) takes a different view.

[2]
> Doun by a floury grene wente
> Ful thikke of gras, ful softe and swete,
> With floures fele, faire under fete,
> And litel used, hyt semed thus;        (398)

such cases[1] is in fact a skilled and accurate technical description of the hunt.[2] The formalized code of chivalry treated the hunt as it treated so much else in the pattern of fourteenth-century courtly living, and enclosed it in a network of rules; hedged about with all kinds of ceremonial, it grew into an 'ars' which was expounded in numerous handbooks on the subject.[3] In interpolating his hunting-scene, therefore, Chaucer was not simply prefacing the knight's seemingly conventional lament with a naturalistic scene; he was drawing upon the stock of traditional chivalry, giving us something appropriate to that world to which the knight belonged.

The hunting-scene serves in relation to the dream-tale as a 'device' leading up to the mourning knight's entry.[4] But it has also a further significance. For it contrasts two elements, the gay eager group of huntsmen,[5] and the single figure turning his back on life. 'The others' i.e. the whole court and the king, are hunting and enjoying themselves; but there, mourning his loss, stands the knight in black, aloof and detached from all this bustle. And it is he himself who puts this contrast into words; when the poet, to sound him, begins to speak to him of the hunt, the knight rebuffs him; he has no thought now for courtly pastimes such as this:

> 'I do no fors therof,' quod he;
> 'My thought ys theron never a del.' (542)

### THE KNIGHT AND THE DREAMER

The conversation between the dreamer and the knight represents the real core of the tale; all that went before simply served to lead up to it. But this long introduction itself contains a good deal of the artistry and the aim of the poem. It is therefore worth

---

[1] E.g. in *Sir Gawain and the Green Knight* and in the *Parliament of the Three Ages*.

[2] The technical expressions in Chaucer's account of the hunt are explained in O. F. Emerson, *Romanic Review* 13 (1922), p. 117.

[3] Cf. H. L. Savage, 'Hunting in the Middle Ages', *Speculum* 8 (1933), *The Gawain Poet*, 1956, Ch. II.

[4] On this function of the hunt cf. Muscatine, p. 103.

[5] Cf. the lines on the 'lust present' of Marquis Walter's passion for hunting, described by him in the *Clerk's Tale*, IV, 80.

while looking more closely at various stages in the roundabout way by which Chaucer leads us. For in this poem 'preparation' signifies 'introduction' and 'postponement' alike. And the dreamer's and Knight's conversation is itself one continuous postponement – the 'preparation', in short, goes on till the very end of the poem. Here and there Chaucer makes some statement, only to veil it again directly. Much of the poem's charm and artistry lie in this play of shrouding and revealing, leading us on and yet restraining us.

Looking first at this conversation[1] as a whole and without going into its detail, we see Chaucer here following divers indirect paths, pursuing several aims at once. The chief object of the knight's story is to give us an elegy on the death of the Lady Blanche. But what sort of elegy? Not an unrelated and literary work of art, not a eulogy uttered by the poet in his own name, but a tale told by the mourner himself, whose hearer, the dreamer, coaxes him to recall step by step the life he had spent with his late wife. In this way a literary artefact becomes a personal account[2] spoken by the sufferer himself, by a man whose state of mind is made quite intelligible to us. For the knight has a hearer, a partner, a stranger to him (and clearly not of his own rank), to whom therefore he can speak here in the depths of the forest more freely and unreservedly than to an acquaintance. This hearer is the poet himself and yet not the poet; for he is lent a certain detachment not merely by the dream but by the rôle which he plays in the *Book of the Duchess* both before he falls asleep and during the dream itself.[3]

But how does all this affect the impact the elegy makes upon us? It is thus placed in a dramatic situation where the reader identifies himself with the hearer in the dream and is thus drawn into the very heart of the poem. At the same time however the

[1] The relationship between the dreamer and the knight, and in particular the dreamer's specific rôle, has been much discussed during the past ten years, for instance by J. R. Kreuzer, 'The Dreamer in the *Book of the Duchess*', *PMLA* 66 (1951); B. H. Bronson, '*The Book of the Duchess* Re-opened', *PMLA* 67 (1952); D. C. Baker, 'The Dreamer again in the *Book of the Duchess*' *PMLA* 70 (1955); St. Manning, 'That Dreamer Once More', *PMLA* 71 (1956); J. Lawlor, 'The Pattern of Consolation in the *Book of the Duchess*', *Speculum* 31 (1956); D. Bethurum, *PMLA* 74 (1959). Cf. also Muscatine, pp. 103 ff.

[2] Cf. Kittredge, p. 39.

[3] Cf. J. R. Kreuzer, *PMLA* 66 (1951).

figure of the poet as the reader knows him contrasts with his other rôle within the poem.[1] And the dream itself reinforces this distinction; for the poet is able to speak of John of Gaunt as it were remotely, behind a veil; the unreality inherent in dreams permits him to speak in some measure indefinitely, ambiguously.[2] The way that Chaucer has chosen to tell his story resembles an offer which one is free to accept or not and which adroitly avoids the rigidity and the obligation implicit in any direct statement.

### ELEGY AND CONSOLATION

This is especially true in the case of the second and important object behind Chaucer's conversation between the knight and the dreamer; namely, that of consolation. This elegy, indeed, was intended to include consolation just as much as lamentation. To achieve this end, however, Chaucer did not choose the traditional type of consolatory speech; the knight's partner, the dreamer, who normally would have spoken this, does not even mention consolation. His sincere avowal of common human sympathy and the attention with which he listens (cf. 749–57), are all that the dreamer offers in its place. And yet it is he who in the course of their conversation leads the other on to relate more and more of his own past and so to realize what blessings and what fulfilment he had enjoyed in the past.[3] The mourner's mind is thus freed from dwelling solely on one single thought, the death of his beloved, and is directed to the *past*, not the *present*. For the duke, moreover, to whom the poem is supposedly addressed, the knight's recital brings back the happiest period of his life, which passes as in a mirror before him; and he realizes once again what 'health' (hele) his treasured wife had brought him by responding at last to his love. The minutely detailed portrayal and praise of his late wife, which form the climax of the knight's recital, served to show the duke how to find strength

[1] Bronson, *PMLA* 67 (1952), p. 879, reminds us that Chaucer was accustomed to recite his poems to his audience who thus unconsciously identified him more closely with the narrator in the poem than is the case with his later readers.

[2] For a similar view on Chaucer's use of the dream in *BD* see C. S. Lewis, p. 167.

[3] Cf. Bronson, *PMLA* 67 (1952), p. 876 f.

and comfort even in the midst of intense grief by reviving her image in his memory.

It is possible to see another reason why the dreamer, affecting not to understand, continues to urge the knight to tell more and more about his love; it might be that he wishes to discover if this love was in fact requited and fulfilled.[1] The knight is thus led on to give a most detailed description of his requited love, the blessing that had crowned his whole life. The duke, too, was therefore able to realize the full measure of this fulfilment, comparing himself with many who have never known it. The knight's wooing of his bride and her final 'response' are described in the familiar phrases and in the tradition of 'fine amour';[2] and Chaucer's description, while it links up with a great tradition and with the lofty ideals already embodied in the 'romances', at the same time gives to these ideals a personal turn and application. The figure of the duke, like Lady Blanche, becomes in some measure an idealized type – by the same sort of process by which the poet had sought a measure of detachment from his second self, the figure of the dreamer.

The praise of Lady Blanche forms the core of the elegy and is indirectly expressed in the knight's recital. But Chaucer's handling of the elegy as a genre which must have been familiar to him is quite unusual. What strikes us first is the absence of certain invariable features in the lament which had become 'topoi',[3] such as reflections on the transience of everything earthly, on death's pitilessness, and above all on the next world. Here, however, death is mentioned on only three occasions (481, 577, 583), and each time the thought passes swiftly

[1] Lawlor (*Speculum* 31) stresses perhaps unduly the contrast between the knight whose love had been fulfilled and returned, and the dreamer, ignorant of love and therefore confined to theorizing, who is represented as 'love's doctrinaire'; and this forms the basis of his stimulating new interpretation of the poem.

[2] Lawlor (*Speculum* 31) shows how in the fourteenth century there was not necessarily any difference between 'amour courtois' and conjugal love. 'The sentiments and stylized attitudes of *amour courtois* can be appropriated by those who have no thought of loving *paramours*, but seek to be united in marriage' (p. 633). Furthermore, cf. D. S. Brewer, 'Love and Marriage in Chaucer's Poetry', *MLR* 49 (1954).

[3] Cf. Wolfgang Clemen: *The Dramatic Lament and Its Forms* in *English Tragedy before Shakespeare*, 1961, Ch. 14. B. Lier, 'Topica carminum sepulcrarium latinorum', *Philologus* 62–63 (1903–04), H. Hengstl, *Totenklage und Nachruf in der mittellateinischen Literatur seit dem Ausgang der Antike*, 1936.

away from it again. The knight's speech contains some of the
other 'topoi' usually connected with the lament: the survivor
longs for death (481, 584, 690), he finds life hateful and wearisome (573, 577), he curses the day he was born (686, 1301);
he attributes his loss to Fortune's envy and treachery. This last
'topos' leads on to Chaucer's long comparison with the game of
chess (618–86), in which Fortune, having cheated the knight at
play and taken his queen, is at once accused and excused. For in
Fortune's place the knight would have done the same himself –
he says so more than once (676, 682): 'I dar wel swere she took
the beste' (684). Thus we are shown something of the paradox
inherent in death which as our opponent acts just as we would
have acted in its place.

The traditional elegy combined both praise and lament for
the dead; the two aspects were constantly present and closely
intermingled.[1] It is significant, however, that during the whole
'praise' in which the knight extols the dead, there is no word of
lament. Lament and eulogy are completely separate; indeed, the
former seems to have been overcome and forgotten by the time
the eulogy follows upon it. But there is a further respect in
which Chaucer mitigates the effect of the lament; many of the
sorrowing knight's phrases and gestures of lamentation (e.g.
563–6) are themselves typical 'topoi' used for the 'complaint' of
love,[2] the language and themes repeatedly echoing the *complainte d'amour*. Some of the 'topoi' used for the lament (the
theme of Fortune for instance), belong to the 'complaint' as well
as to the elegy.[3] A strange state of suspense, too, was induced
by this intermingling of the *complainte d'amour* and the elegy;
and furthermore, its effect was to contribute to the dreamer's
'misunderstanding'. Once again Chaucer's subtle artistry is
clearly seen as he combines the traditional phraseology of love
with the elegy's more serious intention in this way.

To carry out all this required a considerable degree of artistic

---

[1] F. Beissner, *Geschichte der deutschen Elegie*, 1941. Cf. also the article 'Elegie'
in Pauly-Wissowa, *Real-Encyclopädie der Klass. Altertumswissenschaft.*

[2] On the 'complaint' cf. J. Peter, *Complaint and Satire in Early English Literature*,
1956.

[3] The comparison of the game of chess with Fortune, too, was very common in
French love-poetry and it could be made in either context. Cf. the parallels quoted
by Robinson in his notes to 617–709.

sensitivity as well as personal tact;[1] for he had to suggest that consolation was possible, without however putting this into words. Remaining silent in the face of death's overpowering impact, he preferred – as friends do – the mute handshake to the lengthy speech of condolence. For when the knight finally utters the decisive 'She is ded' which makes it impossible for the dreamer to keep up his air of misunderstanding any longer, all he can reply is 'Is that youre los? Be God, hyt ys routhe!' This abrupt and unusual ending to the conversation corresponds to the silence that falls before the majesty of death and the magnitude of the duke's loss. At the end of his poem Chaucer admits that he too can find no direct words of consolation. Lawlor has clearly recognized the dual nature of the answer which this poem makes to the question of consolation: 'In Chaucer's poem something unique is done: we have both consolation and a rejection of it – but not before it has done its work. Neither invalidates the other. . . .'[2]

This survey shows, then, that the poem in a special sense reveals not only Chaucer's artistry but also his human wisdom. Before, however, looking more closely at this conversation we must compare the poem with its French models.[3]

### A COMPARISON WITH FRENCH VERSIONS

In Machaut's *Jugement dou Roy de Behaingne* the poet witnesses a meeting and a dialogue between a lady mourning the death of her lover and a knight whose love is unrequited. The initial situation thus provides a certain parallel with Chaucer; for his own version Chaucer was able to use some of the phrases in Machaut's poem, for there the deceased partner is lamented and the knight gives an account of his love and of his loved one. But

[1] Patch expresses this by saying 'the poem had to be at once intimate and humbly detached' (Patch, p. 28).

[2] Lawlor gives this summary after having pointed out the two conflicting tendencies inherent in elegy as an art form, but also 'present in all experience of bereavement': 'One is the impulse to seek for consolation in the idealization of past happiness; the other the rejection of all consolation in the overmastering sense of loss' (*Speculum* 31, p. 647).

[3] Up to the present, studies have concentrated rather upon individual borrowings and parallels and less on a comparison of the general character of the poems. Cf. Kittredge, *Englische Studien 26* (1899), *MP* 7 (1910), *PMLA* 30 (1915), Mario Praz, *The Flaming Heart*, 1958, p. 41 f., and Robinson's notes.

Machaut staged this meeting solely in order to construct a case of love-casuistry, a so-called 'question of love' to be later put before a 'judge' for his verdict. Besides, both the consolation which the knight at first tries to impart, and also the lady's grief over her late husband are soon superseded by the keenly-reasoned arguments put forward by each party in favour of his own case. The two poets have radically different intentions; Machaut aims at the accurate exposition of a debatable case of love-casuistry, but Chaucer at a portrayal of genuine grief based on an actual experience.

The initial situation in the anonymous *Songe Vert* is in some respects even closer to the *Book of the Duchess* than is the *Jugement*. The poet laments the loss of his loved one and – like Chaucer's knight in black – invokes death. The goddess of love appears to him in a dream, promising him as a consolation the loveliest woman in the world, of whom he then catches a glimpse in a vision. But the goddess goes on to swear the poet anew to her service, expounding its rules to him. Here too, then, we have a grievous experience superseded by an exposition of the rules of love. In addition, past loss is now mitigated by the prospect of a new lady-love.

This optimistic solution of the problem is typical of the other allegorizing dream-poems where similar situations occur.[1] Some personified abstraction or the god of love – or perhaps the poet himself – appears and consoles the suffering lover with instruction on the virtues of love. This close connection between consolation and instruction may possibly go back to the *Consolatio* of Boethius, which influenced the basic design of many allegorical poems of the Middle Ages and of which Chaucer himself made a translation.

Chaucer, however, struck out on a different path, leaving behind him all this consolatory didacticism which was a feature of the French school with its allegorical apparatus of personified abstractions who teach and direct. Later he does make use of comforting advice but only when this is appropriate to the

[1] Froissart's *Le Diz dou Bleu Chevalier* in which the poet encounters a lovelorn knight in a wood, also displays this combination of optimistic consolation and didacticism; and so too does Granson's *La Complainte de l'an nouvel*, where only the initial situation has any real resemblance to the *Book of the Duchess*. (Cf. Haldeen Braddy, *MLN* 52, 1937.)

subject, as in the *Tale of Melibee*. In the presence, however, of that irreparable loss which no ingenious speeches can explain away, Chaucer always chooses some indirect way of consolation. He knows that the grief felt by the knight in black (and through him by the mourning duke) cannot be touched by any didactic speeches; and he has no wish to bring in some helpful allegorical figure who might undertake to comfort the knight in his stead. He rejects the direct speech of consolation not only because for reasons of tact and in view of his noble patron's superior station any direct form of address would be out of the question, but doubtless for the additional reason that he himself no longer believed in this kind of consolation. On the other hand, however, he had no wish to speak of consolation on the religious level by recalling for instance the life the departed enjoy in the next world, as is the case in the contemporary poem *Pearl* or in the German work of about 1400, *Der Ackermann aus Böhmen*, which embodies both disputation and consolation. Chaucer chooses to offer consolation indirectly without actually speaking of it. He makes the knight use such indirect expressions that the dreamer, his hearer, is able to keep up his failure to understand, and furthermore was not obliged to mention Lady Blanche's death. Indeed, the knight's rhetorical digressions and artificial metaphors appear to serve this purpose; for at times (for instance in the chess-passage, 618 ff.) they are so artificial that the dreamer's failure to understand seems only natural.

### THE DREAMER'S 'FAILURE TO UNDERSTAND'

On the other hand it is *before* the conversation takes place that Chaucer makes the dreamer overhear the knight's lament in which he expressly mentions the death of his beloved. The dreamer, then, clearly knows the real cause of the knight's sorrow,[1] but he hides this in order to induce the knight to speak and so to relieve his feelings:

> And telleth me of your sorwes smerte;
> Paraunter hyt may ese youre herte,
> That semeth ful sek under your syde. (555)

[1] Malone denies this; he holds that through 'the device of overhearing . . . the audience' is given 'the advance information they needed' (Malone, p. 38).

# Chaucer's Early Poetry

In this way the role the dreamer assumes, one of apparent misunderstanding,[1] becomes a wise, perceptive action, a tactical move within this relationship between the two – just what we might expect of Chaucer. Every one of the dreamer's later questions and remarks, seeming at a superficial level to show his 'misunderstanding', reveals a deeper psychological wisdom. With each of these questions[2] he leads the other on a step further towards realizing the blessings and happiness that had been his. In fact, these questions and remarks, springing from this 'failure to understand', all draw more of the knight's story from him than any 'sympathetic inquiry' could have done. Furthermore, through this failure to understand, this talk at cross purposes, a dramatic impetus is imparted to a conversation already dramatically conceived. For the reader knows and understands more than the figure of the dreamer in the conversation appears to grasp. And so the knight's and the dreamer's words are lent an ambiguity not to be found in either Machaut or Froissart.

It is not only the dreamer's skill, however, and the sensitive way he has of directing the knight's remarks without his realizing it, that makes it out of the question for us to think of him as naïve, obtuse or unintelligent. We have also those lines, almost a hundred of them, in which *before* the real conversation begins the dreamer describes how he caught sight of the knight in the wood, and how he gradually drew nearer, watching and listening to him. They show how closely and with what sympathy the dreamer observes this newcomer, noting his bearing, his actions and his air, and moreover drawing the conclusions that govern his own behaviour towards him. As the dreamer approaches step by step, feeling his way and trying this and that to induce the other to speak, we see him revealing the 'most delicate tact'[3] which Chaucer himself must have possessed in addition to his diplomatic skill and which his poems so frequently evidence.

[1] There is a wide divergence of views on whether what we have here is a genuine or an apparent misunderstanding or indeed merely a certain degree of awkwardness in Chaucer's presentation. Cf. Kittredge, pp. 48 ff., Tatlock, p. 30, Lowes, p. 100, Bronson, *PMLA* 67 (1952). On the 'discrepancy between the known sophistication of the poet and the obtuseness of the part he has made for himself' see Muscatine, p. 104.

[2] Cf. Bronson, *PMLA* 67 (1952), pp. 816–7. Donald C. Baker (*PMLA* 70, 1956) raises objections to this view.

[3] Shelly, p. 55.

### THE ENCOUNTER WITH THE KNIGHT

The dreamer's wordless encounter with the knight and his approach to the mourner show Chaucer's ability to portray new human situations quite unrecognized as such by his French contemporaries. What Machaut does is to confront two characters abruptly with one another in order to discuss two points of view. But these characters have no contact with one another, nor have they any need of this, for each is conceived as the mouthpiece of some tenet and not as a living person. And so we have a *Discours*, carefully designed and ready-made, flowing on smoothly without references to the other speaker and indeed not addressed to him but to the reader.

But Chaucer had already shown us this meeting as a *process* of gradual mutual approach. A sympathetic human relationship, a sincere readiness to help, is developed before ever the conversation touches on its real theme, indeed before a single word is exchanged. In what a friendly and understanding way, too, does the dreamer note the difference between the knight's present way of speaking to him and his previous despairing monologue:

> Loo! how goodly spak thys knyght,
> As hit had be another wyght;
> He made hyt nouther towgh ne queynte.
> And I saw that, and gan me aqueynte
> With hym, and fond hym so tretable,
> Ryght wonder skylful and resonable,
> As me thoghte, for al hys bale. (529)

It is his partner's observation that clearly impresses some aspects of the knight's personality upon us and leads us to feel attracted to him.

In the *Jugement dou Roy de Behaingne* the knight at once invites the lady to tell him of her sorrow; but this method was too abrupt, too hasty for Chaucer. Sensitively and cautiously his dreamer begins to speak to the knight, trying some roundabout way to sound him:

> Anoon ryght I gan fynde a tale
> To hym, to loke wher I myght ought
> Have more knowynge of hys thought. (536)

And so he begins to speak of the hunt. And it is only when the other's somewhat evasive answer (543) gives him the chance to ask more, that he ventures to put his request. During the conversation, however, the dreamer observes the knight, notes *how* he speaks (529 ff., 558, 710, 1300), reacts to his words and keeps in tune with his mood.

Quite soon after the conversation opens it is made particularly clear to us that the knight has an attentively observant hearer. When the dreamer begs him to tell of his 'loss' more explicitly, the knight replies

> 'Blythely', quod he; 'com sytte adoun!
> I telle the upon a condicioun
> That thou shalt hooly, with al thy wyt,
> Doo thyn entent to herkene hit.' (749)

The dreamer is furthermore required to swear (755 ff.) that he will keep his promise to give his full attention. On his part, too, the knight adjusts himself to his partner and does not forget him even during his longer speeches. *Thou* is now frequently used between them;[1] and it is significant that there is nothing in Machaut to correspond to any of the lines in the knight's speech where he directly addresses the dreamer.[2] The knight's recital is so long – amounting almost to a monologue – that it is astonishing how it still keeps the form of a 'conversation'; it does so by introducing lively dialogue (742–57, 1042–51, 1112 ff.), by taking up a single phrase or word (1045, 1052, 1076, 1115, etc.), by frequent questions, exclamations and interpolations (see page 144). The frequent exclamations in particular make the speech sound like a man repeatedly starting to say something, a 'voice' which we seem to hear speaking. It is typical, for instance, that the knight harks back to his own words and emphasizes them once again (1075), and that he introduces direct speech into his tale, either speaking to himself (1187) or dramatizing some scene of which he tells us (877, 1030, 1219, 1232).

In the *Book of the Duchess*, then, we see Chaucer drawing away from allegorical dialogue, which often amounted to the arbitrary

[1] Malone notes that the knight uses *thou* when addressing the poet, but the poet uses *ye* to the knight (Malone, p. 40; Brewer, p. 45).

[2] 598, 651, 1148, 1152. Cf. also 1020, 1034, 1088, 1181.

opposition of two logically expounded doctrines, and moving in the direction of conversation between real people. The fact, too, that here he was dealing with particular persons well known to him and that a very recent grief was in question certainly had its effect on his style and the treatment of his material.

This is apparent in the many slight deviations from Machaut that we notice in Chaucer. He often interrupts Machaut's bland phrasing with protestations and questions, infusing it with life.[1] In Chaucer, real feeling takes the place of formal correctness; and even where the sense is the same as in Machaut, he is able to put more warmth into the manner in which the knight or the poet speaks.[2] Machaut portrays his knight's indecision of mind in conventionally artificial fashion by making *Bel Acueil* and other personified abstractions address him; in the same situation however Chaucer gives us a soliloquy.[3] And when Machaut's knight does confess his love to his lady, he does so in a mawkish, fulsome speech – matched, too, by the lady's reply. But Chaucer makes his knight say simply

> I seyde 'mercy!' and no more.
> Hyt nas no game, hyt sat me sore. (1219)

And he writes of the lady, 'she sayde "nay" al outerly' (1243). No doubt this aversion of Chaucer's to theatrical speeches at moments when real life makes use of few words, is revealing.

But the matter is not one of style alone; the way the knight's story is built up, the sequence of thoughts and themes, shows that genuine personal feeling was loosening the bonds of rigid convention. An analysis of the speech would show how often certain ideas occur, are dropped, and then recur somewhat later.[4] Instead of a continuous and clearly defined design we have a sequence of thought that is involved and often interrupted, a rapid succession of individual themes, each picture merging easily into the next. And it is typical that the narrative here is

[1] Cf. Machaut, *Dit dou Lyon* (ed. Hoepffner, *SATF*, II), 207–14 with *BD* 1108 ff.; *Remède de Fortune* (*SATF*, II), 363 with *BD* 1159 ff.; *Jugement dou Roy de Behaingne*, (*SATF*, I) 284 with *BD* 810 ff.

[2] Cf. *Jugement* 70 ff., 77 ff. with *BD* 519 ff.; *Jugement* 87 with *BD* 547 ff.

[3] Cf. *Jugement* 457 ff., 480 with *BD* 1187 ff.

[4] Cf. 566, 686 with 573, 580, 584, 690. Cf. 574 ff. and 591 ff., 601 and 688 ff.; 588 and 692; 589 and 709.

punctuated by questions which the knight often appears to be putting rather to himself than to his hearer.[1] For they seem to carry his own thoughts onwards, to dramatize his inner conflict and to project it into the existing situation. The formal rhetorical question, then, which had been merely a rhetorical *device*, has become an anxious self-questioning, as for instance at the close of the monologue at 1187 ff.: Allas! what shal I thanne do? (1191).

### THE PORTRAIT OF BLANCHE

This same personal concern and feeling is noticeable, too, even in that part of the knight's story where convention has the strongest hold, and which reveals the influence of the French poets at every turn – in the description of Blanche. An elaborate system of rules existed for describing a lady, an accepted sequence for enumerating the details of her appearance,[2] a catalogue of feminine virtues and a definite ideal of beauty expressed in an equally stereotyped form.[3] Many of these typical features and conventions reappear in the present portrait of Blanche, and this was natural in view of what this elegy aimed at; Blanche's image was to find its place within the great tradition of ideal feminine beauty and virtue, and a worthy memorial was to be raised to her.[4] To expect 'realism' or any flouting of convention in this connection would be to misinterpret this medieval 'eulogy' completely. On the contrary, in this portrait Chaucer's artistry consisted in his including as many as possible of the conventional themes, commonplaces and approved rhetorical devices already familiar to his public.

Yet compared with its models and parallels, the general effect of this portrait of Blanche is fresh, alive, vigorous, and in

[1] Cf. 670, 810, 1034.

[2] Cf. E. Faral, *Les arts poétiques du 12e et du 13e siècle*, 1924.

[3] Cf. D. S. Brewer 'The Ideal of Feminine Beauty in Medieval Literature. Especially "Harley Lyrics", Chaucer, and some Elizabethans', *MLR* 50 (1955). Rodolfo Renier, *Il tipo estetico della donna nel medio evo*, 1885. Anna Köhn, *Das weibliche Schönheitsideal in der ritterlichen Dichtung*, 1930.

[4] Some of Blanche's attributes here belong not to the 'topoi' for eulogies of women but to poems honouring the dead; in one instance – not found in Machaut – her influence is likened to a 'torche bryght' (963). The praise of Blanche's liberality and charity, too, plainly includes topoi from medieval eulogies of the dead (891 ff., 930, 1013). On the topics of consolatory oratory, cf. E. R. Curtius, Ch. 5, § 1.

some degree personal[1] – and here we touch upon a mystery of Chaucer's art. For while he loves to borrow extensively and to imitate, yet he can convey something quite individual by selecting, transposing, and making trifling changes and additions.

While almost every detail in the description of Blanche's endowments of person and character, then, is taken from Machaut's *Remède de Fortune*, the *Jugement dou Roy de Behaingne*, and the *Lay de Comfort*,[2] there remains to consider the distribution and importance of the details borrowed from these poems. On the one hand, we have in these sources personal description with only slight reference to the relevant virtues, and on the other an exhaustive treatise on the feminine virtues in general.[3] Chaucer establishes an essential connection between these two elements. What counts for most in his portrait is the character, the person; human beauty appears simply as a confirmation of its owner's noble qualities. So Chaucer greatly shortens the catalogue of physical features, more or less exhaustive in Machaut's works; but to his catalogue of good qualities based as it is on the scheme of courtly virtues, he adds a few traits not typically of the court but belonging to Blanche herself, such as human sympathy, friendliness, and goodness of heart. Compared to the traditional ideal of the court lady, Chaucer's Blanche displays less dignity and hauteur, but more natural, friendly serenity and kindliness.

In the description of Blanche's social qualities it is no accident that the only adjective not borrowed from Machaut's *Behaingne* ( 287 ff. ) – which it follows almost word for word – is 'friendly' ( 852 ), and that there is no equivalent in Machaut for lines referring to Blanche's consideration for others, such as:

> But goode folk, over al other,
> She loved as man may do hys brother; ( 891 )

or:

> Therwith she loved so wel ryght,
> She wrong do wolde to no wyght. ( 1015 )

[1] Cf. Shelly, p. 52 f.; Patch, p. 149 f.
[2] Cf. Kittredge, *PMLA* 30 ( 1915 ); *MP* 7 ( 1910 ).
[3] Chaucer took the virtues from Machaut's catalogue in the *Remède*; the introduction and outline of the description are taken from the *Behaingne*.

(and also lines 930 f.[1]). And furthermore we have Chaucer's typically different portrayal of Blanche's attitude to importunate or self-deluding admirers. Machaut's ladies are more coy but at the same time harsher and colder in their rejection, while Chaucer stresses:

> Ne, be thou siker, she wolde not fonde
> To holde no wyght in balaunce
> By half word ne by countenaunce, (1020)

He says expressly of Blanche:

> She ne used no suche knakkes smale. (1033)

and therewith exposes some of the little tricks used in courtly chivalric love. Chaucer must have been anxious to stress this trait in Blanche, for at two points already he had touched upon it in a manner most unlike Machaut's.[2]

In Chaucer's portrait of Blanche, then, typically courtly and conventional qualities are mingled with more general human traits; and what was rigid and artificial in a portrait in the courtly tradition, a strongly idealized likeness, is modified and softened. The ideal is 'humanized', too, by the use of livelier and more varied language and by slight shadings of style which render the description immediate and personal. This is obvious even where the expressions and details are taken word for word from Machaut, as in:

> And which a goodly, softe speche
> Had that swete, my lyves leche!
> So frendly, and so wel ygrounded,[3] (919)

Exclamations like this within a step-by-step description (cf. also 859, 895), protestations, questions, vows, and asides, all thrown in and giving us what the knight himself thinks, feels, perceives and recollects,[4] contribute towards the more personal effect. Machaut's work illustrates how in the 'descriptio' of a venerated

---

[1] See also the instances quoted by Shelly and Patch, in particular 'She used gladly to do wel', 1013; Shelly, p. 53, Patch, p. 150.

[2] 'Algate she ne roughte of hem a stree', 887; cf. also 868.

[3] Cf. Machaut, *Fortune*, 217 f.

[4] 810, 820, 830, 838, 842, 853, 856, 876, 882, 904, 913, 924, 938, 945, 958, 960, 962, 971, 979, 981, 984, 992, 996, 1020.

and noble lady there lay a special risk of monotonous unvaried enumeration. But Chaucer divides his material up into short sections, giving the impression that the knight telling his story is 'beginning afresh' or 'remembering something new'.

## THE KNIGHT'S STORY AS A RECORD OF EXPERIENCE

The striking effect which this centrally-placed description of Blanche achieves depends, too, on its place in the knight's own recital, the record of his experience. We must therefore glance at the stages of this experience through which the knight passes.

At the opening he is deliberately shown to us in the deepest despair and hopeless grief, inconsolable, weary of his life and near to ending it:

> Hit was gret wonder that Nature
> Myght suffre any creature
> To have such sorwe, and be not ded. (467)

> For he had wel nygh lost hys mynde, (511)

– as the dreamer says, watching from his hiding-place. The knight describes his own state:

> I have of sorwe so gret won
> That joye gete I never non, (475)

and firmly rejects all possibility of help and consolation:

> No man may my sorwe glade,
> That maketh my hewe to falle and fade,
> And hath myn understondynge lorn,
> That me ys wo that I was born! (563)

At the same time however Chaucer shows him to be perfectly approachable and friendly. By these means Chaucer acknowledges from the very beginning that he knows how irreparable and grievous is the knight's loss. And since the knight rejects all consolation and those who would bring it, the dreamer considers it out of the question to comfort him in any of the normal ways[1] and is thus almost obliged to try some other means, one which

---

[1] Cf. Lawlor, *Speculum* 31 (1956).

the knight's agreeable, communicative attitude seems to suggest.

The fact that when we first see him the knight is plunged in such an abyss of despair and sorrow increases the effect of what subsequently happens. For as he proceeds to relate the story of his love we see him growing able to free himself from the weight of gloom and to direct his thoughts elsewhere. We are shown, too, how his way of experience brings a two-fold reward with it. In the first place the god of love (Love) hears the knight's prayer, granting him a meeting with the woman who represents the highest ideal (759 ff.).

But even before the knight confesses his love to his lady, the mere permission to catch sight of the loved one brings the healing 'of al my sorwe' (1104). The re-creation of her image in his mind now leads him to reaffirm his own faith that she still lives on unforgotten. For what he states here about his life in the past must apply likewise to a later period, that is to say to the present:

> for be hyt never so derk,
> Me thynketh I se hir ever moo. (912)

he tells us early in the poem; and a hundred lines further on, he twice repeats:

> And yet she syt so in myn herte,
> That, by my trouthe, y nolde noght,
> For al thys world, out of my thoght
> Leve my lady; noo, trewely! (1108)

> Nay, while I am alyve her,
> I nyl foryete hir never moo. (1124)

If one takes the opening lines of the little song which the knight had composed as the lady's undeclared lover and which he now recites to his hearer:

> Lord, hyt maketh myn herte lyght,
> Whan I thenke on that swete wyght . . . (1175)

they too are doubly applicable in the same sort of way. But this happiness gives place to a new abyss of sorrow into which the knight is plunged by his lady's *No* (1243). It is no accident that his grief at being rejected is now expressed in the same detail and in similar terms as his despairing lament on the death of his beloved, which the dreamer had overheard at the beginning (in lines 1181–1261 the keywords *wo, sorwe, sorweful* occur ten times). The knight's final deliverance and happiness when his love is reciprocated is thus brought into still sharper contrast with his former state:

> As helpe me God, I was as blyve
> Reysed, as fro deth to lyve, (1277)

The chief emphases in the knight's story are purposely so placed that we can see him passing from the depths of sorrow to the heights of bliss. He has come to realize that few mortals have been granted such a measure of grace and fulfilment as he, that he now cherishes for ever in his heart an unforgettable image of these blessings. At the same time, the contrast to the words that directly follow and that now tell in plain terms of the death of Lady Blanche, is made sharper and more tragic. The irremediable fact of the most grievous loss the knight could have suffered forms the poignant ending of the poem. Here, then, Chaucer's achievement is two-fold, and it consists of elements seldom so immediately contrasted; he has shown how by reliving the stages of his own past happiness a mourner can find release from the thought of death, while at the same time, far from being conquered, death overwhelms him anew with its relentless finality.

The *Book of the Duchess* does indeed give us a subtle answer to a human problem; and Chaucer has told his tale more vividly than his predecessors. This, however, does not mean that his style has as yet reached the perfect balance between natural ease and conscious artistry which is characteristic of his later work.

### STYLE AND DICTION

C. S. Lewis has been sharply critical of some passages in the *Book of the Duchess*, written in what he calls 'the old, bad manner'.[1] True, in view of numerous 'digressions' and superfluous enumerations, one might accept a criticism that reproaches Chaucer in this poem with 'a lack of poetic control'.[2] But our

[1] C. S. Lewis, p. 164; Lewis quotes *BD* 985 ff.
[2] D. S. Brewer, *Chaucer*, p. 46.

business here is not only to make an assessment but also to recognize the aim that governed Chaucer's style and presentation. For in the *Book of the Duchess* wé can see the beginnings of what grew into the unique combination of stylistic elements which characterize the later works. It may therefore be appropriate to survey here some of the stylistic methods which Chaucer used in the *Book of the Duchess* and to distinguish his various levels of style.[1]

At one end of the scale we have the passages made up of accepted rhetorical conventions displaying a conscious and overt use of rhetoric, striking us nowadays as highly artificial and exaggerated. For instance there is the oxymoron at lines 599–616, where an antithesis is as it were flogged to death.[2] Elsewhere, too, repetition and variation, climax and contrast[3] are overdone; clearly Chaucer is still keen to parade his knowledge and rhetorical skill. And there is sometimes too obvious verbal embellishment;[4] we have classical, biblical and medieval names piled one on the other and used as 'exempla' (close on fifty proper names occur!). As a result what is simple statement is amplified and expanded, while digressions[5] further reinforce the knight's 'roundabout' method of narration. Among such *devices* is the *correctio*, the negative-affirmative statement. When Blanche is described, for instance, what is said of her hair, her look, her qualities, is always prefixed by a negative:[6]

> For every heer on hir hed,
> Soth to seyne, hyt was not red,
> Ne nouther yelowe, ne broun hyt nas,
> Me thoghte most lyk gold hyt was. (855)

---

[1] Cf. B. J. Harrison, 'Medieval Rhetoric in the BD', *PMLA* 49 (1934); Manly, *Chaucer and the Rhetoricians*, 1926.

[2] This goes back to Machaut, the *Roman de la Rose*, but also to Alanus ab Insulis. Cf. K. Hammerle, *Anglia* 66 (1942).

[3] For the resultant figure, *frequentatio*, cf. 1037 ff.; for *superlatio*, cf. 405 ff., 805 ff., 971 ff. Harrison (*PMLA* 49, 1934) points to models in the *Roman de la Rose* and in Machaut's work. In his later work Chaucer is content with short, pithy comparisons, but in the *Book of the Duchess* he shows a preference for ampler illustrations, intended to expand and emphasize each statement at considerable length (cf. 276, 725 ff, 1080, 1117, 1246).

[4] Harrison notes that only two *exempla* (455, 1244) contain one reference alone; the other six bring several at the same time (276, 566, 725, 1115, 1080, 1056).

[5] There is a good example at 1160–71.    [6] Cf. 862, 874, 880, 943.

This kind of statement undoubtedly has its charm. Several possibilities are discarded before the exactly appropriate descriptive word is found – as if the knight were seeking in his memory and only gradually coming upon the correct image. The *Book of the Duchess* was undoubtedly written for people susceptible to such subtleties. It is not astonishing, therefore, that the subtle quality we have already noted in the knight-and-dreamer dialogue is carried over into the use of language. As well as the more obvious *polyptoton*[1] we may in particular note the *paronomasia*;[2] for such 'echo-effects' playing on similarity in sound and difference in meaning postulate a public with a 'keen ear' – even allowing for the fact that medieval treatises on poetry had trained readers to note the use of such artifices. This is particularly true of the puns,[3] the 'most covert' feature of Chaucer's rhetorical style.

Chaucer's diction, however, embraces not only these easily classified rhetorical *colores* but also devices which seem to be more spontaneous and rooted in an innate feeling for language rather than in painstaking application of rhetorical formulae. When he first sees the knight in black, the dreamer describes him:

> so at the laste
> I was war of a man in blak,
> That sat and had yturned his bak
> To an ook, an huge tree. (444)

The repeated 'a' in the first three lines echoes the similar mood of mourning and loneliness of which these lines and their content tell. In other passages, too, assonance and skilfully placed alliteration enhance the picture portrayed in the description.[4]

Key-words are repeated within the poem (*sorwe* occurs thirty times and *swete* twenty), and certain longer passages attuned to some particular basic word (e.g. the word *fals* in the chess-Fortune passage) are among the methods of expression that pass unnoticed and yet achieve a cumulative effect.

---

[1] Cf. 50, 131, 246, 218, 322, 481, 945, 1145, 1199, 1268.

[2] Cf. 175, 262, 381–2, 397, 427–8, 557–8, 629–30, 658–9, 707–8, 931–2.

[3] Cf. 535–6, 614–16, 625, 883. For this and the preceding, see Helge Kökeritz, 'Rhetorical Word-Play in Chaucer', *PMLA* 69 (1954).

[4] Cf. 335–43; 397–401.

We have already noted how in comparison with the French poets Chaucer is able to give the impression of a narrative at once lively and fluent. This continuity, one sentence seeming linked to another and one line to the next, is helped by the rhyme and by the above-noted methods of alliteration, assonance, repetition of single words and word-echoes (Paranomasia), but also by the syntax. The frequent parallel sentences linked by 'parataxis' and giving the effect of the 'spoken word' are a notable feature; the speaker, instead of starting with some preconceived plan, more simply 'appends' further phrases,[1] using the same constructions. (Cf. p. 56.) What we have here, then, is not art but contrived *artlessness*; the speaker forgoes more complex and varied connecting links and always uses the same construction and linking word. Indeed, he repeats not only constructions but sometimes also certain phrases,[2] and at the end of a paragraph he often recapitulates the most important statements in what he has just related[3] – again following up actual habits of speech.

This brings us to the other end of the scale in Chaucer's stylistic method. On the one hand the *Book of the Duchess* contains figures of rhetoric and passages rhetorically heightened to the pitch of exaggeration; on the other it markedly displays a colloquial element evident not only in the sudden cries and pious ejaculations[4] already mentioned, the protestations and assertions,[5] the vows,[6] the modifying asides,[7] and the parentheses, but also in the elliptical phrases where the relative is omitted,[8] 'swallowed' as it were, in the hasty and emotional pressure of the narrative. Naturally, this colloquial element is strongest in the dialogues which often follow rhetorical passages and form

[1] Lines 192–201 afford a good example; *and* introduces each new item in the narration and the same sentence-construction is kept throughout. Cf. 231, 298 ff., 345–8, 350–3, 421 ff., 502 ff., 826 ff., 848 ff., 950 ff., 1038 ff., 1056 ff., 1097 f., 1118–21, 1158 ff., 1211, 1225 ff., 1261 ff.

[2] E.g. 464/87; 714/22; 1054/73; 1240/2; 1262/7.

[3] E.g. 454 (445).

[4] By oure Lord! (544); A Goddes half (370, 758); yis parde (721); allas! Lord!

[5] Cf. the frequently interpolated *certes, soth to seye, by my trouthe, trewely*; also the interpolated 'as helpe me God' (1205, 1235, 1277), 'be thou siker' (1020), 'Hyt ys no nede' (1128).

[6] Cf. 683, 755, 820, 924, 929, 971, 1002.

[7] Me thinketh, me thoghte, I trowe, in my thoght.

[8] E.g. 740 ff., 1045, 1245.

'dramatic interruptions' to the story (519 ff., 539 ff., 714 ff., 742 ff., 1042 ff., 1112 ff., 1126 ff.). But single words and turns of phrase, too, have a colloquial ring;[1] they add to the diction (in which terms taken over from the French emphasize the courtly sphere) a contrasting note of sturdy realism and the racy speech of every day.[2] The transition from one stylistic plane to another does not always follow naturally; the balance later achieved between the different styles is still lacking.

### CHAUCER'S VERSIFICATION

Chaucer's versification, too, displays the same range and delight in experiment which characterize his style in the *Book of the Duchess*. The short rhyming couplet which he uses here, as in the *House of Fame*, had been one of the favourite metres in Middle English poetry; and in Chaucer's own day Gower in particular had perfected this iambic couplet with its four stresses; his lines flow easily along, following the constructions and natural stress of the words; and although they strictly adhere to the iambic metre (keeping invariably to eight or nine syllables) they very rarely relapse into monotony. Gower obviously made a virtue of regularity, a quality which so often constitutes a danger to an artistic use of versification; comparison of his lines with those of some of his predecessors bears this out.

Chaucer however follows a different path.[3] What he is aiming at is not regularity, smoothly-flowing verse, but variety and pungency; and for this reason he is not afraid of harshness or irregularity, his accentuation often running counter to the natural stress of the words; and he frequently omits the initial syllable, changes the rhythm, drops unaccented syllables, elides and uses other means as well[4] to give variety and urgency to his verse, catching and holding our attention as he does so. The reader

[1] E.g. no fors (522, 542), which a fool she was! (734), he wax as ded as stoon (1300); (cf. also 123); I holde that wyssh nat worth a stree! (671, 718); For I ne myghte, for bote ne bale (227); hit ys no nay (147); y not now what. (353.)

[2] On 'Chaucer's Colloquial English: Its Structural Traits', cf. M. Schlauch, *PMLA* 67 (1952).

[3] For a comparison of Chaucer's with Gower's metre, see also G. Macaulay's introduction to his edition of Gower (*John Gower's English Works*, Vol. I, p xvii).

[4] Cf. Paull F. Baum, *Chaucer's Verse*, 1961.

cannot rely on the constant even flow of the verse, as he can in
Gower; it is much more difficult in view of all the irregularity
and freedom Chaucer allows himself, to read his verse correctly.
When it is read aloud, the reader has to keep changing his
tempo; for passages with a rapid, even and almost regular movement alternate with others where the many interruptions and
irregularities require him to read more slowly, indeed at times
to pause. This variety in the tempo of the verse is very frequent
and Chaucer makes conscious use of it to vary his versification
in accordance with the theme and tone of each section.

Of course it is impossible to say how far the frequent irregularities in particular in Chaucer's early verse are a means to an
end and how far a result of negligence or failure to go over
the lines again to polish and correct what was 'incomplete' or
'imperfect'. But Chaucer's own words at the beginning of the
Third Book of the *House of Fame* give us at least a hint – though
he may possibly be also turning his irony on himself:

> Nat that I wilne, for maistrye,
> Here art poetical be shewed;
> But for the rym is lyght and lewed,
> Yit make hyt sumwhat agreable,
> Though som vers fayle in a sillable;
> And that I do no diligence
> To shewe craft, but o sentence. (1094)

Even if we deny any artistic design in the case of some of the
'irregular' lines, compared with his contemporaries Chaucer has
at his command a much greater range of metrical expression. In
his verse he displays an astonishing boldness that exceeds what
had gone before. One has only to compare a dialogue from
Gower's *Confessio* with the end of the conversation between the
knight and the dreamer at the close of the *Book of the Duchess*, to
become aware of this. The conversation between Diogenes and
a messenger from Alexander is one of Gower's most lively and
fluent passages of dialogue:

> The kniht bad speke and seith, 'Vilein,
> Thou schalt me telle, er that I go;
> It is the king which axeth so.'
> 'Mi king,' quod he, 'that were unriht.'

'What is he thanne?' 'That seie I noght,'
Quod he, 'bot this I am bethoght,
Mi mannes man hou that he is.'
'Thou lyest false cherl, ywiss,'
The kniht him seith, . . .

(*Conf. Am.* III, 1243.)

Despite the animated interchange, the metre is kept strictly
regular and the flow of the verse is scarcely interrupted. Chaucer's
lines, however, produce a totally different effect. The abrupt dis-
closure that the dearly-loved Blanche is dead, which brings the
long conversation to a sudden and moving end, takes our breath
away as we read it aloud and makes us pause. The lines before
and after it also are full of subtle and individual modifications by
which Chaucer here – as elsewhere in this poem – achieves
dramatic effects that particularly distinguish him from Gower:

'Sir,' quod I, 'where is she now?'
'Now?' quod he, and stynte anoon.
Therwith he wax as ded as stoon,
And seyde, 'Allas, that I was bore!
That was the los that here-before
I tolde the that I hadde lorn.
Bethenke how I seyde here-beforn,
"Thow wost ful lytel what thow menest;
I have lost more than thow wenest" –
God wot, allas! ryght that was she!'
'Allas, sir, how? what may that be?'
'She ys ded!' 'Nay!' 'Yis, be my trouthe!'
'Is that youre los? Be God, hyt ys routhe!'

(1298)

And what, finally, constitutes the general impression which the
*Book of the Duchess* makes upon us? How does it reveal Chaucer's
poetic artistry? A series of elaborate descriptions and stylized
pictures have passed before the reader's eyes. Despite this conventional framework, however, these pictures breathed freshness
and life. The reader has been led by many a détour; again and
again the essential point seemed to elude him. The basic theme
was enveloped in a rich mantling of elaborate accessories and yet

every paragraph held a hint of it. Throughout the whole poem the reader thus seemed to be urged to follow up these allusions, to seek and to find as he traced the détours and approached step by step the grievous event which was the occasion and the theme of the *Book of the Duchess*. This event, the death of Blanche, is mentioned without disguise only at the very end of the poem. But because then the poem is and must be at an end, everything that had gone before, in other words the whole poem, appears to exist simply in order to prevent this direct statement from having been made earlier. The principle behind the whole presentation clearly lies in this distance set up between us and the death of Blanche. For the poem proceeds only slowly from the adventitious to the essential, and its grave quality only very gradually becomes apparent under the light surface. Over this grave quality, however, there spreads a restrained gaiety and charm, a delicate irony and a rich imagination. Much the same thing happens to the reader as to the knight in black as he tells his story. He comes to realize the extent and depth of grief but as he does so he is helped to master this same grief from which the whole poem has sprung.

# 2

# *The House of Fame*

The *House of Fame* differs radically from the *Book of the Duchess* in tone, intention, and plan. There could of course be no more than rare glimpses of humour and irony in any poem written to extol the dead or comfort the bereaved; but here these qualities break through triumphantly. They are matched, too, by a light-hearted boldness in the treatment of respected, time-honoured themes as well as a zest for experiment and an exuberant delight in fun, together with a gift for telling a number of colourful, crowded incidents in a brisk and amusing way. All this makes for a highly original work; and despite the lack of completeness and unity in it, which constantly embarrasses the critics, it is one of the most entertaining and unusual works which the later Middle Ages has produced.

The *Book of the Duchess* had already shown us the characteristic Chaucerian blend of heterogeneous themes and genres; and we see all this carried a stage further in the *House of Fame*. For the familiar conventions are more than ever used in an entirely new way; we find them serving within a traditional framework to lead on to something quite unexpected and surprising.

For this reason it is essential to investigate what models, conventions, and hitherto accepted poetic traditions underlie the *House of Fame*. The pleasure with which his contemporaries surely read this work must have largely consisted in relating its themes to this same background of recognized models and conventions, and in appreciating the resulting contrasts. The *House of Fame* was certainly written for an audience of *initiates*, that is to say for a public capable of appreciating and following the author as he practised this highly complex art of allusion and reference to the most diverse genres and conventions. In view of so subtle and esoteric an 'art of the initiates', the naïve attitude which the narrator assumes here, as in the *Book of the Duchess*, is a particularly diverting pose; and it still further enhances the irony with which the work is presented.

Chaucer's literary horizon had considerably widened since he wrote the *Book of the Duchess*. By this time he had visited Italy once if not twice and had got to know the works of Dante, Boccaccio, and no doubt Petrarch also. He was widely read in Latin allegorical verse, and by intensive reading he had acquired a knowledge of many branches of literature covering medieval writers in Latin, French, Italian, and English. Indeed, an abundance of the most varied reading underlies the *House of Fame*. There is hardly another work in medieval literature that treats its erudition and its literary models and traditions with such ease, boldness, and assurance, or that shows such supreme confidence in its use of them. The study of Chaucer's sources and influences will have to take this into account. In contrast to previous research on influences, our main consideration here must be the fundamental differences between the *House of Fame* and its 'models', Chaucer's attitude towards literary tradition, and finally how in his own work he achieves a highly individual transformation of such 'influences'.[1] What makes this poem so characteristic, so 'different', can only be revealed if we consider its whole tone, 'spirit', and aim (not merely the individual themes it contains), and compare these with the French works so often wrongly described as its 'models'.

Proceeding, then, along these lines, it is impossible to concur with Sypherd that the *House of Fame* is 'a love vision of the literary genre to which belong such poems as *le Roman de la Rose*, Froissart's *Paradys d'Amour* and Chaucer's *Duchesse*'.[2] The French poems usually centre round the poet's meeting with the love-god or some accompanying personified abstraction – Esperance, for instance. In almost every case the rules of love are then expounded. Should the poet arrive at some 'allegorical spot', this turns out to be the palace of the love-god. Such poems

[1] As a valuable contribution in this matter we would cite Ingeborg Besser's study, *Chaucers 'Hous of Fame'*, 1941 (Britannica 20).

[2] W. O. Sypherd, *Studies in Chaucer's Hous of Fame*, 1907.

frequently take the form of a man's homage to his lady or at least refer to her in some way.

None of this is applicable to Chaucer's poem. It is impossible to claim that its main theme is 'love' (as it so manifestly is in all the French poems), especially if we bear in mind the Second and Third Books.[1] It is true that the author calls himself a poet in the service of the love-god (614 ff.), saying he is seeking 'love's novelties', and that in his dream he awakens in the temple of Venus. All that does not however amount to a 'main theme'. There is not a single personification of love; the allegorical palace belongs to Fame, not to 'Love'; and it is inhabited by living people and not by more of these personified abstractions. Moreover, there is no sign of the inevitable ever-green garden with bird-song and spring air. Chaucer's eagle, 'the poet's guide' that carries him to the House of Fame, might seem to perform a similar function to that of the allegorical personifications of the French poets; seen, however, as Chaucer with his characteristic comic, wry tone has presented him, this creature would be quite unthinkable in the works of these French writers; and he has nothing in common with their stereotyped abstractions.

In the *House of Fame* Chaucer eschews the whole *allegoresis* of love which forms the most obvious feature of the French 'love-visions', and with it the usual exhaustive didactic analysis of the subject. Instead, there is more emphasis on himself and his work as a poet – a theme only rarely touched upon by the French.[2] It is true that in the French poems we often find the poet himself carrying the action forward; but in that case his rôle is that of the 'typical lover', the 'example' demonstrating the general rules governing the theory of love. Chaucer's portrayal of himself, on the other hand, displays unmistakably individual features.

[1] Shelly (p. 73) and others hold this view.

[2] The poet commissioned by his lady or by the god of love to compose new verses, was a convention already favoured by the Troubadours. It is rarer to find the poet himself expressing a wish for fresh themes, for 'matere', as he does in Machaut's *Prologue* (*Oeuvres*, *SATF* I), where 'Amours's' three children, 'Dous Penser' etc. are led before the poet to provide him with new 'matere'. In Froissart's *Le Joli Buisson de Jonece* the poet laments the lack of 'matere', whereupon Philosophy instructs him to open a casket and find his lady's portrait there; and this inspires him afresh. In Chaucer however the wish for new 'matere' takes on a different guise in sharp contrast to the artificiality of the French court poets.

The most significant difference however is this: the French writers' overriding aim was to teach, to point a moral, whereas Chaucer did not wish to instruct but simply to give literary expression to what was in his mind, in an entertaining and amusing way. If it is permissible to speak of 'allegory' at all in connection with Chaucer,[1] it is allegory devoid of all design and didacticism. Unlike the French, Chaucer refrains (both then and later) from interpreting the individual features which he has taken from allegorical tradition. In his treatment of allegorical detail, too, he avoids any of the rigidity or fussy pedantry which is so typical of his French contemporaries. They had analysed and classified, building up the most elaborate system conceivable of edifying material. An entirely different scale of values, however, is apparent in the very structure of Chaucer's poem. Long instructive speeches and abstract deliberations are no longer the main element; instead, much space is allotted to the actual portrayal of happenings and impressions. The 'plot', the external course of events, once more comes into prominence. The result is that we are shown a greater number of incidents in the *House of Fame* than in the French poems. The narrative element is more stressed. Instead of the dry, piecemeal account common in the strongly derivative love-visions modelled on the *Roman de la Rose*, Chaucer gives us a true narrative; he describes things as they strike him, as his own experience revealed them to him step by step. This had been noticeable in the *Book of the Duchess*, and now it is carried considerably further.

In view of this new path that Chaucer's writing takes, it is important to consider whether Italian poetry, especially that of Dante, Petrarch and Boccaccio, might have stimulated him in this respect. Here again however, any influence felt must have been of a very indirect and special kind, far removed from what is understood by 'imitation'.[2] Dante might certainly have opened Chaucer's eyes to the possibilities of accurate, factual and vivid description of events, a concentrated portrayal of dramatic situations, a particular type of realism, which enhanced rather

---

[1] On Chaucer as an allegorical poet, cf. C. S. Lewis, Ch. IV.

[2] Supporters of the imitation-theory include Ten Brink, *Chaucer* 1870, A. Rambeau, *Englische Studien* 3 (1870), Child, *MLN* 10 (1895); E. Koeppel, *Anglia* 14 (1892).

than weakened the underlying thought. From Boccaccio's later work Chaucer might have learned to shun didacticism and a moralizing allegorical treatment, and to employ an easy narra·tive style. But these are influences that operate only at a certain definite level; and besides, it is impossible to deduce them from the borrowing of individual words or themes.[1] The truth is that Chaucer stands a whole world apart from Dante or Boccaccio.

The very general literary pattern to which (with numerous reservations, however) the *House of Fame* might be said to belong, is the allegorical journey. This underlies most of the so-called 'love-visions' as well as many other medieval poems; and it also goes back to a much older tradition. In poems of this basic pattern the poet is usually led in a dream to some allegorical spot; and his guide's duties further include instructing him on many points. The 'allegorical journey' was already a frequent feature of the medieval poetry of the twelfth century;[2] it also occurs in Christian didactic poetry.[3] Dante's *Divine Comedy* is the greatest and most comprehensive example of a work based upon this pattern, already familiar from earlier or contemporary didactic poems.[4] But a glance at these works and above all at the tradition of journeys either into the heavens or to the next world,[5] which constitute a specialized version of the allegorical journey, suffices for us to recognize their fundamental difference from Chaucer's *House of Fame*. What had hitherto always been a serious and noble subject, a theme used for moral edification, serves quite a different purpose with Chaucer; it is as if he

[1] Cf. Lowes, p. 104. On Dante's influence, see also Speirs, p. 43, G. K. Chesterton, *Chaucer*, repr. 1959, p. 23; Coghill, p. 48.

[2] For instance, in the *Architrenius* of Johannes von Altavilla (see Wright, *Anglo-Latin Satirical Poets* I), Architrenius comes in turn to the palace of Venus, the dwelling of Gula, the mountain of Ambitio and the hill of Presumptio.

[3] For example, the 'voie de paradis' poems by Raoul de Houdenc (ed. Scheler, 1879, in *Trouvères Belges*), Rutebeuf (ed. Kressner, 1885) and Baudouin de Condé (ed. Scheler, 1866), and the best known and later example, Deguilleville's *Le pélérinage de la vie humaine* (ed. Stürzinger, 1893–7).

[4] In Brunetto Latini's *Tesoretto*, for instance, the poet arrives on his travels at the palaces of the four cardinal virtues; and in the *Introduzione alla Virtù* (ascribed to Bono Giamboni) Philosophy guides the poet to the palace of the 'Fede Christiana'. Cf. Karl Vossler, *Die Göttliche Komödie*, 1925, p. 478 f.

[5] In his *Chaucer* (2nd edition, p. 778) Robinson mentions F. Cumont, *Le Mysticisme astral dans l'antiquité*, 1909, and Nock and Festugière, *Corpus Hermeticum* I, where many examples of 'intellectual or mental flight' are to be found.

71

reversed the symbols in its scale of values. What had been a sublime translation into unknown spheres becomes a diverting trip, and in the place of solemnity we have comedy or irony (see page 50 f.).

Comparison of the *House of Fame* with the various works cited as its 'models' shows that the poem does not in fact really fit into any of the existing genres or formal traditions, though it borrows features (mostly radically altered) from all of them. Any attempt to pin down the *House of Fame* to a distinct type, to see it as 'true to type', is thus fruitless; on the other hand, it is just as mistaken to ignore its connection with literary traditions and recognized basic patterns.

Similar provisos, too, hold good for the *House of Fame* in the matter of its unity. Repeated efforts have been made to explain the poem in the light of some single central theme. But if we were to require organic unity from a literary work of art and to demand that all its constituent parts shall be directed towards one central subject, we would be thinking along the lines of a modern conception of poetry; and we are not entitled to do this without question in the case of a medieval poem. The allegorical journey in the course of which the poet experiences different kinds of happenings and encounters, was a vehicle for the most varied themes. The mere fact that all these happenings were stages on the way to some constant and definite goal, was sufficient to ensure that the individual parts stood in a mutual relationship. We may find parallels and analogies to link the different incidents of the journey together. Besides, between the individual parts there may be logical connection and sequence. A certain unity may also be achieved – as we see this in the *House of Fame* – by the poet's consistent attitude and the equally sustained wryly-ironical tone and spirit of the whole. But to relate every part of a poem to one single central theme or to seek for some philosophical or conceptual focal point from which every detail can be interpreted – that is an entirely different thing. The perceptive research undertaken along these lines[1] in order to expound the 'unity' of the poem, admittedly

[1] Cf. P. F. Baum, 'Chaucer's the "*House of Fame*"', *ELH* 8 (1941); P. G. Ruggiers, 'The Unity of Chaucer's *House of Fame*', *SP* 50 (1953); G. Stillwell, 'Chaucer's "O Sentence" in the *House of Fame*', *ES* 37 (1956); R. C. Goffin,

includes some stimulating and interesting points of view and some welcome contributions to the interpretation of certain details. But it can construct a 'unity' only by emphasizing certain isolated attitudes or themes found in the course of the poem, while it ignores others. Any conception of unity gained by this procedure has to be wrung from the poem by an excess of ingenuity.

The gay, buoyant spirit of the *House of Fame*, with its consequently somewhat loose construction, its aim to amuse and entertain, its delight in experiment and telling a tale – all these are features which critics have repeatedly stressed;[1] and such features ought to warn us against persisting too stubbornly in any demand for unity and any search for a central theme. Besides, the poem is incomplete. We do not know the end; and as we have here a journey with a definite goal, this surely would have told us much about the conception and aim of the whole poem. Moreover, might our method of interpretation not borrow something of the spirit in which the work itself is written? The eagle's admonition to his attentive hearer, 'Take yt in ernest or in game' (822) may well be meant for us also!

Chaucer prefaced his work with a *Proem* and also a multiple invocation. In so doing he goes beyond many of his predecessors – including the *Roman de la Rose* – in his observance of the regulations governing how a poem should correctly be introduced. Any appearance of pedantry and strictly precise attention to rhetorical usage however is deceptive; and furthermore, it forms an ironic contrast to the real intention of the poem (though it must be admitted that as a rule Chaucer had no quarrel with rhetoric).

### THE PROEM

The Proem begins with a maxim, a pious wish: 'God turn us every drem to goode'; and towards the end of the Proem this is

'Quiting by Tidinges in the *House of Fame*', *Medium Aevum* 12 (1943). On the other hand, the lack of unity and the absence of any central theme are stressed by D. S. Brewer, J. S. P. Tatlock, *The Mind and Art of Chaucer*, 1950; N. Coghill, *The Poet Chaucer*, 1949; and more recently by Paull F. Baum, whose *Chaucer, A Critical Appreciation*, 1958, represents a partial revision of his former point of view.
[1] For instance by Kittredge, Lowes, Patch and Coghill.

repeated somewhat differently (57). To begin a poem in this way with a maxim (and then to recall it at a later stage) was in accordance with the rules of medieval rhetoric. By prefacing his 'mock-serious-poem' with this pious wish, however, Chaucer by no means intends to make fun of it. Medieval literature mingled the pious and the profane, the grave and the gay, more easily than we do today. And yet, as the context shows, Chaucer puts this maxim to an unusual use. It might be said to represent the position to which he clings and resigns himself, after reviewing the many confusing dream-theories in the Proem – without however committing himself to any one of them. The conjunctive 'for' in the second line acts, indeed, as a preparation; with a naïvely innocent pose the poet asks what may really lie behind the business of dreaming.

The French writers often prefaced their dream-poems with theories, to prove that dreams were worthy of belief.[1] When however the French writer opens his poem with some general observation, he means it as a positive statement, an authoritative pronouncement.[2] Chaucer, on the other hand, does not stop at *one* theory of dreams; he gives us a truly bewildering profusion of varied theories; moreover, he does not firmly assert them, he simply puts them before us as possibilities, while he himself remains strictly impartial. The French poets would never have thought of distinguishing between their opening theoretical observations and their own 'personal attitude'. But Chaucer remains aloof:

> but whoso of these miracles
> The causes knoweth bet then I,
> Devyne he; for I certeinly
> Ne kan hem noght, ne never thinke
> To besily my wyt to swinke,
> To knowe of hir signifiaunce
> The gendres, . . .          (12)

---

[1] See the opening of the *Roman de la Rose*, and also Margival's *Panthère d'Amours* (ed. *SATF*, 1883) ll. 41–6.

[2] E. g.Machaut in the *Remède de Fortune* (ed. Hoepffner, *SATF*, III), Jean de Condé in *Li Dis dou Roi et des Hiermittes* (ed. Scheler, 1866), Froissart in *La Prison Amoureuse* (ed. Scheler, 1870); and others.

Disinterested, he stands apart from this theoretical argumentation in which he refrains from taking part. One cannot help
hearing the irony in the whole introductory passage.[1] Chaucer
pretends that all these theories about dreams and the discussion
of them is no affair of his, and yet he brings his whole knowledge
– and he proves more 'learned' than most of his contemporaries
– to bear on the matter. At the same time he reduces all this
learning to a farce; for the conjectures and suggestions crowded
into small compass (indeed into a single sentence!) cancel one
another out, at least in their effect on the reader. Meantime,
throughout these contrivances the poet himself affects innocence
and astonishment, extricating himself adroitly by shifting res-
ponsibility for the questions asked, on to the 'grete clerkys' (53)
and declaring himself to be 'of noon opinion'. (55)[2]

## THE INVOCATIONS

The same sort of thing might also be said of the invocations that
preface the three Books. Chaucer has in all six invocations, a
large number for a short poem. He is at pains to lend his slight
work an impressive apparatus of rhetorical preliminaries, in
keeping with the 'mock-heroic' tone.

The medieval poets addressed themselves to God as well as
to the Muses and to Apollo;[3] they seldom considered very
deeply how far it was in keeping with their subject to address
God, or how far it was inappropriate to call upon the Muses and
the pagan gods. The *Invocatio* had become a rhetorical formula,
and it was no longer necessary to consider whether it was apt in
any particular case. One not uncommonly finds an address to the
Muses side by side with a plea to God or Jesus, without there
being the least element of ridicule or unseemly 'irreverence' in
it.

[1] Cf. Kittredge, p. 75; Malone, p. 48; Muscatine, p. 108.

[2] One is reminded here of Pandarus's sceptical remarks on the interpretation o
dreams (A straw for alle swevenes signifiaunce! *Troilus* V, 362 f.). This does not
however represent what Chaucer himself thought of dreams; for there are other
passages (for instance in *Troil. a. Cris.*) which mention the truth of dreams and their
prognostic qualities.

[3] On invocations to the Muses, cf. E. R. Curtius, Ch. 13; also R. Meissner in the
*Walzel Festschrift*, 1924, pp. 21 ff.; Hennig Brinkmann, *Zu Wesen und Form
mittelalterlicher Dichtung* II, 1928.

Nonetheless the invocations in the *House of Fame* have their humorous and ironical side. The 'Invocation' (66) does not open with a direct address; instead, Chaucer ceremoniously announces his intentions, as if he wishes to draw his hearers' particular attention to the rhetorical flourishes that follow. Even then the invocation does not begin at once; in its place we have an amusing little picture of Morpheus's dwelling. An unusual version of the god of sleep, 'this god, that I of rede' (77) who in this way is made familiar and interesting to us. And thus a note of entertainment runs through the whole invocation. As in Chaucer's treatment of Ovid,[1] the classical material used here serves him to infuse with vivid detail what had in general been a brief and abstract formula.[2] This kind of elaboration with pictorial ornament (noticeable in Boccaccio also[3]) seems to make the invocation at once richer and more spontaneous.

And now Chaucer holds our attention by his breathless and yet circumstantial way of calling for God's blessing on all those who accept the validity of dreams. The humour in the following and contrasting lines is quite unmistakable; Chaucer passionately implores Jesus to visit 'every harm that any man Hath had' on whoever 'misdeems' the dream, whether 'dreme he barefot, dreme he shod' (98) – a comic image which Chaucer calls up in one of his parenthetical phrases.[4]

Furthermore, the three-fold address to Cipris, the Muses and his own 'Thought', with which the second Book opens, has a touch of irony. Cipris (as Venus is called here) calls to mind Venus as the beloved of Mars.[5] And the contrast here is surely intentional; the earnest plea for help which the poet in the lonely desert addresses to Jesus at the end of the first Book is directly followed by an appeal to a lighthearted pagan deity of whose power however Chaucer was well aware. He took this invocation from the *Teseida* (I, 3), while in the following lines he borrows

---

[1] Cf. E. F. Shannon, *Chaucer and the Roman Poets*, 1929.

[2] Cf. for instance the invocations in Froissart's *Li Orloge Amoureux* (86 ff.).

[3] Cf. Boccaccio, *Teseida* I, 1, 3; VII, 32 ff.

[4] On the humour in this invocation, cf. Kittredge, p. 77, Malone, p. 49, Besser, p. 42; Kittredge refers to the convention of cursing ill-wishers, which Chaucer took over from the *Anticlaudianus*, using it however 'to his own purposes'; for 'Under cover of his irony, he is proudly self-assertive'.

[5] Brewer, p. 74.

again from Dante; and echoes of both poets mingle throughout the passage. This carefree, yet selective method is typical of Chaucer. The second Canto in Dante, before the descent into hell, opens with a solemn invocation to 'mente'.[1] Chaucer was well aware of the contrast when he now introduced a slightly expanded form of this solemn invocation, at the very moment when he was about to embark on his entertaining excursion heavenwards to the palace of Fame; and his hearers must have relished the irony in it too.[2] It was characteristic of the 'mock-heroic epic' that the epic conventions, the epic 'adjuncts', were exaggerated and thrust into the foreground in order to stress the contrast between the slender content and the apparatus involved in conveying it. And this is exactly what Chaucer is doing here.

The invocation to the third Book, too, involves contrast of a similar kind. Dante had invoked the Muses in general or (in the *Purgatorio*) Calliope; at the opening of the *Paradiso*, however, he calls for the help of Apollo himself (*Par.* I, 13). He does this because to portray the lofty and divine matter of Paradise he has need of both poetic skill and eloquence. But Chaucer's third Book does not give us this sort of climax within the poem. The castle of Fame is not paradise and no greater inspiration is needed to describe it than for instance the heavenward flight.

Chaucer's invocation for the third Book, too, involves a further divergence from Dante. Dante begins with 'O buono Apollo', whereas Chaucer opens with the much more solemn and ceremonious:

> O God of science and of lyght,
> Appollo, thurgh thy grete myght,
> This lytel laste bok thou gye! (III, 1 ff.)

While Dante, conscious of his own worth, goes on to approach the laurel to crown himself with a wreath, Chaucer acts more modestly; he goes up to the tree sacred to the god in order to offer his thanks.

---

[1] Lowes draws attention to Chaucer's skill here in linking thus the first and second Books together. For just before, in the first Canto, Dante had mentioned the *Aeneid*, and in Chaucer's first Book we have a corresponding reference to Dido's story. (Lowes, p. 107.)

[2] Patch speaks here of 'mock solemnity' (p. 44).

# Chaucer's Early Poetry

We return, however, to the first Book: after the invocation Chaucer begins to tell his dream, making it more credible by a precise reference to time and place – and slipping in, as he does so, yet another ironic innuendo.[1]

Chaucer's manner of description reminds us here of the *Book of the Duchess*. What is seen in the dream is not presented as a complete picture but as if observed by someone gradually growing aware of new surroundings and making discoveries step by step. Chaucer shows his narrative skill by setting before us not only a 'narrator' but a man in the act of seeing and hearing, approaching things in his own way and taking them in by degrees. Instead of the outline of this new scene being sketched in objectively for us, our first impression is that of its strange, bewildering variety (121–7). We are not simply told that this new residence is a temple of Venus; the dreamer only deduces it from catching sight of her picture. In the same way it is not simply stated that there is an inscription hanging on the wall; he only *discovers* it after some time: 'But as I romed up and doun, I fond . . .' (140).

By introducing this temple of Venus here, Chaucer is not attempting an allegorical portrayal of the nature of love; and he does not describe its plan and the details of its construction as the medieval poets had delineated their palaces of love.[2] Instead of the different building materials usually listed together with what they 'signified', only glass[3] is mentioned. And instead of a Venus enthroned amid personified virtues we are given her picture sketched with a few rapid lines. Chaucer's temple is not the dwelling of the god of love; it forms a symbolic background for the summary of the *Aeneid* and for the Dido episode; in fact its plan is not taken from French allegorical poetry but is based on the *Aeneid* itself.[4]

[1] Cf. Robinson's notes to lines 117–8.

[2] Cf. W. A. Neilson, *Origins and Sources of the Court of Love*, 1899; Roberta D. Cornelius, *The Figurative Castle, Study in the Medieval Allegory of the Edifice*, Diss. Bryn Mawr 1930. A list of allegorical descriptions of palaces is given in O. Damman, *Die allegorische Canzone des Guiraut de Calanso*, Diss. Breslau 1891.

[3] Glass recalls the customary crystal, a favoured material for palaces of love.

[4] The model was the temple of Juno in Carthage, on whose walls Aeneas saw episodes from the history of Troy. (*Aeneid* I, 446.)

# The House of Fame

There is a change, too, in Chaucer's use of the device of bringing in episodes from mythology or history as wall-paintings.[1] For with him their function is not to give a full characterization of some personified abstraction as the medieval poets had done when using this same device. Moreover, his readers must have been surprised to find Venus depicted solely by means of the Dido-episode and, to be sure, Chaucer's version of it gives a one-sided picture of Venus.

### THE DIDO-EPISODE

Chaucer's rendering of the *Aeneid* which centres round the Dido-episode offers several instances of his art of taking over well-known material and then going on to disappoint expectations and introduce an ironical contrast to what had been familiar. The effect of surprise is linked with irony and veiled amusement; in addition, the naïve and astonished pose of the dream-narrator adds a particular spice as Chaucer thus skilfully plays with conventions and traditional material, and deliberately influences his audience.

As he himself tells us (378 f.), Chaucer used both Virgil and also Ovid's *Heroides* for his episode. At the beginning, however, it is the *Aeneid* that he recalls by quoting its universally familiar opening lines as the 'inscriptio' on the wall of the temple. This serves to emphasize still further the contrast between his version (which then follows) and the tone and spirit of that great epic.

Chaucer's version of the *Aeneid* falls clearly into two sections. In the first he gives a chronological account up to the beginning of the Dido-episode, which he relates in the second. The first section is an example of his condensing narrative technique, a few bold lines giving a rapid flexible outline of the outward events. Chaucer divides the complex happenings into six sections, each introduced by 'I saugh'; and he 'paints the picture' by portraying

[1] Medieval writers were borrowing from the classics when they described wall-decorations which depicted famous episodes. Alanus de Insulis, too, retold certain tales by the use of wall-paintings. The connection (stressed by medieval writers) between wall-decorations and the allegorical character of the palace described, was lost in early Renaissance times; the symbolical significance of the wall-paintings was forgotten, and they became simply magnificent items in the decoration. A work such as Boccaccio's *Amorosa Visione* illustrates a transitional stage in this development. On the influence of contemporary art on Chaucer's temple of Venus cf. Karl Brunner, *Rivista di Letterature Moderne*, I, 1950–1 pp. 344 ff.

each happening *as* a picture. At the same time the continuous flow of the narrative brings movement into each scene, while numerous verbs of motion carry the story along.

It might seem that this kind of rapid summary, skimming over the surface of things and putting the emphasis on facts, would prevent Chaucer from developing any personal attitude to his material. Yet a characteristic bias does creep in here; the poet abandons his objective attitude as narrator. He does so by his avowals of sympathy (allas 157, 183, dispitously 161, That hyt was pitee for to here 180, 189 etc.), and still more by his familiar address to the two goddesses and his way of describing them (Ther saugh I thee, cruel Juno . . . Renne and crye as thou were wood, 198 f.; Venus, how ye, my lady dere, Wepynge with ful woful chere, 213 f.). This brings the lofty tale of Aeneas and the strife among the gods down from its pedestal into a familiar everyday sphere and presents it with an appeal for the sympathy or disapproval of the public. In this first section there are also indications that Chaucer tends to tone down features at variance with his own attitude; when for instance he relates Creusa's counsel to Aeneas to journey to Italy, he writes:

> And seyde he moste unto Itayle,
> As was hys destinee, sauns faille; (187 f.)

In this context, 'sauns faille'[1] serves to stress not Chaucer's own conviction but – as he later (427) expressly states – a faint doubt about this 'excuse'.

As soon as Chaucer begins the Dido-story itself (239 ff.) it is clear that this was the sole episode of importance to him. He alters his whole method of presentation. The facts and outward circumstances are now given briefly, to allow full scope for the psychological action. No longer content with brief asides, the narrator now steps forward to take his place beside his story, commenting on it, suggesting how it may be applied, plainly taking sides and giving his views. One is struck by this eagerness on Chaucer's part to appear as interpreter of his own story, his readiness in furthering his public's understanding of it and in directing their attention to certain aspects of it. There is an ironic contrast here, one attitude cutting across the other; we

[1] Cf. the slightly comic use of *'sauns faille'* in the *Man of Law's Tale* II, 501.

have the dreamer, naïve about what he notes and relates, and also the busy commentator, passing remarks on what he recounts, pointing out certain details and keen to use this episode for the edification of his public.

What, in fact, is Chaucer aiming at in this Dido-episode? In what tenor does he relate it, and in what light does he show Dido and Aeneas? A few lines are enough to tell how their love to one another came about and what course it took:

> And, shortly of this thyng to pace,
> She made Eneas so in grace
> Of Dido, quene of that contree,
> That, shortly for to tellen, she
> Becam hys love, and let him doo
> Al that weddynge longeth too. (239 ff.)

The '*brevitas*-formula'[1] (often employed here and such a favourite with Chaucer), and the topos of modesty or incapacity (247 f.) are only an excuse to pass quickly, almost scornfully, over this whole part of the Dido story dealing with the birth, upsurge and ecstasy of their love. Chaucer, unlike the poets of 'courtly love', is averse to expressing this love in 'lofty phrases'.

> What shulde I speke more queynte,
> Or peyne me my wordes peynte
> To speke of love? Hyt wol not be;
> I kan not of that faculte. (245 ff.)

He dismisses what Dido felt for Aeneas in a line where alliteration and rhythm emphasize the real intention of the words:

> Made of hym shortly at oo word
> Hyr lyf, hir love, hir lust, hir lord, (257)

In the very next lines Chaucer clearly quite abandons the attitude of an objective reporter, giving his own interpretation and verdict as he says of Dido:

> Wenynge hyt had al be so
> As he hir swor; and herby *demed*
> That he was good, for he such *semed*. (262)

The expressions *demed* and *semed* lead Chaucer on to a long

[1] W. N. Francis, 'Chaucer shortens a tale', *PMLA* 68 (1953).

discussion on 'appearance and reality', using Aeneas as an illustration. And two lines further on, he anticipates the later course of the episode with:

> For he to hir a traytour was;
> Wherfore she slow hirself, allas! (267)

Chaucer seems, then, in great haste to come to what is for him the real point of the tale. He has to leap forward in the story and tell us the end, and only takes it up in its chronological sequence at line 293. Aeneas as a worthless deceiver, a mean fellow who with scornful heartlessness deserts Dido after getting what he wanted; Dido on the other hand as meriting our pity, a tender though foolish and gullible creature easily deceived by a fine show – this is how Chaucer here presents these two famous lovers to us. He continues to break in with his own views and comments, in order to impress this interpretation on his public. He speaks of Dido's 'nyce lest' (287), (her foolish infatuation), states that she loved 'al to sone a gest' (288), and after he has let her lament at length, ends on a dry note:

> But that is don, is not to done;
> Al hir compleynt ne al hir moone,
> Certeyn, avayleth hir not a stre. (361 ff.)

Despite his aim of bringing this love-tragedy to the level of a human and individual story, Ovid had based Dido's lament on genuine feeling common to all mankind. Chaucer however gives us the plaintive lamentations of a girl of middle-class background who has been 'let down' by a man and now bitterly bewails the fact that 'all men are the same':

> Allas! is every man thus trewe,
> That every yer wolde have a newe,
> Yf hit so longe tyme dure,
> Or elles three, peraventure?
> As thus: of oon he wolde have fame
> In magnyfyinge of hys name;
> Another for frendshippe, seyth he;
> And yet ther shal the thridde be
> That shal be take for delyt,
> Loo, or for synguler profit. (301)

Widely applicable banalities of this sort bear no relation whatever to the disillusionment and passionate grief felt by a proud woman of royal blood as described by Virgil. The same, too, applies to Dido's laments at the loss of her good name and her fear of getting herself talked about. People would begin to murmur 'that she will no doubt do with others as she has done now' (358–60). Fame, which appears in Virgil as an independent figure, a mighty personified abstraction (*Aen.* IV, 174) is here reduced to a timorous reflection uttered by Dido herself. Dido's own references to *fama* (a bare hint of Virgil, *Aen.* IV, 321) are expanded by Chaucer into the commonplace anxiety of a woman careful of her good name. Her remarks, like the other passages, show how Chaucer reduces the stature of his lovers, stripping them of all heroism and grandeur. With a kind of shrewd everyday common sense he examines this famous love story under a magnifying glass, subjects it to a coldly disillusioned scrutiny and divests it of the last shreds of romanticism, greatness and magic which the episode may still have possessed at that period.

Chaucer was very well aware that Virgil had represented the episode in quite another way, above all in his unmistakably different portrayal of Aeneas.[1] But when it comes to the most significant point here, the behests of that fateful power which Aeneas was bound to obey before even his love, Chaucer only mentions these in a casual aside thrown out long after he had finished with the whole episode:

> But to excusen Eneas
> Fullyche of al his grete trespas,
> The book seyth Mercurie, sauns fayle,
> Bad hym goo into Itayle,
> And leve Auffrikes regioun,
> And Dido and hir faire toun. (427)

This explanation 'to excusen Eneas',[2] thus woven in at a later stage, throws light on Chaucer's attitude; and this is more clearly expressed in his *Legend of Dido* which deals with the same theme. In Virgil's version, Cupid in the guise of Ascanius

---

[1] Cf. *Aeneid IV*, 331 ff., 340, 361, 393 ff., 447 ff.

[2] For a different interpretation of these lines cf. Muscatine, p. 110.

causes Dido to fall in love (and in Chaucer's eyes this 'excuses' Dido); to this, Chaucer remarks:

> but, as of that scripture,
> Be as be may, I take of it no cure. (*Legend* 1144 f.)

It can of course be argued that in Ovid's *Heroides* Chaucer could see the episode detached from its epic and fateful historical connotation.[1] Ovid had already taken the 'heroism' out of Dido; she had forfeited the tragic greatness of Virgil's *Dido* and had acquired a sweet almost sentimental character. The affecting lament, a feature of all Ovid's *Epistles*, may have stimulated Chaucer to stress these aspects still further in his portrait of Dido, and to express them in her speeches, which form the chief part of the episode.[2] There were also hints here for Chaucer, showing Aeneas in the rôle of a perfidious seducer; these were enlarged upon in the *Roman de la Rose*, by Chrétien and by Machaut;[3] and they were furthermore represented in Germany by the Aeneas Romance and the *Eneid* of Heinrich von Veldecke. But all this is not enough to explain Chaucer's individual portrayal. What he has taken up here is the best-known love-story of the Middle Ages,[4] a courtly theme hitherto treated in a polished and conventional style; and what he makes of it – almost like a ballad-monger singing a murder-ditty – is a very ordinary love-affair, a tale not of some fateful entanglement but of the everyday weakness of men and women.

There is direct contrast to Virgil, then; and there is also noticeable divergence from Ovid. For all that, however, it is neither necessary nor appropriate to regard Chaucer's version as an intentional 'parody of Virgil' or as the 'travesty of a myth'.[5]

---

[1] E. K. Rand, *Ovid and his Influence*, 1925.

[2] Cf. also W. F. Schirmer, 'Chaucer, Shakespeare und die Antike', *Warburg Institute Lectures* 1930–1.

[3] Cf. *Roman de la Rose* 13192, Machaut, *Jug. Navarre* 2104, Chrétien, *Erec* 5342. This conception of Aeneas as a deceiver was supported by a tradition going back to Dares Phrygius and Dictys Cretensis, whereby the Greeks owed their capture of Troy to the treachery of Aeneas and Antenor. On the Dido story during the Middle Ages, cf. D. Comparetti, *Vergil im Mittelalter*, 1875; George Gordon, *Virgil in English Poetry*, British Academy Lecture 1931.

[4] Saint Augustine confesses that on reading the story of Dido he had once been so moved by her death as to forget for the time being to live *in Christo* (*Conf.* I. 1. 53).

[5] Cf. I. Besser, p. 63.

If this were so, then many parts of the *Legend of Good Women*, as well as other re-tellings of classical tales, would also have to be seen as a 'parody' or a travesty. In the case of a parody, some well-known author's typical themes, stylistic traits and conventions are so imitated and used that through radical alteration and exaggeration they offer a comic contrast with the original. But this is not what Chaucer does; he aims at re-telling the story from the very beginning in a new light, on a new plane and with a different intention. What emerges certainly contrasts with tradition and some comic effects may result from it. But the more the hearers or readers were familiar with the Dido story as originally presented, the better they would have been able to appreciate Chaucer's irony that flashes out both here and in the other Books of the *House of Fame*. Moreover, this humoristic effect is only one of many; and to try to see the story from this angle alone would be to take a very biassed view.

Chaucer follows up the Dido episode with a number of further examples of man's duplicity, taken from the classics: Demophon, Achilles, Paris, Jason, Hercules, Theseus. This fact, the narrator's way of expounding and passing judgment, and furthermore the edifying proverbs (272–90) scattered throughout the Dido episode, might lead one to conclude that this, too, is intended as an 'exemplum'. Dido and Aeneas seem both to be set before us as 'instances' illustrating some general truth. Yet although the story is presented to us in this way as an 'exemplum', Chaucer's real aim in narrating it thus was quite a different one.[1] Once more, something different, something new, is cast in a familiar form, and the expectations aroused by the word *exemplum* are only superficially met, while in reality Chaucer's purpose is entirely different.

It is useful to recall here that classical tales when introduced into longer poems almost always served as *exempla*.[2] They were retold so that their moral significance, the lesson derived from the course of events, might be unmistakably clear. The presentation of the medieval *exemplum* was therefore mostly limited to

---

[1] Muscatine (p. 109) notes the 'unsteady' moralization of the episode.

[2] J. Th. Welter, *L'exemplum dans la littérature religieuse et didactique du moyen âge*, 1927. W. Mosher, *The exemplum in the early religious and didactic literature of England*, 1911.

a re-telling of the bare facts; the narrative was in consequence
dry and colourless.[1]

Chaucer himself enters more into his Dido episodes than do
the authors of most medieval *exempla*. He does not merely limit
himself to facts; indeed, he puts things in such an individual light
that the atmosphere, the pitch, the manner of expression tell us
much more than the bare facts do. Another difference is that
whenever classical tales are used as *exempla*, we are always told
explicitly *why* they are brought in. The speaker or narrator
begins by clearly stating the proposition to be demonstrated,
and the wider context always makes it logically evident where
the *exemplum* is relevant. But there is no such explicit connection
in Chaucer. He does not tell us why man's *untrouthe* is to be
demonstrated here. We have as it were an *exemplum in vacuo*,
and are left to put the question 'why' for ourselves.

For Chaucer's *audience*, instances of man's – or woman's –
faith or inconstancy formed part of a controversy which had
become fashionable since the *Roman de la Rose* and in which
authors took sides. From this point of view the Dido episode
could be taken as an anticipation and prelude leading up to the
*Legend of Good Women*, in which Chaucer (often in similar
terms) gave further examples of innocent and patient women
shamefully abandoned by their husbands. As they heard Dido's
lament about men:

> O, have ye men such godlyhede
> In speche, and never a del of trouthe?
> Allas, that ever hadde routhe
> Any woman on any man! (330)

Chaucer's audience must have recalled this controversy and
realized that the rest of the examples added were part of that
dispute. It is obvious, however, that Chaucer himself did not
take this controversy seriously.

But this connection affects no more than the outermost of the
many layers which went to make up even Chaucer's earlier
works. If we look more closely, the verdict of *untrouthe* which

[1] Gower however is capable of making an *exemplum* live. At the same time it is
always quite clear why he narrates it. As well as Gower, Jean de Meun, Machaut
and others have included the Dido episode as an *exemplum*.

Chaucer like other medieval authors applies to the Dido episode, fits in with the derogatory and almost casual way in which he both treats and tells the story. Just as despite his fair-seeming actions, Aeneas is revealed as a miserable swindler, this whole familiar and cherished classical tale of love, when looked at with a keener eye, proves to be an instance of pitiable weakness. Chaucer is faced here with a story frequently idealized and romanticized; he surveys it now, drily and without illusion. Though humour and irony are present also, there is no doubt about this deeper basic intention. It does more than merely fit in with how Chaucer treats famous classical material elsewhere in his works. We can see the question of *trouthe* running through his whole poetry; it becomes a *leitmotif* in many of the *Canterbury Tales*, and it occupies a high place in his hierarchy of values. Chaucer has a light touch and knows how to entertain and amuse; but that does not mean that there is not any graver intention present beneath the surface. And this is already true of the *House of Fame*.

After Chaucer has quoted the examples of man's inconstancy which he appended to the Dido episode, he returns to the narrative technique of the first section.[1] Briefly and with obvious anxiety to finish with this task as soon as possible, he covers the rest of the *Aeneid*. He concludes his summary with a prayer addressed to Venus; and this brings us back full circle to the Venus temple at the beginning, reminding us of the presiding deity of the whole story. It would be an error however to assume from these and other references to Venus, either that Chaucer wishes to be regarded in the *House of Fame* as purely a love-poet,[2] or that the whole poem is a typical love-vision.[3] This pious address too – like all that had gone before – is not without its ironical side; once again, it is a convention with its symbols of value reversed.

[1] Paull F. Baum notes the alternation between portrayal and narration, *ELH* 8 (1941), p. 250 n. 3.
[2] Shelly, p. 73.
[3] Sypherd, *passim*.

## THE DESERT SCENE

A reversal like this of a typical convention occurs, too, in the following scene. When the dreamer has looked at everything in the temple, he marvels again at the 'noblesse of images' he has been contemplating 'in this chirche'. But he knows neither 'whoo did hem wirche, Ne where I am, ne in what contree!' (474). He therefore decides to go outside to find out something about it. Chaucer gives us here a typical dream-situation; it is only after he has looked at everything that the dreamer notices that he has no idea where he is; he then tries to get out. At this point Chaucer's public, familiar with the French love-visions, were faced with an unexpected development. For the temple of love stands in an expanse of desert, not in a splendid ever-green garden as tradition had it and as Chaucer represents it both in the *Parliament of Fowls* and (if we accept the glass room as corresponding to it) in the *Book of the Duchess*. The poet however does not state this fact outright, he arrives at this conclusion by induction and by taking up certain isolated hints. There are occasional instances in Italian and French literature of desert or inhospitable regions out of which the poet is led by a guide; yet one can hardly imagine a greater contrast to what one would expect for a temple of love than this setting.[1]

Chaucer steps, then, out of this magnificent temple of Venus; and finding that it stands in a desert, he is overwhelmed with a feeling of loneliness and impending disaster. This sequence speaks for itself. The scene is already a symbolic one, even without any allegorical interpretation or specific reference to its symbolism. The French poetry of Machaut and his contemporaries contains no such scenes with a direct and obvious symbolic content, frequent though they were in French romances of the twelfth century; nor does it contain scenes in which a situation is portrayed so vividly as something seen and experi-

---

[1] Cf. H. R. Patch, 'Chaucer's Desert', *MLN* 34 (1919). Patch does not arrive at any particular source for this situation in the *House of Fame*; similar themes can be traced, but in a different connection. For in the 'love visions' we have mostly a quickset hedge whose thorns prevent further progress. Dante's burning sandy plain in the *Inferno* (XIV, 8), and the 'selva oscura' at the beginning of the *Divine Comedy* are closer parallels. Comparison might also be made with Boccaccio's *Amorosa Visione* and *Corbaccio*.

enced at the time of writing. Here Dante's influence and perhaps that of twelfth-century poetry is again noticeable.

The Bible had already invested the desert with such a depth of symbolism that it is impossible to think that Chaucer set his temple of love in a desert without any reference to this episode. To see the desert as simply a suitable place from which the eagle may bear the poet heavenwards is to miss the symbolism here.[1] The desert in fact hints retrospectively at Chaucer's disillusionment over the famous classical love-story. But as an 'intermediate stage' too, on the poet's journey in the *House of Fame*, the desert has symbolic value. It expresses – as does the poet's appealing upward glance to heaven – helplessness and expectancy, a search for some escape from the present situation.

A certain solemnity hangs over the whole scene which ends with the appearance of the golden eagle, a greater seriousness than is the case with any other section of the poem. This is brought out, too, by the ejaculatory prayer to Christ, 'that art in blysse' (492). There are no ironic asides in this section; the earlier nervous restlessness in the style and presentation has given way here to an impressive poetic concentration. The first sight of the golden eagle in the height of heaven, close to the sun, and the vision of his overwhelming splendour, are described with an urgency and conviction that recall Dante, and indeed there are turns of phrase and images that echo the *Divine Comedy*. Yet this scene is in ironic contrast to the one that follows. In his distress, the poet utters a cry for help to Christ Himself; and what answers this cry is no heavenly messenger but the eagle of Jupiter. Besides, this bird reveals itself as a strange 'saviour in need'; a jovial, talkative and facetious guide, it brings the poet a peculiar kind of 'deliverance' in the shape of an entertaining excursion into the heavenly regions.[2]

Once more the question arises, can this ironic contrast – undoubtedly present – entitle us to deny the serious tone of the scene and to see nothing but a humorous intent in it? An antithesis of this sort between two mutually exclusive possibilities is common in present-day poetry. To be sure, Chaucer often mingles the grave with the gay and it appears that in his age

[1] Kittredge, p. 84.
[2] Cf. Malone, p. 54; Besser, pp. 85 ff.

the transition between them was easier, and the connecting links more close, than some later periods had assumed. Each of the three great poems considered in the present volume exemplifies this in its own way.


## THE SECOND BOOK

The second Book[1] is the most successful part of the whole poem. Its theme and presentation gave scope for some of Chaucer's particular talents of which there had so far been no more than occasional hints. Here we have instruction in a most entertaining and amusing form. Chaucer displays, too, his gift for letting observations and remarks spring naturally from an actual event – in this case a heavenward flight – as the result of a man's experience. At every stage this experience is shaped by the dramatic contrasting of eagle and poet; and the soliloquies, dialogues and speeches give it a directness very rare in the poetry of that period. But even this directness has something behind it; for this Book – even more than the first – draws upon the most divers models and themes, transforming them and linking them together in a very unexpected way. Behind the numerous lightly and as it were casually scattered allusions is an extensive literary tradition; instead of being a pompous, burdensome background, it is a plane to which Chaucer can refer back for his ironical contrasts and subtle effects. Nowhere in the work of Chaucer's early period do we ever again have so varied and amusing an instance of the poet's self-depreciation. As well as this delicate and often veiled irony however we have broad humour expressed in droll and comical effects. Every time we read it, this second Book delights us afresh.

When the eagle plunges from the heights to seize the poet in his talons, we see this happening from the standpoint of the dreamer who is thus caught up. It is worth noting, however, that the scene also includes what the eagle notes and does – and later what he feels and thinks. Surely Dante's influence must underlie

[1] The division into three Books was first made by Caxton and Thynne, not by Chaucer; he does however refer to what is now called Book Three as 'this lytel laste bok' (1093). On this matter, cf. Paull F. Baum, *ELH* 8 (1941), p. 249.

this description at once so precise, so realistic and yet so truly a part of experience. What influenced Chaucer in the *Divine Comedy*[1] was not the basic conception, the thoughts, the 'content'; it was Dante's method of presentation, the intensity, precision and perception with which he reproduced sensuous detail, visual impressions of movement and light for the most part, but also of sounds. Chaucer must have been impressed at discovering a poet who portrayed marvels and visions as if they belonged to reality, yet expressed his own reactions so vividly that everything seemed to be happening at that very moment and to himself. This in particular must have been what Chaucer was looking for, to further his own art; but it was not to be found among his French contemporaries. He gives us more of marvels and visions than they do. Yet at the same time he is at pains to make his marvels seem real. Dante preserves the sublime and lofty element in the rare wonders he relates, but with Chaucer they lose their remoteness in an atmosphere of everyday realism and semi-comic intimacy.

We can observe this process in the poem under discussion. The sublime spectacle of this eagle of unequalled splendour (501 ff.) and his swift descent like a thunder-storm in its might, cause amazement and fear and awake lofty expectations. Hardly however does this majestic and heavenly eagle open its beak, than it stands revealed not as some 'higher being', whose sublimity inspires fear, but simply as a bird whose behaviour and vigorous speech are clearly of this world. The 'descent', then, in this case represents another disillusionment, though of a different kind from that of the Dido episode.

Chaucer takes some time over the description of this mutual approach, before the eagle's first longer speech explains the significance of the abduction. There is some resemblance to the meeting between the dreamer and the knight in the *Book of the Duchess*; a human relationship is first set up and the speeches that follow are thus in context, not *in vacuo*. While it does away with the distance between the awe-inspiring figure of the eagle and the alarmed poet, however, and creates an atmosphere of general intimacy, this process of 'humanizing' the situation involves a

[1] On Dante's influence on Chaucer cf. J. L. Lowes, 'Chaucer and Dante', *MP* 14 (1917).

certain touch of irony. In the second Book this takes various forms and acts as it were at different levels.

At the very beginning the poet's self-depreciation was noticeable as something not to be found anywhere in contemporary or earlier French literature. Chaucer puts himself into an intentionally comic, almost ludicrous situation. In great alarm he hangs like a human rag-doll in the eagle's talons; from the start, then – and despite the eagle's reassuring remarks – he is in a position of pitiful inferiority where he hardly dares to contradict his companion. The poet's distress of mind is further underlined by the way in which the eagle roughly domineers over him (Awak! and be not agast so, for shame! 556–7), calling him a wearisome burden (Thou art noyous for to carye/And nothyng nedeth it, pardee! 574–5), and by his own fearfulness also (594). Irony of a different sort is introduced too in the poet's wordless prayer to God that Jupiter might spare him and not 'stellyfye' him, seeing that he was neither 'Ennok, ne Elye, ne Romulus ne Ganymede'. For to be translated to the stars was the very pitch of honour, and Chaucer is here declining it as a 'troublesome' distinction.[1] In this way he deliberately contrasts his unheroic self with the heroes of old. At the same time these lines bandy about mythological figures and honoured biblical names in one breath in a serenely ironical way; the theme of 'stellification' is boldly introduced here within the framework of the strange heavenward journey.

This dialogue between the eagle and the poet takes on further significance, moreover, when compared with Dante and Virgil in the *Divine Comedy*. (This work had of course already influenced the description of the visionary eagle descending out of the heavens.) Many of Chaucer's readers will have recalled the significance of the eagle-symbol and the mysterious and noble context in which it appeared in Dante; and they must have been aware of the incongruity between this lofty symbol (at the end of his first Book Chaucer had closely followed Dante) and the odd, comical role played by the eagle. Hardly has this 'disenchantment', this 'descent' taken place, however, when the bluff, friendly eagle who tries to soothe the poet with kindly words, is linked with another honoured figure in the *Divine Comedy*, with

[1] Cf. his renunciation of renown in Book III.

Virgil.[1] The somewhat harsh opening words with which the eagle shakes up the poet, half-dazed with fright (556), correspond to Virgil's admonitions to Dante to banish his fear;[2] and the eagle also shares with Virgil[3] his ability to read the thoughts of his protégé. There is more than one echo in what follows, too, of Virgil's part as comforter[4] and guide, as he tells Dante in advance of the great things he will be privileged to see on his journey through hell.[5] Moreover, the eagle's first reassuring words (556 f.) recall not only Dante but also the opening situation in Boethius's *De Consolatione*.[6]

In addition to this covert irony, the verses also contain an ironic reference to what lies close at hand. The eagle's first words to Chaucer echo Virgil's encouraging words of comfort; but their cadence also reminds the poet of 'oon I koude nevene' (562) – perhaps a reference to his wife. A comic touch is moreover added to the allusion by what is appended:

> For hyt was goodly seyd to me,
> So nas hyt never wont to be. (565 f.)

Chaucer's self-depreciation is very obvious here, in the eagle's first longer speech; and he gives it dramatic expression through his partner's words. In the four lines all beginning 'although', the eagle directs little home-thrusts at his opposite number. Despite a meagre understanding and a meagre reward (619, 621), the poet has been constant in the love-god's service; he was without practical experience however of the god's art (Although thou haddest never part, 628), and indeed was among those rejected by him (Although thou maist goo in the daunce/ Of hem that hym lyst not avaunce, 639 f.). The comic image of the poet, 'domb as any stoon' (656), sitting nursing a headache in his study (632) and obviously gleaning everything from books and nothing from life, together with the final ironical thrust

---

[1] The comparisons are made by Rambeau (*Englische Studien* 3, 1870); but he exaggerates their importance and draws faulty conclusions. Cf. also, for what follows, Besser, p. 96 f.

[2] *Purg*. IX, 46.

[3] *Inf*. X, 18; XXIII, 25; *Purg*. XIII, 76.

[4] *Inf*. II, 43 ff., 121 ff., *Purg*. IX, 46.

[5] *Inf*. I, 115 ff.

[6] Cf. in particular: 'Quid taces? Pudore an stupore siluisti . . . Nihil, inquit, pericli est . . .' (1, 2).

(Although thyn abstynence ys lyte, 660), is surely a most delightful humorous self-portrait, although admittedly a partial and artistic one.

There is self-depreciation, too, as well as irony directed against his partner, in the poet's terse and not over-grateful reaction to the eagle's pompous instructions. A monosyllabic 'Yis' (864) and 'Wel' (888) is his answer to the bird's polite questioning; and he rejects the further generous offer of instruction about the stars (Wilt thou lere of sterres aught? 993) by asserting: 'For y am now to old' (995). When the eagle makes another offer, he shows no interest whatever, even in a chance to see the stars for himself, saying that he can learn as much from his books and that moreover the dazzling light from the stars up there is injuring his eyes (1010–17). In thus professing himself satisfied to 'learn from books', the poet is of course contradicting himself, For he had said shortly before that having seen things for himself made him now able to believe what 'Marcian' and 'Anteclaudian' had written (985 ff.).

This same self-depreciation now[1] appears at yet another level; for during his heavenward journey – and here Chaucer uses quotations, allusions, contrast and comparison – the poet comes into contact with the most diverse figures from myth, history and literature, with Dante, Ganymede, Scipio, Boethius, and the Apostle Paul; and all serve for comparison or contrast. In this gay, colourful blending we can appreciate Chaucer's serenely playful attitude to even the most revered models.[2]

The eagle is not infrequently hailed by critics as a masterly creation of Chaucer's humour;[3] and this figure, as well as the role he plays, are shot through with irony of different sorts. This, Chaucer's first great comic figure, as he has been called,[4] cannot be reduced to a single formula, for his various qualities are in contrast with one another. He is a good-natured friend, concerned in a fatherly way for its protégé's well-being; but he

---

[1] On the particular type of irony present in this 'self-depreciation' cf. Earle Birney, 'The Beginnings of Chaucer's Irony', *PMLA* 54 (1939).

[2] Cf. Besser, p. 105.

[3] Kittredge's chapter on the *House of Fame* (Kittredge, pp. 86 ff.) contains what is still the best portrayal of the comic role played by the eagle. Cf., too, Muscatine, pp. 110–13.

[4] Shelly, p. 70.

is also a rough fellow, quick to take advantage of his 'hearer', hanging helpless in its talons. For now he can give rein to his passion for lecturing people; loquacious and tireless, he proceeds to indulge in this with comic complacency. He imagines, of course, that with his patronizing speech and innuendoes he is taking the poet down a peg or two. But that is just what the poet tersely and with a final rebuff is doing to the eagle; and in default of the right applause from his hèarer he is now obliged to sing his own praises (A ha . . . 865). Yet on the other hand the poet himself with his questions, ignorance and doubts 'malgré lui' repeatedly gives the eagle the chance to regale him with fresh information. It is most entertaining indeed, to watch these two, each in his role unconsciously working the other up. There is irony, too, in the eagle's gleeful satisfaction at having been able to explain the laws of sound so simply to his pupil:

> Withoute any subtilite
> Of speche, or gret prolixite
> Of termes of philosophie,
> Of figures of poetrie,
> Or colours of rethorike? (855)

For his own speech was not without 'subtilite' and 'prolixite'. Research has shown[1] that despite his contention, the eagle used no fewer than six of the ten tropes under the head of 'ornatus difficilis'; and in view of the fact that the 'ornatus difficilis' is only suited to noble and lofty themes, and not to 'laws of sound', this constitutes another instance of irony. It must however be said for the eagle that he does not obtrude his rhetoric; and on the whole he can congratulate himself on having given instruction that was simple to understand. Finally, a further ironic effect is contained in the eagle's protestations; though the messenger of Jupiter, he prefers to invoke the Christian saints. In the end the eagle himself shows that there is no need to take his pompously uttered proofs too seriously, for he concludes by directing the irony against himself and remarking 'Take yt in ernest or in game' (822).[2]

---

[1] Florence E. Teager, 'Chaucer's Eagle and the Rhetorical Colours', *PMLA* 47 (1932).

[2] H. L. Levy, 'As Myn Auctour Seyth', *Medium Aevum* 12 (1943).

It is only against the background of the heavenward journey – the main theme and framework of the second Book – that the irony in the portrayal of these two partners can be fully grasped. Chaucer himself refers with his 'Marcian' and 'Anteclaudian' (985 f.) to the great medieval models who had provided the pattern of such journeys. But there were others which served some great philosophical and noble aim, among them the heavenward journeys of Martianus Capella (*De Nuptiis Philologiae et Mercurii*, esp. Book VIII) and Alanus (*Anticlaudianus*), as well as the *De Universitate Mundi* by Bernhardus Silvestris, a work of prime importance in the Middle Ages. In Alanus's work for instance the journey signifies an ascent to the archetypes and the principles governing the creation of earthly things. Besides these models and the *Divine Comedy* already mentioned, Chaucer was able to draw upon journeys beyond this present world which the Middle Ages ascribed to great and holy men (Aeneas, Scipio, Alexander the Great,[1] St Brendan etc.). Wherever journeys to the heavens appear in medieval literature however, they always serve some specific noble aim and are treated as a 'lofty' theme.

There is no need to stress the fact that Chaucer's journey contrasts ironically with such models as these. No specific principle underlies it, nor is it built up on any system. It does not lead the poet into 'regions divine', but brings him to the 'Palace of Fame', a strange, grotesque place hardly suited to the heavens. What we have here is a complete reversal of the way in which this poetic theme had hitherto been treated; in a 'mock-heroic' vein it is now brought down to the level of the temporal and the trivial. We had seen heroes and saints caught up in ecstasy, but now we have a most unheroic character taking a pleasure-trip with a comic companion as his guide.

Not only the whole tone and mood, but also the express statement in the eagle's first longer speech, reveal that this was the purpose of the journey. The eagle states that Jupiter wishes to reward the poet with a journey to the House of Fame

> To do the som disport and game,
> In som recompensacion (664)

[1] Cf. F. P. Magoun jr., *The Gests of King Alexander of Macedon*, 1929.

and it therefore bids him be 'of good chere' (671). The eagle's jovial:

> Be seynt Jame,
> Now wil we speken al of game! (885)

is quite deliberately placed as an introduction to the very part of the journey which grants the poet an extensive view of the heavens from a height never attained by Alexander, Scipio or Daedalus (915). For its gay mood of enterprise contrasts all the more sharply with the later references to famous journeys either to the next world or flights into the heavens, to Cicero's *Somium Scipionis*[1] (906), Boethius (972), Martianus Capella (985) and Alanus de Insulis (968, 986). In his anxious uncertainty about his own situation the poet breaks out in phrases that almost directly echo St Paul's words in II Corinthians about being 'caught up to the third heaven',[2] while in the very next line we find (983) Chaucer following Dante.[3] Here again we have a passage that might sound blasphemous today but where the audience of that age saw nothing but a permissible degree of ironic light and shade.

The heavenward journey as newly conceived by Chaucer in this way also brings a novel feature, the 'interest of the journey', to the forefront. The poet spies eagerly about to see whatever is to be seen in and from the heavens. But what he sees is not linked up with any philosophical or didactic material; Chaucer was now concerned simply with observation as such, not with knowledge deduced from what might be perceived. When for instance the poet, looking down from the vault of heaven, says that the earth is no larger than 'a prikke' (907), this might have been an echo of the *Somnium Scipionis*.[4] In that work, however, the earth's minuteness is stressed solely to show how futile it is to strive for earthly fame. Chaucer makes his observation for its own sake.

[1] In view of Chaucer's reference to 'kyng Scipio' (916), it is possible that at this stage he was only indirectly acquainted with the *Somnium*.

[2] *II. Cor.* 12, 2: 'I knew a man in Christ above fourteen years ago (whether in the body, I cannot tell; or whether out of the body, I cannot tell: God knoweth;) such an one caught up to the third heaven.'

[3] When he mounts the hill of purification Dante admits to Virgil that his understanding was never so clear as at that moment (*Purg.* IV, 76).

[4] *Somnium* VI, 12. 'Prikke', however, might also derive from the *Consolatio* (II, Prose 7) cited at line 972.

Wherever any more serious speculations beyond the mere 'interest' of the journey are mentioned (985–90), the eagle interrupts these with an impatient:

'Lat be . . . thy fantasye!' (992)

It must be admitted that this observation and description of things seen during the journey through the heavens only begins after the eagle has spoken for 280 lines on the aim and purpose of the journey and has finished its exposition of the laws of sound. Only then are we reminded of the flight (And with this word upper to sore/He gan . . . 884). The journey, in fact, begins with a speech about the laws of sound and the topographical situation of the Palace of Fame; and it corresponds to the didactic moralizing explanations which formed the core of traditional journeys to the world beyond. But what a difference in the treatment of the didactic element! Not only are we concerned – as regards the material – with something totally unconnected with morals or philosophy or edification of any kind; in addition, the didactic material is offered in a light and entertaining form entirely in keeping with the spirit of the poem.

There is irony, besides, in the fact that a pure invention, a product of the unreal wonder world of allegory, should here derive support from scientific proof and the laws of physics. Science and logic are brought in to lend colour to a pure figment of the imagination; real factual observation is used to substantiate a castle in the air. Admittedly there are occasional instances in medieval writings of mythological conceptions being rationalized; but Chaucer is here carrying to ironic extremes the contrast between rational factual observations and what the imagination creates.[1]

In the eagle's speech Chaucer has achieved two things at the same time. He has parodied the bird's zeal to instruct (and there-

[1] H. L. Levy ('As Myn Auctour Seyth' *Medium Aevum* 12, 1943) considers that Chaucer's aim here is to criticize the favourite medieval mixture of science and poetic imagination; in particular he holds that the final rejection of the eagle's offer (to show him in reality each one of the constellations familiar to him from poetry) represents the poet's new attitude 'which refuses to mingle science with poetry and sees poetry as a realm of its own' (p. 34). But Chaucer himself goes on to blur this distinction – in so far as he makes it at all – by making science the subject of poetry.

fore medieval didacticism as well) on the score of complacency, prolixity and exaggerated self-importance. But at the same time he has managed to make the speech so entertaining and to convey its 'message' so unmistakably that there is nothing dry or difficult about it. We, too, much enjoy listening to the eagle; what he says has the directness of something addressed to a partner, both speakers being constantly present during this disquisition. Not only does the eagle season his remarks with emphatic phrases such as 'out of doute', 'withouten drede', 'parde' and 'ywis' and proudly stress the proofs he has to offer (loo thys ys my sentence etc.); he is also continually turning to his monosyllabic hearer, urging him to listen (Now herkene wel – take hede now), reminding him of what he already knows by experience (loo, thou maist alday se – Thou wost ful wel this – wel wost thou – thow shalt see wel), and recalling what he has already shown him (As I have before preved the 839, cf. 814, 823, 850); furthermore, he voices in advance any possible doubts or reactions the poet may have (e.g. Although thou thenke hyt a gret wonder 806). The 'thou' to whom he speaks comes alive, too, through his jocose and genial manner of address (beau sir, Geffrey, brother, my leve brother); and at the same time the many references to himself and his repeated 'I' (e.g. 725, 742, 750, 772, 782) bring him vividly before us as, consumed with zeal to instruct, he smugly pushes to the forefront. Though the poet speaks rarely and briefly, the form of dialogue is preserved and we can trace Chaucer's dramatic skill throughout; even during the long didactic speeches we always seem to see this strange pair before us.

In the final words of his exposition of the laws of sound the eagle refers with satisfaction to the 'empirical proof' (preve by experience 878, cf. 787) which is to follow and provide the needed support for what has been postulated. He had already mentioned many observations and experiments which anyone can make for himself in the world of nature (737, 774, 777, 788, 814). On the other hand the eagle makes use of the medieval method of logic, priding himself on his 'conclusions' 'skilles' and 'sentences', and basing his assertions on the authority of classical writers (Aristotle and daun Platon/And other clerkys many oon; 759). The exposition he gives is constructed like one of those 'problemata dialogues' which open with the question to be discussed (here, typically, it is the eagle himself who poses the question) and proceed with a sequence of logical 'conclusions' leading on to the final clarification. In his speech the eagle thus unites what are in fact two contrary methods of proof; and we find Chaucer being slightly ironical about each of them.[1] Moreover, he does not merely place them paradoxically side by side. When the eagle triumphantly concludes with:

> 'A ha!' quod he, 'lo, so I can
> Lewedly to a lewed man
> Speke, and shewe hym swyche skiles
> That he may shake hem be the biles,
> So palpable they shulden be. (865)

in reality he is involuntarily making fun of his own proof which he terms 'lewed'; for 'skilles' that are so palpable that one 'can shake them by the bill' amount to a comic contradiction in the sphere of abstract logic. We see, then, that Chaucer achieved a number of aims at once by his portrayal of the flight undertaken by these most dissimilar partners. Behind the talk between these two – highly entertaining even at surface-level – there flash out allusions, sly hints and overt references of many kinds. Yet all this contrives to appear as if happening by the way, only just touched upon in passing.

### FAME AND THE THIRD BOOK

At the end of the second Book the eagle, having put Chaucer down in front of the House of Fame, left him with a parting blessing; and the third Book follows straight on with Chaucer approaching the house which is then described.

The question of how the parts of the poem are connected recurs here once more. At the start of their flight the eagle had promised to bring the poet to the 'House of Fame' where he would hear 'moo tydynges' than one could possibly imagine (672 ff.). It had already been made clear that the main purpose

[1] Petrarch had already mocked at the 'conclusiunculas' of the dialecticians. (*Epistolae de rebus familiaribus* I, 6); cf. H. L. Levy, *Medium Aevum* 12 (1943), p. 35.

of the journey was to reach this source of 'tydynges'.[1] According to the eagle, this was how Jupiter proposed to reward the poet for his 'labour', his service of the love-god – especially as the poet had lived so secluded in his study that no 'tydynges' could penetrate to him, not even those of his immediate neighbours (647). After enumerating these 'tydynges' the eagle had added that Fame's palace was so situated that everything that was spoken was bound to reach it. The eagle's 'And so thyn oune bok hyt tellith' (712) had reminded the poet of the passage in Ovid where the 'arx' of Fame is described in detail (*Met*. XII, 38). So when in the third Book Chaucer now proceeds to describe the house of Fame, we expect him to portray this place to which everything that is spoken penetrates. Once again, however, we are disappointed; for *this* house of Fame does not contain those many 'tydynges' promised to the poet; it is the allegorical dwelling of Fame who is then described with the court she keeps. The 'tydynges' are in another house not far off, the revolving 'House of Rumours'.

At the end of his visit to the house of Fame the poet himself admits that in a sense he has come to the 'wrong' place:

> For certeynly, he that me made
> To comen hyder, seyde me,
> Y shulde bothe here and se,
> In this place, wonder thynges;
> But these be no suche tydynges
> As I mene of. (1890)

There is, then, some contradiction between what the second Book announces and what the third proceeds to offer. The use Chaucer makes of the passage from Ovid already cited, indeed, bears this out; for in the second Book Chaucer began by borrowing from Ovid for his house of Fame, but in the third he now uses this same passage for the house of Rumours and not for the house of Fame.[2] All this throws light on Chaucer's way of going to work; the composition of the *House of Fame* is clearly based on experiment and improvisation. It was only while he was

---

[1] R. C. Goffin's contention is that by 'tidinges' Chaucer meant 'new stories' ('Quiting by Tidinges in the *House of Fame*', *Medium Aevum* 12, 1943).
[2] Cf. E. F. Shannon, *Chaucer and the Roman Poets*, 1929, p. 81.

writing that it seems to have occurred to Chaucer that he could insert a description of Fame and her court before he came to the end of the journey (the house of 'tydynges'). Fame appears, however, to signify glory and renown rather than rumour; her palace is an allegorical picture representing the transitory and delusive quality in all earthly renown.[1] So we find that Chaucer has split the idea of 'fame' into the two chief meanings always implicit in it.[2] By describing Fame's palace he could at one and the same time enrich his poem, prolong his journey,[3] link up again with a well-known literary convention of medieval allegorical poetry, and materially expand the critical and ironic gloss on human weaknesses and common situations which runs through his whole poem. Though Chaucer probably owed his nearer acquaintance with the idea of Fame to the Italian Renaissance, his portrayal contrasts with the Renaissance conception of it. And this divergence throws so strong a light on Chaucer's own basic attitude that it is worth while comparing his conception of fame with that of the Italian Renaissance.

'Fame' was not one of the typical personified abstractions known to the medieval world. In art, which faithfully mirrors the range of allegorical conceptions, Fame does not appear until the close of the Middle Ages,[4] and most representations date from the fifteenth century. The Middle Ages knew the personified figure of Fame only through Ovid, Virgil and Statius; and this figure represented not so much renown 'Gloria' as rumour, reputation, report.

It may have been in Italy that Chaucer first met with this new conception of Fame.[5] He may have gained some idea there of what renown, and the desire of it, meant to writers, and he may

[1] The palace stands on an icy rock – that is, on an unsure foundation; on one side the sun has already melted away the names inscribed there. The palace is built of 'Beryll' which makes everything appear larger than it really is (1290).

[2] Cf. the article on 'fama' in '*Thesaurus Linguae Latinae*', and 'fame' in the *NED*.

[3] In the Middle Ages allegorical journeys were not so composed that the travellers might arrive at their goal as soon as possible; they were expected to see as much as they could on the way!

[4] Cf. R. van Marle, *Iconographie de l'Art Profane*, 1932, p. 124 ff. Supplementary references to representations of Fame on fifteenth-century 'Cassoni' are given by P. Schubring, *Cassoni*, 1915, Nr. 201, 209, 583, 589.

[5] Cf. Jacob Burckhardt, 'Modern Fame' in *Civilization of the Renaissance in Italy*.

perhaps have heard of the ceremony at which Petrarch received the poet's crown. Yet when he came to portray Fame he clearly dissents from this glorification of personal renown; he does not see Fame as something splendid, an object of aspiration. Once again, he probes the real content of an ideal notion and brings it down to earth.

The difference is obvious in the very construction of Chaucer's palace of Fame.[1] This is no 'temple of renown' like the later versions of Mount Parnassus and 'Walhalla'. Chaucer does not place the poets in the House of Fame by virtue of their own renown (though they are called 'folke of digne reverence'), but because they serve Fame by handing on and keeping alive the record of 'fame', the remembrance of celebrated episodes and figures. Chaucer repeatedly stresses this (1435, 1461, 1472) by saying that these poets are there 'to bere up the fame'.

In placing his poets on pillars made of various metals which stand for the different content of the 'matere' each of them treats, Chaucer is portraying the medieval conception of the poet. The poet and the historian both hand on the 'record' of great events and famous men; but for them we should know nothing of Achilles, or Troy, or Caesar.

If however we look at comparable Italian versions we shall not find the poet fulfilling this subservient role. Here he is exalted in his own person. Boccaccio for instance in the *Amorosa Visione* describes the poets and heroes in magnificent wall-paintings with the object of extolling them; and in his gallery of poets (*Inf.* IV, 76) Dante had assigned them a place of honour within the semicircle ringed with fire, by virtue of their *posthumous renown*. For the most striking instances of this conception of renown in the sense of personal glorification we may look to the Italian *trionfi*;[2] these aim not so much at presenting the allegorical personified abstractions as at introducing the famous figures in their suite.[3] Behind the ranks of illustrious kings, heroes and statesmen which pass before us in both Petrarch's *Trionfo della Fama* and Boccaccio's *Amorosa Visione*,

---

[1] On parallels between this palace and medieval art cf. Karl Brunner, 'Chaucer's *House of Fame*', *Rivista di Letterature Moderne I*, 1950-1.

[2] Cf. Werner Weisbach, *Trionfi*, 1919.

[3] Cf. Viscardi, *Petrarca e il Medio Evo*, n.d., p. 79 ff.

we can discern the concept of 'greatness'; it is a concept belonging to more recent times than Chaucer's age, and he would never have accepted it. Petrarch[1] portrays his famous figures in a spirit of wrapt reverence for their illustrious greatness; but Chaucer adopts a sceptical attitude and is critical and matter-of-fact towards the numerous figures in his palace of Fame. It is true that in the case of the strange and motley collection he brings together here one thinks not so much of 'gloria' as of 'note', 'notoriety', 'publicity'. Besides Orpheus, Orion and other harpists in the niches on the outer wall, there is a countless multitude of players on pipes, flutes, horns and trumpets. Here, in other words, we have (in pictorial form) the 'trumpet of renown', the 'blazing abroad of tidings'. In addition there are also tumblers, jugglers, magicians, and witches, among them Medea, Circe, Calypso, Simon Magus, etc. This swirling bustle with the most varied callings and names is not there to glorify any particular single individual, but to give us an entertaining picture of the motley throng that makes up Fame's huge retinue. Many of these retainers act indeed as Fame's servants. Like the great poets from Homer to Claudian who later appear within the palace, they help to spread 'reports', to create excitement, arouse interest, and extol the 'famous ones'. Obviously, then, Chaucer's idea of 'fame' puts the accent as much on 'report' or general 'reputation' as on genuine 'renown'.[2] For among the many figures he names Chaucer mentions only two who are genuinely there by virtue of their 'renown', 'Of thoo that hadde large fame: Alexander and Hercules' (1412 f.). These two however stand on Fame's shoulders; they have no need of the poets to spread their 'fame' abroad.

How differently, too, Chaucer describes Fame herself! She is no august and noble lady, like Boccaccio's Gloria or Petrarch's Fama, but is represented as a capricious creature commanding no respect whatever and indeed a laughing-stock for the poet. Her ugliness, her fickle and uncertain character, were of course traits already to be found in Virgil's description of Fame. Besides, the medieval figure of Fortune, similar in some respects

---

[1] For Petrarch's views on renown, cf. H. W. Eppelsheimer, *Petrarca*, 1926.

[2] On the contrary, Petrarch's *Trionfo della Fama* shows that for him the central idea in fame was 'gloria'.

to Chaucer's Fame, served to bring these traits into greater prominence;[1] indeed, Chaucer himself draws attention to the likeness when, speaking of Fame, he mentions 'her sister, dame Fortune' (1547). After all, however, these elements represent only the material from which Chaucer built up something essentially his own – a spiteful, fickle woman, a very strange object indeed in the gallery of personified abstractions to be found in medieval literature.

Fame is the only personified abstraction – besides Nature in the *Parliament* – which Chaucer describes in any detail; and yet the 'Fame' that he gives us has ceased to be a personified phantom and has become a strange, slightly grotesque and common creature, envisaged as a quite ordinary human being. She, like the golden eagle, is a 'character'; there is a touch of humour about the way she is presented. A glance at the allegorical presentation of personified abstractions in French poetry is enough to make the distinction clear. Chaucer has none of the accompanying figures usually symmetrically grouped around, no speeches designed to expound the *allegoresis*, no systematic interpretation of allegorical detail, no admonitions and no didactic injunctions to either the poet, the petitioners or the 'subjects'. Instead, we have the comic pungent retorts of a shrewish scold; and they sound most strange in the mouth of a personified abstraction. Not even the speeches of *Vieille* or *Faux-Semblant* in the second part of the *Roman de la Rose* can be said to equal this creature's coarse abuse:

> 'Fy on yow,' quod she, 'everychon!
> Ye masty swyn, ye ydel wrechches,
> Ful of roten, slowe techches!
> What? false theves! wher ye wolde
> Be famous good, and nothing nolde
> Deserve why, ne never ye roughte?
> Men rather yow to hangen oughte!
> For ye be lyke the sweynte cat
> That wolde have fissh; but wostow what?
> He wolde nothing wete his clowes. (1776)

[1] W. O. Sypherd, p. 117 f. On the contrast between Fame and the conventional and 'high' context cf. Muscatine, p. 114.

Chaucer must have been prompted by his artistic temperament to move these abstract personifications into living persons realistically portrayed; but this line of development is evident also in the French literature of the following century.[1] We can trace it already in Langland (e.g. Sloth). It exemplifies a late medieval tendency already remarked upon by Huizinga;[2] this was to reduce every concept to a tangible form, to find specific images that would express the world of their ideas. Chaucer's Fame deserves to rank with Langland's personified abstractions as one of the first examples within English literature of this development. On the other hand Lydgate, who gives us many personified abstractions, is at pains to preserve the artificial and didactic qualities of the older allegories. Later, about the turn of the century, Skelton's upsurge of new realism finally shattered the rigid mould in which the allegorical figure had set.[3] The personifications in his *Bowge of Court* are typical characters from everyday life envisaged as real people; the only thing about them that recalls their allegorical origin is their names.

Chaucer's treatment of Virgil's well-known passage on Fame can well illustrate this 'humanization of allegorical concepts'. Virgil wrote:

> parva metu primo, mox sese attollit in auras
> ingrediturque solo et caput inter nubila condit.
>
> (*Aen.* IV, 173)

and Chaucer alters this to:

> For alther-first, soth for to seye,
> Me thoughte that she was so lyte
> That the lengthe of a cubite
> Was lengere than she semed be.
> But thus sone, in a whyle, she

---

[1] There are examples in Chastelain, Jean Molinet, Charles d'Orléans, Francois Villon etc. In Charles d'Orléans, for instance, Mélancholie is represented as an old nurse leaning on a stick, Soupir as a beggar, etc. Cf. P. Champion, *Histoire poétique du XVe siècle II*, 1923, pp. 42 ff.

[2] Huizinga, *Waning of the Middle Ages*, Ch. XII.

[3] On this aspect of Skelton cf. Schirmer, *Geschichte der englischen Literatur* I, 1959, pp. 174, 194. On the whole development of allegory in this connection, cf. C. S. Lewis, *The Allegory of Love*.

Hir tho so wonderliche streighte
That with hir fet she erthe reighte,
And with hir hed she touched hevene,
Ther as shynen sterres sevene. (1368)

It is characteristic of him to omit the *metu* which in Virgil is so significant. However, Chaucer indicates the varied gradations of size more precisely, with a real delight in noting and measuring. Virgil's Fame, an imposing mythical figure flying far and wide by night, is turned into a grotesque creature; what had been strange becomes merely freakish, and the impressive grandeur of Virgil's Fame is quite lost. Chaucer's Fame remains seated on her throne, too, with the result that the constant changes in size which had suited Virgil's portrayal now have a comic effect. The same thing happens as in the case of the golden eagle; Chaucer brings the creatures of his poetic imagination into our very midst, right down to everyday level, and reduces the super-human to our human proportions.

He is not content however with simply describing Fame to us; he goes on to portray her dramatically by means of several scenes in which different groups of petitioners appear before her. What we have here is one of the best examples from Chaucer's early poetry of how he takes various abstract items and trans-poses them into a succession of highly entertaining, amusing and lively events. Kittredge has drawn attention to the precise design, 'a model of schematic precision', underlying these delightful scenes, systematically graded to exploit all the variations of Fame's capricious behaviour. At the same time, however 'we forget the schematism in the liveliness of the narrative'.[1] Chaucer certainly did not merely wish to amuse us, to make us laugh; he wanted to illustrate a moral fact, to portray a 'living truth'. But he disguises his intention in so subtle and entertaining a way, he so rivets our attention by the realism and humour in each of his scenes, that we are scarcely aware how all this while a comprehensive and exact criticism of various varieties of human weakness is going on beneath the surface.

The dramatic element is not limited to the picture of Fame confronting her petitioners. We have a 'three-cornered' drama,

[1] Kittredge, pp. 94-6.

indeed; for at this point Aeolus, the god of the winds, is brought in; the different kinds and colours of smoke that issue from his trumpet serve as 'illustrations' to Fame's abstract pronouncements. But Aeolus has first to be fetched by a messenger of Fame; and this allows for a description both of his dwelling in Thrace (where he holds the winds so forcibly in check 'That they gonne as beres rore' (1589), and also of how he is summoned. We find this opportunity to bring in a comic touch at once exploited:

> And he anon
> Tok to a man, that highte Triton,
> Hys clarions to bere thoo,
> And let a certeyn wynd to goo,
> That blew so hydously and hye
> That hyt ne lefte not a skye
> In alle the welken long and brod. (1595)

Here, as in the Ceyx episode from the *Book of the Duchess*, or in the Dido episode, the gods of old appear in a comic light; Chaucer gaily works his own playful will with the apparatus of mythology and strains its themes and devices till they become grotesque.

Throughout this scene the poet is present both as narrator and as witness. He wonders at Fame's capricious behaviour (1543), expresses his sympathy for the seekers after fame who are so unjustly treated (1631), and shows what he thinks of Fame's decisions by an apt gesture (with that aboute y clew myn hed, 1702). At the end, however, he is drawn into the action, for he is asked what is his own attitude to the all-important question at issue. When a friendly stranger inquires 'Artow come hider to han fame?' (1872), he replies:

> I cam noght hyder, graunt mercy,
> For no such cause, by my hed!
> Sufficeth me, as I were ded,
> That no wight have my name in honde.
> I wot myself best how I stonde;
> For what I drye, or what I thynke,
> I wil myselven al hyt drynke,
> Certeyn, for the more part,
> As fer forth as I kan myn art. (1874)

This passage forms as it were the serious epilogue to the humorous scenes which had gone before. Speaking for himself, Chaucer renounces the fame which the whole preceding portrayal had been designed to prove as vain and fortuitous. He has no use for a Fame so capricious, unreliable and incalculable.[1] 'I wot myself best how I stonde' is perhaps the most personal statement that Chaucer makes in the whole poem. It witnesses to a natural self-reliance which Chaucer here puts in the place of personal ambition or self-glorification. However this self-confidence is also characteristic of a new era.

In this work, however, it is not renown but 'tidings' that the poet is seeking. At the close of the scenes in the palace of Fame we now see him joining in the action, raising an almost peremptory voice to express this as yet unsatisfied demand (see the quotation on page 153). In this way Chaucer reminds us again of the real 'aim' of the journey. His unknown friend therefore leads the seeker to the House of Rumours. Here Chaucer's portrayal reaches a pitch of inventive imagination. The palace of Fame had drawn upon medieval tradition in the description of allegorical palaces; but this wickerwork house has nothing in common with traditional allegorical detail.[2] The House of Rumours belongs at once to fancy and to reality. With that 'realism of the unreal' so often evident in his early work, Chaucer describes this house for us with such a wealth of factual detail and such vividness that the poet seems to be speaking from his own experience.

Many possibilities have been advanced about the nature of these 'tidings' which quite obviously were to have been revealed at the end of the poem by the 'man of gret auctorite'.[3] One theory frequently put forward is that Chaucer wished to retail some precise news of the court – possibly some scandal – and that for

[1] Kittredge (p. 97) has warned us not to read this passage outside its context and imagine that Chaucer 'renounces fame altogether'.

[2] Sypherd points out that there were indeed wickerwork houses and also (in saga and folk-tales) those that constantly revolved. But the combination of these elements with an allegorical aim and with Ovid's descriptive material is without precedent.

[3] Cf. A. Brusendorff, *The Chaucer Tradition*, 1925; R. Imelmann, *Englische Studien* 45 (1912); John Koch, *Englische Studien* 41 (1909); B. H. Bronson, 'Chaucer's *House of Fame*: Another Hypothesis', *Univ. of California Publ. in English*, 3 (1934); F. C. Riedel, *JEGP* 27 (1928).

this reason the poem remained unfinished. But Chaucer repeatedly stressed the extraordinary variety of the things to be heard in the House of Rumours (674 ff. 1960 ff.). The 'tydynges' enumerated in the second and also in the third Book read like a colourful survey that covers every conceivable event and theme in human life. Love is spoken of, but is by no means the only theme mentioned.

### THE HOUSE OF FAME: A GENERAL APPRAISAL

It is impossible either to deny or specifically to prove that the *House of Fame* was written as an 'occasional poem' and concerned with some precise situation at court. The possibility must be borne in mind – again, proof is out of the question – that in the conclusion which has not come down to us, Chaucer said something that could be linked with a piece of 'court news' or even with the actual occasion that prompted the poem. Yet even if some day the explanation of these allusions should rise beyond the level of mere conjecture, this would have no more than a superficial effect on the work and would do little to further our understanding of its poetic aim and significance. The *House of Fame* continues to live and have its own manifold meaning for us even though the problem of what actually prompted it should never be solved.

We are more likely to give this poem its rightful place in Chaucer's whole output if we do not limit the question of the news which the poet is to learn at its close merely to some 'court news'. We ought to give due weight to the arguments and details which when referring to these 'tydynges' Chaucer himself provided (644 ff., 2007 ff.) through the mouth of his eagle. These seem to suggest that in this poem Chaucer was giving expression to his longing for new material which should be taken from life itself. It is significant that as their journey begins the eagle reminds Chaucer how he does not even know the news about his own neighbours, who live 'almost at his doors'; for he is no sooner back from his 'rekenynges' than he buries himself in his books again and lives like a hermit (649 ff.). The design of this first Book, indeed, appears to suggest this point. Immediately after he has retold the *Aeneid* episodes, one of the best known pieces of 'literary material', the poet is borne upwards by the eagle to regions where he sees and experiences something entirely new. We may further submit that at this time Chaucer's thought was beginning to turn in the direction of the *Canterbury Tales*; indeed, he may even have had the general scheme of that work in his mind. And the *Canterbury Tales* are stories which despite a good deal of borrowing from literary sources spring in the main from Chaucer's own experience and seek to seize and hold life's colourful abundance – exactly the sort of material that he gives us here in the second and third Books. It would of course be too much to read into this 'wish for new tidings' any idea that Chaucer is turning altogether away from 'books'. (In any case this would hardly be conceivable in a medieval writer.) But Chaucer does realize that books can only speak to the man who brings some experience of life to them. He seeks to supplement the wisdom culled from books by bringing it into contact with the reality of life.

We must keep this basic intention in mind when we consider some specific features of the revolving house of tidings and rumours. All the 'tydynges' reach that house directly, in a fresh, unmixed condition. The poet is here at the fountain-head, as it were, and can experience everything for himself. But he can also see how the false and the true are mingled, how on arrival rumours are at once blown out to gigantic proportions. Moreover, once the 'tydynges' leave the revolving house, they pass on to Fame who treats them 'after hir disposicioun', further adulterating and exaggerating them or perhaps suppressing them altogether (2110 ff.).

What the poet sees and learns in the house of rumours and tidings is in tune with the disillusioned, cynical and critical attitude displayed by Chaucer in some form or other in all three Books. The palace of Fame was a 'Vanity Fair'; and now the house of rumours again shows us the way of the world, how truth and falsehood are almost inextricably mingled. Each time some piece of news is passed on it is distorted (2065). Although they swear they are speaking the truth (2051), those who make up the huge bustling throng, whispering or openly telling one another some piece of news, are not genuinely trying to find out the real truth; they are all merely adding to the general confusion and distortion of facts. In spite of all the humour in these scenes with their lively dialogues, there is real and sometimes cutting satire here, a criticism of human weaknesses that runs through the whole poem. The poet's journey is over and he has gained what he had wanted; and yet a certain paradox remains: He is now in the midst of a vast mass of tidings, and he has received at least part of what the eagle had promised him. He realizes, however, to what an extent deceit and guile prevail even here. The longing for 'truth', it seems, cannot in the last instance be satisfied.

We were led to the view that in the *House of Fame* Chaucer was expressing his desire for fresh material, for a poetry to a greater degree shaped by actual experience. Yet this does not mean that we should think of the work as a pronouncement of a new literary aim or an attempt to explain the whole poem purely along those lines. There are more personal traits, more 'self-portrayal', in Chaucer's early poems than in the works of his contemporaries; he was not the man, however, to think of writing a 'confession'. What we have here is a wish-dream compounded of a mixture of grave and gay, its *action* built up on a journey to the house of Fame but its *content* going far beyond these limits.

If, however, we look at the *action* of the poem from this point of view, we can see how the first Book sets the stage at the beginning for the journey to the house of Fame, the second gives us the journey itself with a preparatory explanation of the topographical situation, and the third describes the arrival and the two-fold goal of the journey – the palace of Fame and the house of tidings. A scheme of this sort would establish sufficient connection between the individual parts; and the design of the allegorical journey itself (see p. 137) ensures continuity of incident within the poem. Much has been added however to this basic structure – in rather the same way as the copious variety of late Gothic decoration often shrouds and masks the shape of a late medieval building. The *House of Fame* is an example of the typical style of an outgoing period, one that derives a wealth of themes and elements from the rich cultural and literary tradition behind it.

It would therefore be hopeless to attempt to reduce the content or the aim of the *House of Fame* to some common denominator.[1] We have already noted (see p. 106) that neither love nor the 'poet of love' can be considered adequate as a central theme. Nor does the 'search for tidings' suffice as the sole and principal theme; for we cannot see it as a logical reason for either the elaborate portrayal of Fame in the third Book or the eventful journey and the conversations during the flight in the second Book.

Finally, what about Fame itself? Dido's own words about 'wikke Fame' (349) establish some connection between the Dido episode and Fame as represented in the third Book; but the link is too feeble for us to see Chaucer's re-telling of the Dido story as an instance of what Fame can bring about.[2] Chaucer seems to touch on this theme at the end of the Dido episode purely for the sake of linking up again with the title and the aim of his poem. Besides, our interpretation surely demonstrated that his real aim in recounting this episode lies on a different plane. Furthermore, how are things seen in heaven and on earth, the 'observations' made during the journey, to be explained if one remains strictly limited to the theme of Fame? None of these attempts to interpret along the lines of *one* single theme can do more than carry us some part of the way. They cannot satisfy, because when he began his poem and as he continued to write it, Chaucer's mind was quite obviously occupied with more than one idea. There are several sides to his intention, and it cannot be reduced to any simple formula such as 'Love', 'Fame', or 'Tidings'.

The *House of Fame* relates an amusing adventure; yet beneath the surface we can clearly distinguish the conflict between *auctoritee* and *truth*, between what is handed down and a man's personal experience; this is a theme that runs through the whole of Chaucer's early work. The early poems start from a background of literary tradition, conventional subjects, themes already moulded by much treatment in the past; yet all this material is presented in a spirit directly contrary to convention. Undoubtedly there is more than a humorous or ironic intention

---

[1] 'It could be worse than churlishness to comb this fascinating poem for incoherencies, were it not that incoherency is the central fact of its character.' Muscatine, p. 114.

[2] Cf. Paul G. Ruggiers, 'The Unity of Chaucer's *House of Fame*', SP 50 (1953).

in all this; for in itself it postulates a new critical attitude to poetry, a new consciousness, a new freedom. In other words, the *House of Fame* is a typical poem of a transitional period. A new content is to be expressed within a traditional framework; and fresh motives replace what had governed the use and purpose of former themes.

### STYLE AND MANNER OF PRESENTATION

This process is also evident in the style and manner of presentation; and to this we now return in conclusion. A specific technique of presentation had so far dominated allegorical poetry. Each theme was taken separately, and treated according to a very definite plan. Descriptions were not usually given from the observer's point of view; the poet did not put himself in the place of someone gradually becoming aware of some new object step by step, and relating what he has to say as if from personal experience and observation. Instead, description followed a plan already laid down, the items following one upon the other. Medieval treatises on 'Poetics'[1] provided this method of description with certain specific models as well as a theoretical basis. In the Middle Ages it was adherence to these precepts rather than faulty artistry that divided not only allegorical poetry into strictly segregated sections in which each theme was sharply distinguished from its neighbours. This kind of subdivision was fully in line with the need for a clearly regulated and systematic type of presentation; but a story told just as it came without method or plan and dealing with several themes together, could not possibly come into being in these conditions.

Chaucer was perfectly familiar with medieval descriptive techniques and knew how to apply them.[2] In this field too he represents a transitional stage. Several passages in his work make it clear that he was seeking new methods of presentation and was trying to replace strict order and sequence by a principle

[1] Cf. Faral, *Les Arts Poétiques du XIIe et du XIIIe Siècle*, 1924. Claes Schaar, *The Golden Mirror, Studies in Chaucer's Descriptive Technique and its Literary Background*, 1955. This last cites other relevant works.

[2] Cf. Manly, *Chaucer and the Rhetoricians*, 1926; Cf. Schaar, *The Golden Mirror*, 1955.

of freer associations, easy transitions, and constant variety in the method of presentation.

At several points – when the poet wakes in the temple of Venus, or when he is borne off in the desert – we had seen how Chaucer describes everything that happens to him just 'as he sees it'. He tells us how he himself grows aware of something, drawing nearer to it step by step. He projects himself into the state of someone gradually getting to know something completely new to him, observing it at first in a detached way, then pondering and noting what he is seeing, and finally drawing his conclusions. The process of seeing and observing also recurs again and again in the episode of the flight. 'Now see . . . yond adoun,' the eagle admonishes the poet, who in turn obeys this injunction with the same expressive words:

> And y adoun gan loken thoo,
> And beheld feldes and playnes, . . . (896)

This is repeated again and again (912, 925, 927, 933, 935, 964); we seem to be present as the poet follows the eagle's orders and looks now upwards, now down, observing things far and near.

In this connection the poet's method of describing the palace of Fame is particularly revealing. Chaucer breaks up the rigid pattern of stereotyped and systematic allegorical description,[1] transmuting it into a free narrative style. He singles out smaller individual features from the usual continuous description of the palace and makes use of them here and there in the course of his tale.

Much of the description of the palace had been anticipated in the eagle's preparatory speech. The poet divides the well-known passage from Ovid on Fame's dwelling into a succession of concrete items and inserts one from time to time until the whole of Ovid's description has been utilized. The first hundred lines of the third Book which deal with the poet's arrival at the palace of Fame offer a very clear example of this kind of portrayal

---

[1] For instance, in the description by Alanus de Insulis of the house of Fortuna we have a long antithetical passage, 'magnificent' matched with 'wretched', 'rich' with 'poor', and a whole succession of contrasting pairs of words. (Alanus ab Insulis, *Anticlaudianus*.) Chaucer's description contains only one such antithesis that could recall Alanus, namely the contrast between the sunlit and the shaded sides of the rock of ice.

'from the subject's point of view'. Chaucer painfully climbs up the rock and tries to find out what kind of stone it is made of. In the end he sees that it is *ice*, and thereupon he reflects:

> 'By seynt Thomas of Kent!
> This were a feble fundament
> To bilden on a place hye.
> He ought him lytel glorifye
> That hereon bilt, God so me save!' (1131)

Here we see Chaucer allowing the allegorical significance as it were to come by chance to light as a result of supposition and observation.

The additional 'allegorical' features of Fame's palace interspersed here and there (1136, 1288, 1297) are also evidence of this new and unobtrusive manner of presenting allegorical material. The allegorical element fades before the interest in fanciful description and witty invention, much of it apparently based on actual experience. Indeed, it must surely have been an eye accustomed to late Gothic architecture that built up the castle with its countless turrets, pinnacles, galleries, windows and other elaboration of detail.[1]

Even Fame's allegorical nature seems a by-product of her behaviour, of the 'action'. Chaucer makes no attempt to follow usual practice; this would have set this personified abstraction before us and interpreted all her peculiarities, using her appearance and her 'courtly state' to illustrate each of her essential characteristics in turn.

With Chaucer it is the speaker, the 'I' himself, who observes events and objects for himself, who presents them as impressions, not as facts. This comes out in the little personal asides with which the poet tells us what he supposes and expresses his amazement and his opinions in general. When he is swept up into the air by the eagle, we are told for instance:

> How high, I can not telle yow,
> For I cam up, y nyste how. (547)[2]

This acuteness in perceiving and observing is matched by the

---

[1] Cf. Joan Evans, 'Chaucer and Decorative Art', *RES* 6 (1930).
[2] Cf. 582, 499.

wealth of impressions received. Scarcely any other of Chaucer's poems is so rich in concrete detail. Caught up on this unusual heavenward journey, the poet observes and sees more than his predecessors had done on their flights. The third Book in particular with its description of the palace of Fame and the house of rumours conveys an impression of amazing and colourful variety, a flashing, whirling abundance of objects that alternate strangely between what strikes us as very curious indeed and what is in fact true. There are two devices in particular that strengthen this impression; first, there are the long lists in which the strange and the familiar are piled one upon the other (1187, 1217, 1260, 1301, 1960), and strange names and categories keep recurring. Then in the second place, the idea of a vast number, of an almost overwhelming variety, is conveyed to us by the use of numerical comparisons to express an 'innumerable' profusion.[1] In the third Book this accumulation, this mass of impressions, objects, names and words has become the dominant principle governing both style and presentation.[2]

Let us take some examples of this vivid presentation by the 'piling up' method, drawing from both observation and imagination, and mingling the grotesque, the fanciful and the real. We have the descriptions of the pinnacles and turrets (1188 ff.), the pillared entrance gates with the decorated capitals (1301 ff.), the musicians' instruments (1209–40), and not least the sounds that issue from Aeolus's two trumpets:

> That thrughout every regioun
> Wente this foule trumpes soun,
> As swifte as pelet out of gonne,
> Whan fyr is in the poudre ronne.
> And such a smoke gan out wende
> Out of his foule trumpes ende,
> Blak, bloo, grenyssh, swartish red,
> As doth where that men melte led,
> Loo, al on high fro the tuel. (1641)

[1] Moo than sterres ben in hevene (1254) As grasses growen in a mede (1353); For as fele eyen hadde she As fetheres upon foules be (1381). Cf. also 1216, 1389, 1516, 2119.

[2] For further examples of the technique of enumeration in the second Book, cf. 676, 856, 897, 915.

It would be vain to look in French allegorical poetry for descriptions at once so forceful and so uniquely imaginative (cf. also 1598, 1684, 1801, 1865). Chaucer makes fantastic descriptions like these seem real by the precision with which he records the sounds and smells and by the use of comparison to bring out their qualities (1025–42, 1521, 1589, 1654, 1685, 1927, 1931).

Chaucer's own particular artistry – for which 'realism' is too vague a term – is most evident, however, when he is portraying action, incident, and dialogue; for this gives scope for his dramatic gift. The description in the third Book of the bustling, thronging crowd offers a particularly good instance of how Chaucer breaks up mass movement into dramatic scenes. He takes Ovid's lines:

> Atria turba tenet: veniunt leve vulgus euntque;
> Mixtaque cum veris passim commenta vagantur
> Milia rumorum, confusaque verba volutant.
>
> (*Met.* XII, 53)

and transposes them to make a highly entertaining scene, where action and swift dialogue (2052 ff., 2097) flash and turn, and where Ovid's generalized account is turned into real live figures, conversations and events.[1] He puts something concrete and precise in the place of a generalized statement and makes it real by providing some indication of scale or number, or by adding some factual comparison. This is a process that runs through the whole poem. At the end of the second Book, for instance (1025 ff.), Chaucer follows Ovid in describing the sounds that come from the house of Fame. Chaucer breaks up Ovid's statement:

> Qualia de pelagi, siquis procul audiat, undis
> Esse solent;                                  (*Met.* XIII, 50)

into a dialogue between the eagle and the poet.[2] By adding 'Whan tempest doth the shippes swalowe', however, he makes his 'lyke betynge of the see ayen the roches holowe' – which

---

[1] Cf. W. F. Schirmer, 'Chaucer, Shakespeare und die Antike', in *Warburg Institute Lectures*, 1930–1, p. 86.
[2] Cf. Shannon, p. 82.

might be said to correspond to Ovid's 'pelagi . . . undis', – seem
much more real and vivid. His:

> And lat a man stonde, out of doute,
> A myle thens, and here hyt route; (1037)

gives graphic concreteness to Ovid's 'siquis procul audiat'; and
where Ovid indicates the tiny proportions of Fame as she is first
seen, Chaucer is more precise:

> That the lengthe of a cubite
> Was lengere than she semed be. (1370)

At the end of the second Book the poet says that he and the
eagle have come as close to the house of Fame 'as men may
casten with a spere' (1048). Again, the throng in the house of
rumours is said to be so great that there is 'scarcely a foot-
breadth' (2041) of space. Speaking of the crowd of heralds,[1] we
hear:

> Men myghte make of hem a bible
> Twenty foot thykke, as y trowe. (1334)

Where crowds are mentioned, indeed, it is usually with some
such comparison added. It might of course be argued that this is
a case of the 'imago' and 'comparatio' of the medieval rhetoricians.[2] Yet few images in the *Roman de la Rose* are so real and
concrete as are the comparisons in the *House of Fame* ( *HF* 691,
1192, 1254, 1353, 1382, 1390, 1516, 1806, 1946, 1984, 2078).

In speaking of the Dido episode, we have already referred
to Chaucer's colloquial style which is almost like everyday
language. We see it even more clearly in the third Book. We
have already noted Fame's speech as being couched in crude and
downright terms; and such expressions as 'But wite ye what?'
(1618), 'What . . . and be ye wood?' (1713), 'What? false
theves!' (1779), 'anon; and wostow how?' (1791) demonstrate
the everyday quality of this colloquial language. The rapidly
flowing dialogue – that between the eagle and the poet, for

---

[1] Cf. 1216, where the musicians are said to be 'Many thousand tymes twelve';
and the rumours at line 2119 are said to be 'Twenty thousand in a route'.

[2] 'Comparatio' however is not included among the figures 'recommended'.
Matthew of Vendôme gives a particular warning against it, and Gaufred of
Vinsauf sanctions only brief comparisons.

instance, or the one between Fame, Aeolus and the petitioners, and also the one among the people in the house of rumours – for the most part adopts a plain and forthright tone.

It is impossible to reduce the style in the whole poem to any single formula. The ambivalence that characterizes all Chaucer's poetry is again evident here in the alternation – the contrast, indeed – between high-sounding rhetorical phrases and passages where the construction is loose and almost careless. Taken as a whole, however, the language of the *House of Fame*, unlike the *Parliament of Fowls*, strikes one as not yet fully perfected and rounded; and it betrays the poem's characteristically experimental quality. It gives the impression of having been rapidly conceived and written down. In regard to syntax, it is noticeable that phrases are often added on like afterthoughts, by the use of *and* and *that*; it is as though while he was writing it down, this or that occurred to the author and he wanted to add it at once. This impromptu, often rapid and hasty way of writing makes the style in places appear restless, nervous, breathless. Chaucer rarely builds up a long, involved period; he relies on accumulation, adding short co-ordinate phrases and stringing them together. This nervous, restless and rapidly-flowing style – like the metre, to be considered later – is of course suited to Chaucer's basic aim of amusing and entertaining, to his often humorous way of presenting his material, to the 'confidential tone' he often employs. The frequent exclamations and comments, the parenthetical asides with which the poet interrupts the flow of his own narrative and indeed himself too, likewise serve this end, though they are characteristic of Chaucer's later style also. The same is true of his frequent protestations; he assures us that he must not linger over something more than is necessary, that he must eschew lengthy or detailed descriptions, that he cannot do justice to the abundance of what he sees. Such turns of phrase (which correspond to the rhetoricians' 'occupatio' and 'praecisio') are very frequent in all Chaucer's poetry and are put by him to various uses.[1] In the third Book they strengthen the impression of overwhelming profusion and of amazement.[2] For they make us think that the poet's description is only one portion

---

[1] Francis, 'Chaucer shortens a Tale', *PMLA* 68 (1953).
[2] Cf. 1179, 1255, 1282, 1299, 1329, 1341, 2055.

of a limitless field. This is an artistic device well known to painters, to create an impression of abundance and variety. In addition, however, such formulae also intensify the feeling already mentioned of hurrying impatiently on without a pause.

Chaucer's style, in other words, is also transitional in character. He is seeking a new manner of presentation to convey what cannot be adequately expressed within the traditional forms.

The poem is written in the octosyllabic couplets which Chaucer had already used for his *Book of the Duchess*. This metre is particularly suited to the fresh and entertaining character of the whole work. It had been employed in English poetry for over a century[1] and Chaucer uses it with great freedom. In actual fact the octosyllabic couplet is particularly prone to produce a monotonous and droning measure of wearisome uniformity. But Chaucer infuses its unvarying note with variety by frequent 'enjambement' and by irregularities in the verse (the first metrical foot often has only one syllable, there are unexpected inversions, a trochee or an anapest is used for an iambus, etc.).[2] It is, however, in passages such as the Dido episode, where this droning measure is consciously used to underline and reinforce what is said. The artistry in Chaucer's use of metre is very clearly seen when one notices how he adapts it in every case to the basic character of what he has to say. In the desert scene, for instance, the rapid tempo of the lines slackens; they are more ponderous and weighty here than in most other passages. In dialogue, too, the metre is particularly versatile and flexible, and at other times the natural even tone of the lines is intentionally underlined by parallels in phrasing and wording.[3] Chaucer's metrical artistry has not yet received the attention it deserves.

[1] Cf. Charles Langley Crow, *Zur Geschichte des kurzen Reimpaars im Mittelenglischen*, Diss. Göttingen 1892.

[2] Cf. Ten Brink, *Chaucers Sprache und Verskunst*, Leipzig 1920; Paull F. Baum, *Chaucer's Verse*, 1961, pp. 27 ff.; E. F. Shannon, 'Chaucer's Use of the Octosyllabic Verse in the *BD* and in the *HF*', *JEGP* 12 (1913).

[3] E.g. 1538 ff., 1960 ff., 2151 ff.

# The Parliament of Fowls

In the *Parliament of Fowls*,[1] as in the *House of Fame*, the poet is seeking and exploring. This is at once made clear in the opening stanzas where the poet tells how he has been reading all day in an old book, 'a certeyn thing to lerne'. As the poem proceeds, too, he continues to seek and to inquire. What he sees, experiences and hears is put in such a way that it leads him and us to ask questions, many of which remain unanswered. We, the readers, are thus infected with his questioning spirit; though we are quite prepared to dwell on the delightful and charming tale as it is told, at the same time we wonder and ponder over the hidden purposes and unsolved problems that underlie these stanzas. In the *House of Fame* this seeking had led to a series of experiments, proceeding by sometimes abrupt turns; in the *Parliament* we find it rounded into a conscious work of art; for the attitude of exploration and inquiry has here found its convincing artistic expression.

## CHARACTERISTICS OF CHAUCER'S ARTISTIC PRESENTATION

The art of suggestion and allusion, already a noticeable feature in the *Book of the Duchess*, takes on a new and subtler form in this poem. The essential point is hardly ever expressed; it is conveyed 'by implication'. The poet remains a seeker throughout the whole poem, and on waking from his dream in the

[1] Two detailed and extremely informative interpretations of the *Parliament of Fowls* have recently appeared (J. A. W. Bennett, *The Parlement of Foules, An Interpretation*, 1957; *The Parlement of Foulys* ed. by D. S. Brewer, 1960); these exhaustively deal with several fundamental questions, as well as with numerous minor points. Any new treatment is therefore bound to use and build upon the material, results and suggestions contained in these works. The present chapter, while offering its own approach, has been greatly stimulated and owes many observations to these two commentaries, whose authors have sanctioned the omission of acknowledgment over each individual point.

last lines of the *Parliament* he admits that he must go on reading, seeking and hoping:[1]

> I hope, ywis, to rede so som day
> That I shal mete som thyng for to fare
> The bet, and thus to rede I nyl nat spare. (697)

In other words, although his experiences on his journey have given him a deeper insight into it, he has not yet found the answer to the question touched upon in the opening stanzas about the nature of love. The wooing of the three noble eagles, too, which forms part of the argument among the birds, remains inconclusive, and the formel eagle postpones her decision for a year. In a way, this symbolizes the whole poem. The poet avoids committing himself or taking any definite line, but provides a context of pictures and incidents within which we are brought to consider the various problems, and in particular the central question about love. In the course of his eventful journey he shows us the ingredients, the elements which go to make up the complex and essential problem. The grouping and sequence of the contrasting or complementary scenes and symbols hint at various tendencies and possibilities[2] which are not followed up, however, or explained within the poem itself. This kind of presentation is different from that to be found in most medieval literature which for all its *allegoresis* was explicit and expository; perhaps Chaucer felt that a complex situation taken from real life can only be expressed in this way, and not by a definite attitude or a simple alternative.

Reflections such as these must not, however, tempt us to read some profound philosophy of life into this poem. Indeed, the *Parliament* itself places limits on the weight that can be put upon it, for it appears in the guise of a courtly occasional poem[3] – light, charmingly artificial, full of subtle humour. One must not – indeed, one cannot – attribute too much philosophical significance to it[4]; the poet can do no more than touch on profounder

---

[1] Cf. Bennett, p. 185; Brewer, *PF*, p. 25.

[2] Cf. Brewer, *PF*, p. 16.

[3] On the *Parliament* as a 'St. Valentine's poem' dealing with the institution of the 'Cour Amoureuse' etc., see Brewer, *PF*, p. 3 ff.

[4] Muscatine (p. 122): 'There is no doubt that a serious view is involved with the poem, but the poem cannot support the theory that makes of it a sober philosophical tract.'

problems in passing. The form and aim of the poem allow him only a hint at these fundamental questions concerning the place of love in human life; they do not permit him to state them explicitly or to follow them up. The particular form which Chaucer invented for the *Parliament* was admirably suited to his natural liking for holding aloof, for playing hide-and-seek with his reader. Indeed we realize that there are many reasons why questions are 'left open' in this way.

This poem ranges from the exalted vision of heaven and the grave moral exhortations in the *Somnium Scipionis* to the droll dispute among the birds, from Scipio Africanus to Priapus, from the sublime goddess Nature to airily-clad Venus, from Diana to Tristan and Isolde, from Cicero to Alanus de Insulis. But as well as including names and themes of such heterogeneous origins and kinds, in his *Parliament* Chaucer has blended the most divers traditional genres, forms and elements. His early work shows no clearer instance of his gift for combining several literary traditions, for building up in a new style on older foundations. Again and again we are struck by the ease with which Chaucer recalls past conventions or imitates former models, but then proceeds to reverse what had at first appeared to be his intention. Much as his contemporaries, with their knowledge of literary tradition, admired it, however, this art of combining and apparently imitating is only a means to an end. Chaucer makes use of these various literary themes and genres to find symbols which fit and indeed illustrate the experience or meaning he wishes to convey. He could thus rely on what his readers were bound to expect and associate with these themes, and so he was able to employ an abbreviated, inferential style to present his ideas – an advantage enjoyed by all poetry rooted in tradition.

The content of the *Parliament* is complex and even contradictory; and the presentation is correspondingly varied. At the same time, however, the restless style of the *House of Fame* has been replaced by a remarkably even tone which masks the subtle alterations. The more elaborate construction of line and stanza (the seven-line stanza, the 'rime royal') imposed a clear structure on the content, and we find that most stanzas introduce some new thought or theme. The presentation takes on a more condensed and finished form, the whole poem is more clearly subdivided and constructed than either the *House of Fame* or the *Book of the Duchess*; and it also shows more control, more deliberate subordination of language to subject-matter.

This artistry in the use of language serves in its turn to under-line the division of the poem into a number of longer sections employing differing techniques. In addition, too, there are subtle gradations in cadence and rhyme, and in the pace of the narration, which all help to emphasize the different significance each section possesses.

Let us glance at these diverse techniques[1] in the three chief episodes within the poem – the account of the *Somnium*, the love-garden, and the parliament of the birds. In the shortened account that Chaucer gives of his reading of the *Somnium*, we notice how the poet, usually so involved in the action, effaces himself completely. He makes no comment; there is no elabor-ation of detail, the stress is laid on making the ideas plain and there are few occasions for the 'actualization' at which Chaucer so often aims. The account moves forward rapidly in a monotone broken by few emphases. As we read it – even without having pondered on what significance the *Somnium* may have in this connection – we feel we are covering a 'long mile', whose sole purpose is one of indirect preparation.

In the middle section description and narration replace what was a simple account. At the same time there is now more variety in both style and syntax. We notice that the language is more intense, poetic, rich in images, the verse is handled with great skill, cadence and rhythm are subtly shaded. Changing emphasis, caesurae and contrasts match this ampler conception and more varied content. Chaucer discards the dry indirectness of a 'synopsis' in favour of the greater urgency of what has actually been felt and witnessed by himself. The poet's 'I' dispels the objectivity of the description, and gives us what he himself has experienced.

The stronger contrasts of the middle section now develop into a spirited drama when it comes to the dispute among the birds. For dramatic treatment is the best for expressing the opposition of different standpoints, allowing as it does of the most telling contrasts in style and diction and also of the greatest vividness.

[1] Cf. R. W. Frank, 'Structure and Meaning in the *PF*', *PMLA* 71 (1956).

Besides, it enables the poet to take up a position of unprejudiced objectivity, above party differences, and to present the different points of view so as to do justice to each one. We have here a basic attitude typical of Chaucer's whole work. The little 'drama' which gives its name to the poem and which brings it to an end, is indeed the logical climax and crown of all the artistic possibilities of which Chaucer has made use in his *Parliament*. Furthermore, it constitutes the form of presentation most suited to his own particular gift. In regard to its stylistic pattern and in the sequence of the techniques employed, the *Parliament* displays more consistent development than either the *Book of the Duchess* or the *House of Fame*.

### THE ROLE OF THE POET

The part played by the poet within the poem, too, is a more subtle one. As in both the *Book of the Duchess* and the *House of Fame* he is not only the narrator, he is also a participant, personally and directly involved in what he has to tell, although he does not interfere in the 'action'. His reactions to what happens to him or to what he observes go far to explain the different episodes. Right at the beginning the poet appears involved in some uncertainty and at a later stage this situation is repeated outside the gate of the love-garden (with its contradictory inscriptions); these features, like the 'attitude of seeking' already mentioned, are important pointers to the significance of the whole poem.

Africanus leads the poet into the love-garden (154 ff.); and his words serve Chaucer to adopt an attitude above either party and to play the astonished, disinterested innocent, and at the same time to be present at the scene. The feelings of heartfelt joy (171), of unequalled delight (198), of distress followed by relief (297), of respectful admiration (298), and of emphatic approval (484) which the poet expresses at various points in the story in each case suggest and foreshadow the significance of the relevant passages, and are usually conveyed through the cadence and tone of the language chosen. Yet it is most revealing, too, that at the conclusion of the birds' debate the poet is silent and refrains from making any comment at all.[1]

[1] Cf. Dorothy Everett, p. 111.

# The Parliament of Fowls

The *Parliament*, like the *Book of the Duchess* or the *Complaint of Mars*, has been regarded as an 'occasional poem'; and this being so, research was concentrated for a long time upon this 'occasion', that is to say upon the historical personages and circumstances which underlie the birds' wooing. Just objections were soon raised to this kind of interpretation;[1] but it is only in the last twenty years that the essential link between the several parts, the 'meaning' and 'unity' of the whole poem, have become the main object of critical studies, and here the most contradictory hypotheses have been advanced. Research[2] has ranged from interpretations along philosophical or sociological lines to analyses which regarded the poem as united by some consistent comic or ironic strain. Though these works have placed many details and essentials of the *Parliament* in a new light, it seems that no definitive answer to the question of the meaning and unifying factor of the poem has been found, and it is unlikely that the discussion will ever be concluded. It appears more probable that this question will continue to remain open, just as Chaucer leaves the result of the birds' dispute an open one at the end of his poem. Perhaps Chaucer may have wished to play at hide-and-seek with his commentators also![3] It is surely better to confine oneself to a more modest aim – instead

---

[1] J. M. Manly, 'What is the *Parlement of Foules?*' *Studien zur englischen Philologie* 50 (1913). Cf. also J. L. Lowes, *Chaucer*, 1934, and Robinson's notes. For a list of further literature on the 'historical allegory' in the *PF* see Ch. O. McDonald, *Spec.* 30 (1955) printed by Wagenknecht, *Chaucer, Modern Essays in Criticism*, 1959, p. 327. For more recent historical interpretations cf. also H. Braddy, *Chaucer and the French Poet Graunson*, 1947, and Ethel Seaton, *Medium Aevum* 25 (1957).

[2] B. H. Bronson, 'In Appreciation of Chaucer's *PF*', *Univ. of Calif. Pub. in Engl.* 3 (1935); R. C. Goffin, 'Heaven and Earth in the *PF*', *MLR* 31 (1936); R. E. Thackaberry, *Chaucer's PF: A Reinterpretation*, Diss. Univ. of Iowa, 1937; R. M. Lumiansky, 'Chaucer's *PF*. A Philosophical Interpretation', *RES* 24 (1948); G. Stillwell, 'Unity and Comedy in Chaucer's *PF*', *JEGP* 49 (1950); B. H. Bronson, 'The *PF* Revisited', *ELH* 15 (1948); M. Emslie, 'Codes of Love and Class Distinctions', *EC* 5 (1955); C. Clark 'Natural Love in the *PF*' *EC* 5 (1955); D. Everett, 'Chaucer's Love Visions, with Particular Reference to the *PF*', *Essays on Middle English Literature*, 1955; D. Bethurum, 'The Centre of the *PF*', *Essays in Honour of Walter Clyde Curry*, 1954; Charles O. McDonald 'An Interpretation of Chaucer's *PF*', *Spec.* 30 (1955); R. W. Frank, 'Structure and Meaning in the *PF*', *PMLA* 71 (1956); also relevant chapters in the works of Patch, Muscatine, Malone, Tatlock, Baum, Coghill, Bronson.

[3] The latest estimate of the *Parliament* admits that 'It is too nimble for criticism, which always hops behind'. (B. H. Bronson, *In Search of Chaucer*, 1960, p. 46).

of producing some new thesis – to co-ordinate the observations prompted by the text and to link them up with literary tradition.

## STRUCTURE AND COHERENCE

Starting, then, from this literary tradition, the conventions, the past history of the genre and theme, we can note some typical features in the general structure of the poem which at once and at least outwardly bind the individual parts together. Behind this surface-relationship, more essential links are forged, most of which Chaucer allows us only to guess at. We are always concerned with meaning and relationships on two planes at once – one at surface-level, where everything appears plain and is largely governed by existing convention; the other deeper and embracing the admittedly vexed question of fundamental aims. When it comes to this level, neither 'logical sequence' nor a supposed single pivot holding all the different parts of the poem together, can really help us. Chaucer's *Parliament* brings it clearly home to us that we must work out quite new categories if we are to begin to understand how many medieval poems are constructed.[1]

Some typical features in this structure become clearer if we proceed from the chief section, the birds' dispute about love. This dispute involved an enumeration of all the birds and a description of Nature conducting the debate. Following Alanus,[2] Chaucer placed Nature in an ever-green garden full of delights and very closely connected with the 'love-garden' which in any case was an integral feature of any dream-poem dealing with love. The pattern of the *Roman de la Rose* and its successors had laid it down that the poet had to go through a gateway into the love-garden and be led by a guide. Furthermore, as the subject was a dream, this dream had to be introduced; and Chaucer achieves this here, as in the *Book of the Duchess*, by making the poet take up a book and read it before falling asleep. This book, in its turn, tells of a dream, and so Africanus, Scipio's guide,

[1] Cf. D. Bethurum, 'The Centre of the *PF*', *Essays in Honour of Clyde Curry*, 1954, p. 48 f.

[2] Alanus ab Insulis, a Latin poet of the twelfth century, had given a long account of Natura in his work *De Planctu Naturae* (Migne, *Pat. Lat.* 210, pp. 431 ff.).

who figures in it, also acts as guide to the poet in his own dream.

We have, then, a conventional link affording an extrinsic connection between the individual themes; but this does not solve the question of any essential coherence in the thought. The present preliminary survey however may be of use as a reminder that some of the principles underlying the composition of a medieval poem differ greatly from the structural laws which obtain in the case of a modern work.[1]

Thus, long introductions are typical of all Chaucer's allegorical dream-poems. It is as though we were being led by devious routes towards the principal room in a house. The trend of the period in regard to style was not towards simplification, but baffling complexity and intricacy. Ornamental and decorative elements were not confined to any recognizable external zone surrounding the core; they covered the whole, and sometimes constituted the essence of the work itself. In literature as in other arts, there was frequently no clear line between essential expression and additional ornament.

There is a further element in the subtle and original kind of 'indirect approach' that we find in the *Parliament*. For the themes treated in these preliminary 'introductions' are for the most part very familiar ones indeed. What Chaucer added 'out of his head' he built up on a broad basis of traditional material. What he himself had to say thus acquired a greater measure of authority and weight, springing as it did from accepted convention. The 'original', 'individual' element was not some newly-created separate item; it consisted in the novel combination or use of familiar themes and formal features.[2] And this 'individual' element was allowed expression only after the basic plan and framework had been firmly grounded on a basis of tradition. We have this type of structure in all three poems, which open with the re-telling of a classical tale in a setting composed in the first place of several conventional elements.

[1] On this point, cf. also Hennig Brinkmann, *Zu Wesen und Form mittelalterlicher Dichtung*, 1928.
[2] Cf. D. Everett, *Essays on Middle English Literature*, 1955, p. 107.

## THE OPENING STANZAS

This type of structure is obvious in the very first lines of
the *Parliament*. For it begins in accordance with the rules of
rhetoric with a maxim, the well-known 'Ars longa, vita brevis'.
Yet the conventional correctness of this opening is at once
toned down, as it were; for the maxim leads on to the poet's
own musing reflections. The other rhetorical figures of these
first two stanzas, too, are unobtrusively woven in.[1] From the
point of view of rhetoric, these stanzas are an extension of the
opening maxim; yet if one reads them aloud, the whole passage
has an unusually free, impromptu air and strikes a personal note.
As so often with Chaucer, we do not quite know where he is
leading us. The 'Ars longa' which generally refers to life and
study, is suddenly applied to something else – to the nature of
love, in fact. We only realize this afterwards, however, thanks
to the characteristic transitional line which recalls and explains
those that preceded it. (Al this mene I by love. . . .) The
dualistic nature of love, as has been pointed out already,[2] is
suggested in these very first stanzas, which also look forward
to the two-fold inscription at the gateway to the love-garden
(127). Furthermore, this first stanza is particularly important
because the dual nature of love finds an echo in the poet's own
uneasiness and induces in him a feeling of uncertainty which his
pondering only makes worse (that whan I on hym thynke,/Nat
wot I wel wher that I flete or synke. 6). The commonly-used
formula Chaucer chooses to describe this helpless and unsure
feeling, 'wher that I flete or synke', has a special significance
in this context. Not only does it tell us of his inward dilemma;
it also contains a *contentio*[3] – a rhetorical figure which often
recurs in the course of the poem and reflects even on the smallest
scale and on a purely linguistic level the basic polarity of the
poem.

The personal note in the first stanza is continued as Chaucer
confesses his own inexperience in the matter of love – he had
done the same in his two previous dream-poems.[4] Here it serves

---

[1] Cf. D. Everett, p. 104 f.    [2] Bennett, p. 29.    [3] Cf. D. Everett p. 104, 149 ff.
[4] See Bronson's interpretation in *Univ. of California Publ. in Engl.* 3 (1935),
p. 197.

to lend the poet an air of impartiality (and of naïve astonishment); and this air is at once important and typical of his role in the poem. The paradoxical nature of love is the theme of this stanza also (11); and we are reminded that love is inescapable, compelling, brooks no rival, and involves suffering – traits which all acquire significance as the poem proceeds. These brief references open up a wide horizon; but once again Chaucer breaks off in his strange but customary way; with a pious 'God save swich a lord!' he as it were silences and dispels all future questioning and doubts while avoiding committing himself. The sigh 'I can na moore' which ends the stanza quite simply and plainly expresses the poet's dilemma and perplexity that had underlain both these stanzas. The poem abounds in expressions that mask their meaning and disingenuous statements placed side by side and serving to emphasize its contrasts.

In the next stanza, too, we do not know exactly how the poet means to deal with us. The sudden interruption 'But wherfore that I speke al this?' (17), seems to echo his reader's unspoken question – a device Chaucer employs in his other poems also. His reading of the 'bok' follows naturally and more or less casually, just as a story-teller might describe himself walking along and coming by chance upon what in fact he means all the time to relate. These lines seem as if lightly tossed off, yet they serve to place the poet, lost in delight and curiosity over what he reads, in the actual setting of a particular day (21, 28), and they enshrine those other lines where a simile explains the 'germinative significance' of a classical tale of this sort:

> For out of olde feldes, as men seyth,
> Cometh al this newe corn from yer to yere,
> And out of olde bokes, in good feyth,
> Cometh al this newe science that men lere. (22)

These lines could indeed stand as a motto for all the rest of Chaucer's work; except for adaptations or translations, the *bok* of some *auctour* almost always formed his starting-point. The *Book of the Duchess* began with Ovid, the *House of Fame* with Virgil, and the *Parliament* opens with a classical work equally well-known to the Middle Ages. But the *Somnium Scipionis* was not merely an outstanding source of knowledge; it was also the most famous dream in classical literature and naturally Chaucer could place his own dream under its shadow. His poem would carry greater weight if it was built up on a foundation of such accepted authority and significance.[1]

## THE SOMNIUM SCIPIONIS

The same Africanus who in the *Somnium* tells Scipio the meaning of what he is seeing, also acts as guide to Chaucer through the love-garden in the subsequent dream. There is a further link, too; for before his dream Scipio had been thinking about Africanus (who had been mentioned when Scipio was conversing with King Massinissa), and he then went on to dream of him; so this further explains how Africanus came to reappear in Chaucer's dream.

These connections and links only serve, however, to emphasize the essential difference between the two dreams. For the view of life in the *Somnium* is in sharpest contrast, is indeed diametrically opposed, to the world opened up to us by Chaucer's dream of the love-garden and the birds' debate on the subject of love.

Macrobius had interpreted the *Somnium* in a Christian sense as a warning to live virtuously here below, and as a reminder of eternal life in Heaven and of the Day of Judgment. The references it contained to the futility and vanity of all human efforts to attain fame here on earth, to the punishments threatening those who yield to the pleasures of the senses, and the counsel given to despise the things of this world – all this was so consonant with the Christian idea that the *Somnium* (as Macrobius presented it) came to be regarded as an outstanding example of classical doctrine embodying Christian teaching.[2] Chaucer's version, too, which omitted numerous details and personal touches and gave only Africanus's essential admonitions and

[1] R. C. Goffin, discussing the significance of the *Somnium* for the *PF*, goes much further, holding the view that Chaucer wished to establish his 'alibi' by means of the *Somnium* (*MLR* 31, 1936). For a comparison of the role of the *Somnium* in the *PF* and in *Troilus* V. 1807 ff., see Bronson, 'In Appreciation of Chaucer's *PF*', pp. 198 ff.

[2] For a recent English translation see W. H. Stahl, *Macrobius; Commentary on the Dream of Scipio*, 1952.

teaching, is wholly Christian in outlook. Not only does his selection make it quite clear that Chaucer is relating the *Somnium* for the sake of Christian doctrine and not because of the view of heaven which it affords; certain slight deviations and shiftings of emphasis also demonstrate this plainly. For instance, Chaucer speaks of the earth as not merely small (quae si tibi parva ut est . . . ), but also as 'ful of torment and of harde grace' (65),[1] echoing the Christian notion of the 'vale of woe'. Besides, the words *torment* and *grace* are taken up later in the poem. Similarly, in place of 'in caelo definitum locum' Chaucer inserts 'a blysful place' (48), an important expression repeated (for 'hunc in locum') at line 83 which links up with 'into that hevene blisse' (72) and with 'to that place deere/That ful of blysse is and of soules cleere' (76), and recurs in the inscription on the gateway to the love-garden (127). This last phrase in particular where he is rendering Cicero's 'animus velocius in hanc sedem et domum suam pervolabit . . . ' shows how Chaucer's Christian outlook has expanded and coloured Cicero's vaguer and more prosaic statements.

Furthermore, this praise of the 'place deere that ful of blysse is and of soules cleere' appears in a section in which Chaucer has significantly altered the language used in the *Somnium*. After he has learned enough about the 'way to Heaven', Cicero's Scipio is eager in his assent ('tanto praemio exposito enitar multo vigilantius', VIII); not so Chaucer's Scipio, however, for at this point he expressly begs again for instruction (to telle hym al/The wey to come into that hevene blisse 71); and this gives Africanus the chance to repeat lines 46–9 and 55–6 with emphasis and in part word for word. In this passage spoken by Africanus Chaucer passes from the indirect speech hitherto employed to direct speech; he thus reinforces the immediacy of the personal admonition (and loke ay besyly 74, and thow shalt not mysse 75). In the last stanza, we hear Chaucer speaking more deliberately and urgently and inserting explanatory phrases (soth to seyne 78, out of drede 81), giving a Christian version of the

---

[1] Brewer reads here 'And disseyuable, & ful of harde grace', which he takes from *MS* Gg, advancing good reasons for his reading. The present writer however adheres to the hitherto accepted reading found in most of the *MSS* and adopted also by Robinson.

punishment meted out to the 'likerous folk' whom Cicero mentions in section nine of the *Somnium*. Cicero makes the souls achieve their self-purification (IX), whereas Chaucer speaks of forgiveness (82) and of grace (84); neither of these ideas is found in Cicero. Furthermore, in the first revelations which Africanus makes to Scipio about life in Heaven, Chaucer's version expands Cicero's purely individual promise to the dimensions of established Christian belief. It is only by omitting the prophecy about Scipio's future which shows him as especially singled out and therefore able to learn of the prospect of life in Heaven[1] that Chaucer can extend the promise till it is universally valid. This promise moreover does not refer, as in Cicero, to any particular circle, the 'leaders of society' (harum [i.e. civitatum] rectores et conservatores'), but to *all* men 'what man lered other lewed' – a considerable alteration indeed!

These and other details[2] make it clear that far from producing merely a systematically shortened version of the much longer Ciceronian text, Chaucer selected what from his point of view was of significance and presented it in a modified form and with emphasis at certain points.

But even a close study of Chaucer's version of the *Somnium* cannot begin to answer the question why this sort of general view of the world should be placed at the beginning of a poem dealing with love. For it reflects, in an acute form, the medieval Christian-ascetic contempt for this world, there is no room in this conception either for love or for the appreciation of the beauty of this world as God's handiwork. The world is 'ful of torment', life is 'but a maner deth', the whole of man's endeavour is fixed solely upon the next world. The only means moreover than can open the way to Heaven, 'commune profit', has little to do with the opening question about love.[3]

Reading the *Somnium* is in fact of no use to the poet and indeed only increases his perplexity – so much is clear from the

---

[1] '. . . tu eris unus in quo nitatur civitatis salus' etc. II, 2.

[2] To which Bennett (p. 40) refers.

[3] Some have seen in 'commune profit' a reference to marriage and the founding of a family – an interpretation that cannot with any certainty be proved. This sort of connection between the subsequent debate among the birds and their choice of mates is too slender and artificial a construction.

lines in which Chaucer begins to speak of the effect the *Somnium* makes:

> And to my bed I gan me for to dresse,
> Fulfyld of thought and busy hevynesse;
> For bothe I hadde thyng which that I nolde,
> And ek I nadde that thyng that I wolde. (88)

The wearisome search hinted at in these lines, the perplexity and dilemma in the poet's mind, are expressed again and again in the course of the poem and form as it were the climate of the entire work. This in turn throws a light on the role of the *Somnium*; it represents something contrary, a 'détour' which can be of no use as it only heightens the dilemma – the very effect which Chaucer wanted to convey. In this way the 'unre-solved' and difficult quality of the problem is emphasized and the questioning and seeking seem more natural.

Those aspects of the *Somnium* however, with which Chaucer dealt, were far from 'irrelevant' by medieval standards. They represented the Christian conception of the 'contemptus mundi', proclaimed from many a pulpit and no doubt both valid and obligatory in the minds of large numbers of Chaucer's contem-poraries. If he wished to keep his poem within the orbit of Christianity – and all we know substantiates this – the most direct way was to begin by considering the point of view pre-sented in the *Somnium*, and then (with the help of Africanus) to lead on to a different conception, one which by means of the goddess Nature, 'the vicaire of the almyghty Lord' (379), assigned a place in God's creation to love. Besides, each of these conceptions could claim the support of one of the great philo-sophers, either Cicero (in the Macrobius version) or Alanus de Insulis, both equally revered by medieval Christianity. It was not a question of descending from the heights of Christian metaphysics to the dark depths of paganism; it simply meant passing from one philosopher's province to that of the other – although admittedly the latter region was more extensive and varied than simply that of Alanus himself. The section of the *Parliament* containing the *Somnium* does however come nearer to Christian metaphysics than does the second part. Short as it is, by beginning in Heaven and ending on earth the poem can lay some claim to universality, to a concern for heavenly as well as for earthly matters, even although everything takes place within the light and charming framework of a 'love-vision'. Medieval poetry could pass more easily from what was serious to comedy, from a gloomy to a serene and light-hearted view of life.[1]

Finally, it seems an important point that while he is reading the *Somnium* the poet himself does not feel that he is following a useless or 'devious' path. As he tells us:

> To rede forth hit gan me so delite,
> That al that day me thoughte but a lyte. (27)

(and see also line 21). Reading the *Somnium* can satisfy and engage the poet, gives him food for thought and a good measure besides of the *lore* which – with the 'lust' (15) – is his customary reason for turning to books in order 'a certeyn thing to lerne' (20).[2]

But the view of the world taken in the *Somnium* is too lofty and remote to be of use to the poet in his present situation. Chaucer is aware, too, that the sublime truths which the *Somnium* had revealed must be radically altered and indeed freshly interpreted, in the light of his successive experiences as he wanders through the love-garden. With delicate irony, then, and skilfully echoing a phrase here and there to suggest subtle links and contrasts he weaves elements of his version of the *Somnium* into the two-fold inscription on the gateway to the park of love and into subsequent passages in the poem.[3]

[1] Machaut, for instance, in the *Jugement dou Roy de Navarre* (in the main a 'demande d'amours'), begins with grave and gloomy reflections on the Great Plague, as a chastisement from God. Our modern taste can hardly appreciate the transition from the pious solemnity of this opening to the amusing love-allegory.

[2] 'a certeyn thing' has usually been taken to refer to Chaucer's questions about love (cf. R. C. Goffin, *MLR* 31, 1936; R. M. Lumiansky, *RES* 24, 1928; B. H. Bronson 'In Appreciation of Chaucer's *PF*', 1935; Stillwell, *JEGP* 49, 1950, Ch. O. McDonald, *Spec.* 30, 1955). A new interpretation of 'a certain thing' was advanced by one of my students, Brigitte Thaler: 'certeyn' is to mean here 'precise, definite'; in that case 'a certeyn thing' would refer to the true and reliable wisdom contained in Christian philosophy, resting on a sure foundation, and not subject to the mutability and contradiction of love which had been the poet's theme in the first two stanzas.

[3] Cf. 'welle of grace' (129) with 62, 84, 319; and 'the wey to al good aventure' (131) with 72; also 'sped thee faste' (133) with 76. And see also Everett, p. 106, and Bennett, *passim*.

# The Parliament of Fowls

## THE DREAM

In the stanzas covering lines 85–119, as the poet passes from his reading of the *Somnium* to telling his own dream, he gives us yet another example of a complexly allusive transition taking place on different levels at the same time. In the first place, the incidents of going to bed and falling asleep are treated more naturally and with greater realism than in the *House of Fame* (112 ff.) or in the *Book of the Duchess* (270 ff.) – for here darkness has begun to fall and has prevented the poet from reading on; his day's 'labour' has tired him and so he comes 'to slepe faste'.

But the dream which he begins to tell at lines 92 ff. and which also brings the reappearance of Africanus, is twice interrupted (99 and 113) for the sake of interpolating something which is of importance for the 'transition to the dream-state' and also for an understanding of what happens once it has begun. In fact the 'insertions' as well as the 'Invocatio' to Cytherea and the list (taken over from Claudian) of possible causes for the dream, represent rhetorical devices[1] which recall the introduction of the dreams in the *Book of the Duchess* and the *House of Fame*. But these insertions also have a more important aspect, namely their special function within the context. The stanza 99 ff. gives instances of what had occupied the dreamer during the preceding day now recurring in his dream that night. This provides a natural reason in accordance with 'dream psychology'[2] for the reappearance of Scipio Africanus, who now in the poet's own dream resumes the role of 'guide' and interpreter which had been his in the *Somnium*. The same noble interpreter of the heavenly cosmos now conducts the poet through the park of love; but any scruples about this ironic inconsistency are as it were routed by the mention, in the same stanza, of the 'logic of dreams' which after all ignores any such differences in status. It is obvious that here – as with the golden eagle in the *House of*

[1] Cf. Malone, p. 68. Malone sees a link between the stanza at 99–105 and the *Proem* of *HF*.

[2] Although Macrobius uses the term 'insomnia' for dreams of this sort, it is unlikely that Chaucer classified his individual dream-poems in line with these rigid theoretical 'types'. Cf. Curry, *Chaucer and the Medieval Sciences*, 1926, p. 233, and Bennett, p. 53.

*Fame* – Chaucer means to indicate an ironic contrast between noble origins and present function; so much is clear from the parallels between Africanus's first words to the poet (109 ff.) and the lines in which Virgil had spoken to Dante in the *Inferno* (I, 83 ff.).[1] Yet it would be erroneous to interpret this solely as a 'comic effect', an intentional 'shock'.[2] Chaucer's art is to a far greater degree one of subtle allusion than of grotesque contrast for the sake of 'comic' effect alone. Africanus has more than one function; the 'ironic contrast' between his own role in the *somnium* and the Virgilian figure represents only one side of him.[3]

But irony is indeed involved here; it is clearly revealed when Africanus speaks to the poet (109–12; 155–68), and furthermore in the manner in which Chaucer thus paints his own portrait, that of the 'poet'. Africanus's kindly announcement that the poet is now to be 'rewarded' for his 'labour' in reading the *somnium*, creates a genial, amicable transition from prospects of heaven to those of earth, and recalls the golden eagle's jovial words as he tells how Jupiter has decreed that as a reward the poet is to be snatched up and taken to the House of Tidings and News[4] (*HF* 661 ff.). We are reminded too of the golden eagle's speech once again, when at the very start of the poem (8), having taken up the attitude of ignorance in the matter of love, the poet allows Africanus to confirm this (160 f., 162 f.) with a sly side-thrust, and submits to playing the helpless, hesitating dullard who needs a strong arm to push him along. Finally, in view of what was to follow, Africanus's image of the wrestling-bout (with its vigorous expressions, 163–6) is not without a touch of irony; for this comparison, somewhat startling in this context, contributes to the poet's portrait of himself.

In addition, other themes and features in this same section prepare us for what is to come. The 'Invocatio', the solemn and

[1] And see further parallels between 142 and *Inf.* III, 12; 155–6 and *Par.* IV, 10 f.; 157–8 and *Inf.* III, 127; 169 and *Inf.* III, 19. See also Lowes, *MP* 14 (1917), Brewer, *PF*, p. 105.

[2] Cf. R. W. Frank, *PMLA* 71 (1956), p. 534.

[3] On the 'ironic point' implicit in Africanus's dual role, see B. H. Bronson, *In Search of Chaucer*, 1960, p. 45.

[4] The theme of 'quiting by tidinges' is treated by R. C. Goffin, *Medium Aevum* 12 (1943).

ceremonious address to Cytherea (the planet Venus) which interrupts Africanus's first words, quite unequivocally prepares us for the poem's 'central theme' of love; and line 115, 'And madest me this sweven for to mete', with its suggestion of Chaucer as the 'poet of love', lends added piquancy to Africanus's somewhat later remarks. It must be admitted that even this, the poet's respectful salutation to 'Cytherea' is subsequently tinged with irony when he adds 'As wisly as I sey the north-north-west' (117) – whether we follow Manly in reading 'north-north-west' as 'in an unpropitious position' or agree with Bronson that it means 'hardly at all'.[1] Besides, it is Chaucer's way to use a convention involving a high tone of lofty solemnity and then to treat it ironically; his work abounds in examples of this treatment.

### THE GATEWAY TO THE LOVE-GARDEN

The inscriptions on the entrance-gate to the park of love and the poet's subsequent reaction to them also illustrate features which recur in the poem and are strongly characteristic of its author's methods; for here we see him opposing two contradictory possibilities while leaving the decision between them open, harking back to models belonging to a different and higher plane, reviving ideas in some entirely new context.

What these two inscriptions provide, which underline their message by a liberal use of metaphor and symbolism,[2] is not, as has been supposed, a contrast between 'natural' and courtly' love,[3] but between the possibilities inherent in love itself. Both paths – towards happiness or sorrow, good or evil – lie open to all who enter this domain. The conflicting nature of love, one of the themes of the whole poem, is here most clearly expressed. Chaucer emphasizes the ambiguity and yet also the parity of

[1] Manly, *Studien z. engl. Philologie* 50 (1913); B. H. Bronson, *Univ. of California Publ. in Engl.* 3 (1935). On the possibility that this stanza may be a later addition, cf. Bronson, *ELH* 15 (1948), p. 249 f. Cf. Brewer, *PF*, p. 104, and Koch, *ESt* 55 (1921), Braddy, *PMLA* 46 (1931). For a critical attitude to existing dating theories see Bronson, *ELH* 15. Cf. also C. O. McDonald, *Spec.* 30 (1955).

[2] Bennett, p. 63 ff.

[3] Cf. C. O. McDonald, *Spec.* 30 (1955), p. 447. Bennett (p. 65) on the other hand points out that the phrases and symbols of *both* inscriptions are applicable to earthly love and in particular to 'amour courtois'.

the two inscriptions by beginning them both in the same words
– with a cadence that recalls the famous phrase spanning the gate
of Hell in Dante (*Inf.* III, 1.). In this way the first inscription
which obviously promises blessing and happiness, includes an
undertone of ironic reference to the acute contrast contained in
that message. We see how Chaucer has characteristically trans-
formed the Homeric theme of the two gateways[1] (closely akin
to the primeval, old theme of the choice between two paths
[Hesiod]) in order to bring out the essentially dualistic nature
of love. For he is not concerned with two gates or paths of
which one has to be selected, but with *one* entrance bearing *two*
inscriptions. No 'choice' then is possible; whoever goes through
the gateway accepts both possibilities.

The antithesis between the two inscriptions is repeated in a
shortened form in the contrastingly parallel verbs and descriptive
phrases[2] with which the poet expressed his indecision. Chaucer
gives us the contrast in various ways, and uses several means
(culminating in the vivid comparison at line 148) to prolong
the poet's state of rigid fascination over all but two stanzas,
stressing his inability to come to any decision, his almost
crippled condition. Once more we have a state of mind – in this
case the poet's own dilemma – which practically rules out any
decision, transposed into a strikingly symbolic *external* situation.
Moreover, we have here an emotional dramatic climax within
the 'course of the action'; for what we are shown is a complete
deadlock only resolved by Africanus, the poet's guide. It therefore falls to Africanus not only to speak but to act; and when with
an encouraging handshake he passes out of the poem at the gate
of the love-garden, he has been more than merely a companion
and an interpreter.

Throughout the 'Africanus episode' we have noted a dramatic
method involving both preparation and suspense; this was
brought out in the dialogue between Africanus and the poet
by means of the hesitation and indecision of the latter, caught
in the toils of the contradictory inscriptions, then by delay and
deadlock, and finally by the resumption of the 'action' when
Africanus takes a hand in it. As soon as the poet has passed into

[1] Cf. *Odyssey* 19, 562.
[2] On the rhetorical figure 'contentio' in *PF*, cf. D. Everett, p. 104.

the park of love, however, and is thrown upon his own resources, the emotional situation and with it the method of presentation undergo a change. The web of introspective dubiety and hesitation is broken; and now we can relax and gaze our fill, absorbing and lingering over the wealth of impressions spread so profusely and in such vivid detail before us.

### THE PARK OF LOVE

The happy, spontaneous cry of 'But, Lord, so I was glad and wel begoon' (171) sounds in this context like a sigh of relief as it ushers in the description of this region of love; and it is one of the choicest poetic pictures to be found in Chaucer's work. If we compare these stanzas with the equally vivid and detailed descriptions in the *House of Fame* (in particular from the third Book) we shall see clearly how in this present case Chaucer has mastered his rich material. Instead of random impressions piled up in almost bewildering profusion, what we have here is a succession of carefully balanced stanzas of which each as a rule treats a new theme, alternating visual and oral effects subtly varying sight with hearing and touch, the cumulative impact at the same time creating an 'overall atmosphere'.

Recent commentaries have already dealt so fully[1] with the origin and 'significatio' of the various themes in Chaucer's description of the park of love, that there is no need to enlarge on these again. The individual items derive from a host of typical conventional details mostly belonging to the 'locus amoenus',[2] the 'paradis terrestre', and the 'natural opening';[3] and description taken from Boccaccio's *Teseida* provided Chaucer with further conventional material. To trace the origin of these 'topoi' back however to the ideal landscape and the paradisal pleasance serves to divert our minds from Chaucer's own artistry rather than to stress it. For the secret of these stanzas does

[1] See particulars in Bennett Ch. II and Brewer, *PF*, which have largely superseded the references in my *Der Junge Chaucer*, p. 177. And see also R. W. Frank, *PMLA* 71 (1956); C. O. McDonald, *Speculum* 30 (1955), and R. A. Pratt, *PMLA* 62 (1947).

[2] Cf. E. R. Curtius, Ch. 10, § 3.

[3] Cf. D. Scheludko, 'Zur Geschichte des Natureinganges bei den Trobadors', *ZfFSL* 60 (1936).

not lie in their blending of many typical traits but in Chaucer's way of giving new life to what is characteristic and conventional; he links it with the dreamer's own life and experience, and combines these heteogeneous elements in a definite sequence that forges a single chain of impressions.

The dreamer's personality is kept present to our minds; we also follow as he sees and takes in what goes on around him, and we share in his astonishment and delight, his doubts and comments.[1] From the very beginning the reader is led on to see as it were with the eyes of the dreamer, and when 'that joye was to seene' (175) rounds off the first stanza of this section, the reader's feelings are voiced at the same time.

The catalogue of trees that now follows is another case in point. This enumeration of various species – a familiar convention[2] – gives point, as it were, to the dreamer's delight at the richness and variety of the magnificent park – an impression which is reinforced when animals, colours, personified abstractions and species of birds are also mentioned. The epithets applied to the trees do not make us 'see' them any better, but they have associative value and thus enhance the plastic image we gain of each individual tree.[3] For a mere list of names would not have impressed each individual species on the reader's consciousness.

### CHAUCER AND BOCCACCIO

In each of the following stanzas instead of enumeration Chaucer gives us a self-contained picture or some special theme; and they are closely modelled – with characteristic alterations – on Boccaccio's *Teseida*. Boccaccio's art of poetic description came so near to what Chaucer was aiming at that such extensive borrowing seemed natural. Boccaccio's influence on him, however, did not result in more or less fortuitous borrowing of

[1] Cf. 172, 183, 190, 194, 198, 200, 208, 211, 218, 223, 224 etc.

[2] In addition to Robinson, p. 793, cf. Bennett, p. 73 f., Brewer, *PF*, p. 106, and Root, *MP* 15 (1917), and Lane, Cooper and Sedgwick, *The Classical Weekly* 22 (1929).

[3] Schaar's verdict, 'This description is a predominantly abstract one' (*The Golden Mirror*, 1955, p. 370), is surely too negative. For a contrary view see Malone, p. 70. Bennett interprets the catalogue of trees at several 'levels', finding it tinged with a 'sense of ambivalence and indeterminacy'; but this surely reads too much into this stanza. (p. 79)

formal and stylistic elements from the works which served as models; it amounted to a conscious expansion of a poetic technique which Chaucer could learn from Boccaccio. Guillaume de Lorris whose *Roman de la Rose* Chaucer had translated, had described his love-garden and the personified abstractions who lived in it in order to build up an action; he had sought to represent a love-story in an allegorical form by means of the interaction of chosen personified states of mind. But what Boccaccio does is to present this whole allegorical world merely as a charming and static picture, limiting himself to tracing the picturesque outlines of this peopled scene. The individual personified abstractions have ceased to do anything at all; they are silent, neither uttering didactic speeches nor indeed engaged in any kind of conflict with one another. Boccaccio looks back over a century of the *Roman de la Rose* tradition, and condenses in a few stanzas the cumbrous apparatus of personified abstractions which had formerly taken up thousands of lines of verse. In place of an *allegoresis* that analysed and expounded, he offers us a charming and decorative picture.

Like Boccaccio, Chaucer has abandoned this world of allegorical forms and introduces his love-garden as a picture, a decorative and appropriate setting, a prelude to the birds' subsequent debate about love. And it is typical of Chaucer that this debate, the 'drama' played out in the love-garden, is enacted by the various birds and not by the customary personified abstractions; in this way a totally different world is introduced into Chaucer's allegorical dream-poem.

Like Boccaccio, Chaucer favours description which though concise and concentrated, can absorb a wealth of individual features. As the former didactic application and analytical *allegoresis* decreased, new elements in the art of presentation could come into play.[1] Boccaccio developed an acute sense of the picturesque beauty and wealth of plastic detail that lay in these allegorical themes. He thus acted as a vigorous stimulus to Chaucer's gift for vivid detail and picturesque description. Machaut and Froissart had had little to offer in this field. Moreover much of the liquid warmth, the music, the 'swetenesse' of Italian poetry seemed also to have permeated Chaucer's

[1] Cf. C. S. Lewis, *The Allegory of Love*, passim.

language. The mellifluous lines in which he delicately and meticulously paints the natural scene for us is indeed something new in English poetry. His contemporaries and successors were also aware of this and were particularly responsive to this aspect of his art; poems such as *The Flower and the Leaf*, *The Cuckoo and the Nightingale* or Lydgate's *The Complaint of the Black Knight* indeed bear witness to this fact.[1]

This survey has been necessary for a proper estimate of Chaucer's description of the park of love, not only as regards the poem itself but also in the larger context of the development of English literature. Turning now to textual detail we see Chaucer, in the stanzas which he takes from Boccaccio, stressing and developing these same elements which we have noted. An instance occurs in the stanza which immediately follows the list of trees:

> A gardyn saw I ful of blosmy bowes
> Upon a ryver, in a grene mede,
> There as swetnesse everemore inow is,
> With floures white, blewe, yelwe, and rede,
> And colde welle-stremes, nothyng dede,
> That swymmen ful of smale fishes lighte,
> With fynnes rede and skales sylver bryghte. (183)

Comparison with Boccaccio[2] shows mostly slight alterations or additions resulting in what we take to be typically Chaucerian diction. For instance, whereas Boccaccio writes '. . . d'ogni fior novello' (VII, 51), Chaucer names the individual colours 'with floures white, blewe, yelwe, and rede' (186). He expands Boccaccio's line 'E fonti vide e chiare vi surgieno' to give us a picture that is more vivid and colourful, by peopling the waters with glistening little fishes 'with fynnes rede and skales sylver bryghte'. Indeed, he sometimes adds concrete detail and bright colouring to Boccaccio's more condensed but also more general description, in order to give a minutely detailed picture. This sort of medieval 'miniature technique'[3] is typical of Chaucer, and

[1] Cf. various fifteenth- and sixteenth-century assessments of Chaucer in C. F. E. Spurgeon, *Five Hundred Years of Chaucer Criticism and Allusion*, 1925.

[2] Cf. recent investigations by R. A. Pratt, *PMLA* 62 (1947).

[3] Schaar speaks of the 'pointilliste technique – dissolving the visual impression . . . into bright particulars' (*The Golden Mirror*, p. 393).

corresponds to the pictorial art of his day. He tends, to be sure, to use more words in rendering a passage by Boccaccio than are to be found in the original. But to describe him as being 'more profuse' than Boccaccio would not do him justice. For most of his additions and expansions are in the direction of a more vivid and detailed description.

Chaucer's expansion of his model, Boccaccio's *Teseida*, is not however limited to the above traits; we have already indicated that he also adds further conventional features to his park of love. The stanza at lines 197–210, for instance, introduces the 'earthly paradise'. The hint given earlier in the birds' angelic song (191) is now expanded and emphasized – possibly under the influence of Dante's description of the earthly paradise (Purg. 28, 9–15) and of the *Anticlaudianus* (I, 3).[1] The description of the constantly mild and temperate air and the evergreen foliage fulfils what the first inscription on the gate had promised: 'There grene and lusty May shal evere endure' (130). And the two phrases 'blysful place' and 'welle of grace'[2] (127–9), likewise mentioned in the inscription, are also elaborated in the features of the 'earthly paradise' taken and expanded from the *Teseida*. The 'ideal landscape', now enhanced, has become the 'earthly paradise' – not by a random or merely decorative enrichment of conventional detail, but by skilful and deliberate expansion. Furthermore, it enhances the special effect this description makes within the whole poem. And this effect is what we must now try to define.

The dominant impression is one of growing delight at the loveliness of the park (cf. for instance 208). We, like the poet, are intended to share in the feast of beauty and splendour for eye and ear. The charm, the enchantment of earthly beauty had never before been so eloquently presented in English poetry. Surely it is impossible to doubt that Chaucer himself

[1] We may also recall Granusion, the dwelling-place of Physis, described by Bernardus Silvestris, as a medieval version of the paradisal evergreen garden (*De mundi universitate* 9, 15 ff.). Further material is given by H. R. Patch, *The Other World*, 1950. Cf. also Bennett, p. 70 f. For the love-garden as depicted by medieval miniaturists, cf. Kuhn, *Die Illustration des Rosenromans*, 1912.

[2] Various explanations have been offered of the significance and symbolism of the 'welle of grace'. Cf. Bennett, p. 66; D. Bethurum, *Essays in Honor of Walter Clyde Curry*, 1954, p. 42.

responded eagerly to this paradisal and yet earthbound world of the senses.[1]

Chaucer gives us what appears to be a repetition of the development of the ideal landscape into a love-garden; this had already been exemplified in the 'locus amoenus' as interpreted by Servius, Virgil's commentator.[2] For it is not clear until line 211 that what we have here is a garden of love and not simply an evergreen earthly paradise. Chaucer follows accepted tradition in peopling his strange park with the personified abstractions of 'fine amour' and with mythological figures; and, like Claudian long before him[3], he places the temple of Venus within it.

### CUPID AND VENUS

Richly allusive and detailed stanzas are introduced by a picture of Cupid as the poet catches sight of him, 'under a tre'. This reminds us that the poet has not passed into some new region; he is still in the same park whose individual trees had been enumerated at the outset of the description.[4] The personifications of love which are now mentioned and which derive for the most part from figures in the *Teseida*[5] bring love's whole circle and compass before us in the shortest possible form; we see all that goes to make up her attributes and phases, her facets and attendant phenomena, her resources and methods.[6] 'Meede' (bribes) and the 'Craft that can and hath the myght/To don by force a wyght to don folye' (220), introduce the questionable and negative aspects of love, and we seem to be being prepared for what the *second* inscription had warned of and threatened as a possibility. But it would be dangerous to try to read any direct

[1] Here, too, opinions have differed. Brewer, *PF* (p. 44), writes: 'Both Boccaccio and Chaucer, like Spenser after them, wished to describe what they deplored in rich and luxuriant terms as a set-piece of beautiful description. . . . Beautiful evil is still beautiful' – Brewer is however referring here solely to Venus and her temple. For a contrasting view cf. Bethurum, *loc. cit.* p. 45.

[2] Cf. Curtius, Ch. 10, § 3.

[3] *De Nuptiis Honnorii et Mariae*; cf. also Neilson, *The Origins and Sources of the Court of Love*, 1899, p. 15.

[4] Boccaccio's rather different version has 'among the bushes' (Fra gli albuscelli, *Tes.* 7, 54).

[5] For details, cf. Bennett and Brewer, *PF*, and also Pratt, *SP* 42 (1945), *PMLA* 62 (1947), and McDonald, *Spec.* 30 (1955).

[6] Cf. D. Bethurum, *loc. cit.* p. 45.

contrast into what Chaucer has given us, any antithesis between pure natural love and its sinful unnatural counterpart, between 'fine amour' and the natural choice of a mate; for both aspects are mingled and blended in the personified abstractions he delineates.[1] Where, indeed, could the line be drawn betweer them? Are Beauty and Youth 'sinfully-sensuous'; and where does the innocuous 'Dame Pees' (240) belong? Has the 'ideal' and 'natural' lover (and the commentators obviously take it that this kind of love represents Chaucer's own requirements) no concern, then, with 'Cupide, oure lord' (212)? And what of Venus, the central figure in the picture, standing there 'in a prive corner in disport', half-naked and with 'gilte heres', keeping company with her 'porter Richesse'? Does this really mean that she stands for licentiousness, vice and unchastity? It is true that the episode ends with the names of those whom love has brought to disaster. Boccaccio gives a list of them too, but with Chaucer they are placed more conspicuously at the end, like a warning epilogue to the whole passage; he has also added some important names. Here, then, we have the fulfilment of the dire threat in the second inscription; but no explicit moral judgment is passed on those named, nor is a moral assessment made of any particular kind of love.

Besides, this whole scene passes before the poet's eye like a 'spectacle', a dumb-show, a series of 'tableaux vivants'. He wanders through the park, 'learning' and 'seeking', and sees around him the wide range of love's manifold experience symbolically reproduced within a small compass. Chaucer's aim here was not to take sides or to contrast two 'poles' of love from some moral point of view; what he wanted was to represent the contradiction in love's whole complex range, its shifts and compromises, but also its happy potentialities.

Chaucer, like Boccaccio, in only a few cases qualifies or describes the personified abstractions of the park of love in any way, as a rule he simply names them.[2] This gives particular importance to the few details that we *are* given; and their form

---

[1] On this vexed question, see McDonald, *Spec.* 30 (1955); B. H. Bronson, 'In Appreciation of Chaucer's *PF*', *Univ. of California Publ. in Engl.* 3 (1935) and Bennett, *passim*.

[2] McDonald uses this observation among others in support of his contention that

and their altered arrangement are typically Chaucerian, though the stanzas themselves derive from the *Teseida*. It is worth while noting the irony (not present in Boccaccio) which shows us Dame Patience sitting on a 'hil of sond' (243) – an incongruous image, quite apart from any symbolic significance it may have. And, referring to Venus, we have 'But thus I let hire lye' (279) – a favourite transitional formula, too, in Chaucer's later works – which ends this magnificent description on a note of irony.

Having contemplated these images of unhappy lovers, the poet has now passed from his first feeling of relief and delight on entering the park of love, to one of despondency. The line 'Forth welk I tho myselven to solace' (297) expresses this. It also carries us over to the recovery of spirits, indeed the exultation, which result from the sight of Nature enthroned, and which find expression in the incomparable lines, 299–301. These contain one of the few 'poetic comparisons' in the whole poem; indeed, there is not a trace of satire or irony, not a tincture of realistic disillusion, in the entire passage. We feel after these lines that something new and important is about to begin now.

### NATURE

The advent of Nature marks the climax of the 'Parliament'. For it is Nature who will preside over the birds' parliament; besides giving its name to the poem, this parliament occupies its latter half, to which the preceding episodes had all led up. In a poem true to the tradition of the 'love-vision' and mainly concerned with a 'love debate', it is Nature and not the god of love or some kindred personified figure who presides over the debate. This important extension of the framework hitherto accepted is of the greatest significance for the whole poem.

In his portrayal of Nature Chaucer cites Alanus as if to justify himself for not giving any detailed description. Not only does this reference demonstrate that after nearly two hundred years Alanus's influence was still an active one, and testify to the

---

*all* the personified abstractions illustrate the second inscription (Disdayn and Daunger), that they hinder growth and fertility, and are therefore opposed to 'Nature'. But this ignores the fact that the description of the love-garden represents the fulfilment of the *first* inscription also.

intellectual range of Chaucer's audience; we also see Chaucer once more bowing to an 'authority' whose brilliant portrayal of one of the most difficult and at the same time central themes could not be bettered. Indeed, when Spenser came to undertake a description of Nature in the *Faerie Queene*[1] he cites this very passage from Chaucer.

Chaucer expressly refers to Alanus from whose work the Middle Ages derived their conception of Nature. And the fact that he does so has led commentators of the *Parliament* to interpret the character and significance of Nature in Chaucer's work for the most part in terms of this general conception as defined by Alanus. It is true that when he was writing his poem Chaucer had Alanus's Nature and also that of Jean de Meun in mind; certain of her attributes indeed constitute direct parallels or borrowings. Without doubt it is most significant that it is not Venus but Nature whom the poet reaches at the end of his wanderings through the park of love. It is also no accident that Nature, the 'mater generationis', the embodiment of the generative principle, the symbol of fertility, of the continuous abundance of God's creation, should preside over the birds' great assembly and their choice of mates on St Valentine's day. The linking of this conception with that of courtly chivalric love, so different in origin, lends a peculiar charm and subtle dramatic tension to the birds' debate. Possibly Chaucer chose this way to pose a problem which may have had some special topical significance.

Even so, however, one is not necessarily justified in drawing all the conclusions which, on the basis of Alanus and the thirteenth-century school of Chartres, would see Nature in the *Parliament* as evidence that Chaucer takes any definite line over this problem of love. It has been amply demonstrated[2] to what extent Alanus's Nature is a poetic symbol for the conquest over an exclusively other-worldly philosophy based on the 'contemptus mundi'. Furthermore, we have read how Nature assigns its due place in God's creation to sexual love within the marriage bond, and how the twelfth century developed a theory of earthly

---

[1] *Faerie Queene* VII, 7, 9. When speaking of Nature, Lydgate also cites Alanus's portrayal (*Ballad on the Forked Head Dresses of Ladies*).

[2] Bennett, Ch. III; Brewer, *PF*, pp. 26 ff., p. 43; cf. also E. R. Curtius, Ch. 6.

beauty as an 'outward and visible sign' of the miracle of His divine creation. Such a view, however, would mean that in Chaucer's poem Nature represents an attempted solution, a formula offered by the poet, which would reconcile the conflict between a philosophy which excluded love (such as that mirrored in the *Somnium*) and an erotic sensuality (seen at times within the confines of Venus's temple) that leads to disaster. But this kind of moral-philosophical interpretation is obliged to take its arguments from what the Middle Ages associated and connected with Nature rather than from Chaucer's own text; this offers very few points of contact in this respect. Chaucer had quite deliberately exercised restraint in his portrayal of Nature. His careful way of omitting or at best barely hinting rather indefinitely at what might lead on to further conclusions, might well inspire a like restraint on the part of his commentators.

Some reservation is needed, too, in following the development of allegorized Nature from Alanus by way of Chaucer and on into the fifteenth century.[1] What Alanus aimed at was to give expression to his complex, philosophical conception of Nature by means of a comprehensive and detailed allegorical portrayal of her dwelling, her clothes, figure and actions. He regarded the allegorical guise as mainly a means of imparting and conveying his thought. No poet after Alanus, however, ever again attempted such an exhaustive portrayal of Nature. For Nature – like so many other conceptions – then became secularized and popularized. Certain isolated features were picked out from Alanus's large canvas while its philosophical content faded into the background. The portrayal of Nature in the second part of the *Roman de la Rose* illustrates how much of the complex philosophical material had already been whittled away. By the fifteenth century Alanus's Nature, so nobly conceived as the principle that rules the spheres, the 'vicar of God', had become a charming goddess of springtime and love, a conventional figure in the elegant poetry of the court.

Chaucer, the first to portray Nature in English poetry, stands midway in the course of this development. In his usual manner he

[1] Cf. Elsa Berndt, 'Dame Nature in der englischen Literatur bis herab zu Shakespeare', *Palaestra* 110 (1923); E. C. Knoulton, *JEGP* 20 (1921); Marie Gothein, 'Der Gottheit lebendiges Kleid', *Arch. f. Religions-Wissensch.* 9 (1906).

tosses in here and there a trait from Alanus, but he does not attempt to give any systematic picture of Nature. Certain important basic conceptions from Alanus are suggested in a word or two. The easy grace and nonchalance with which he grasps the essentials of this complex intellectual inheritance without attempting to give a complete or detailed presentation, allows us to guess at the new poetic freedom which had replaced the circumstantial didacticism of former times.

The kindly human character with which Nature is endowed by Chaucer is also typical of his manner. As in Alanus, she is called the 'vicaire of the almyghty God' (379) and therefore occupies the highest position in the poem. But at the same time she is represented as a human being, an attractive and likeable person who can however if need be intervene in good round terms (521). Chaucer never had any liking for lofty condescension or haughtiness either in people or in the sphere of myth or allegory; and so he never represents these qualities except in an ironic vein. Like the golden eagle, like Fame, like the god of love in the Prologue to the *Legend of Good Women*, Nature is delineated along the familiar lines of all mankind. Machaut and Deschamps do something in this direction too, but they lack Chaucer's humour, the light touch and the skill which make his figures so charmingly alive for us. Indeed, Chaucer's whole description of Nature on her flowery hill amid the birds, radiates both intimacy and freshness.

## CHAUCER'S ART OF DESCRIPTION

A few words must now be said about this art of description and the manner in which Chaucer presents his material. He describes, narrates and comments; and all three methods overlap, alternate and combine to form a single whole, like a mosaic built up piece by piece of tiny individual stones. The very first stanza for instance, after the introductory metaphorical phrases of praise and delight (298–301), gives us a clear-cut picture of Nature enthroned in a 'launde' on a flowery hill in an arbour of deftly-twisted branches. After these first four lines, all sorts of birds are mentioned which crowd round Nature 'To take hire dom and yeve hire audyence' (308); and this is an important observation.

The contrast between Nature and her vast feathered retinue is developed in the next stanzas. Chaucer has contrived to define the real and multi-dimensional situation in one single sentence. What is said of the noise all these birds were making leads on to a survey of the wide scene (earth, air, tree and lake, 313). Next, the impression of this jostling and thronging is linked up to this; and now the poet can relate from his experience what had merely been hinted at in the preceding stanza (307):

> And that so huge a noyse gan they make
> That erthe, and eyr, and tre, and every lake
> So ful was, that unethe was there space
> For me to stonde, so ful was al the place. (312)

The next stanza turns again to Nature, this time not immediately and directly, but with reference to Alanus's portrayal. At the same time the action takes a step forward; the 'noble emperesse ... Bad every foul to take his owne place,'; and we are again reminded of the St Valentine's Day rites (321–2). After the five stanzas crowded with names, listing and characterising the individual species of birds, we return to the overall picture and plunge once more into the 'action':

> And everich of hem dide his besy cure
> Benygnely to chese or for to take,
> By hire acord, his formel or his make. (369)

Chaucer's description does not flow on systematically or regularly. He darts forwards and backwards, interrupting it with lists and digressions, with observations by the narrator, with repetitions of details or circumstances, throwing in reflections, comments or ejaculations; he condenses and expands, now crawling and now leaping forward, so that the story is forever moving to and fro, his portrayal switching from one category to the next. But it is just this absence of calm and system, this frequent intercalation of the most incongruous methods of telling or elaborating the story, that give it life and variety. Besides, in this way we have the impression of hearing it all being spoken – and indeed Chaucer's work was primarily if not exclusively intended to be heard. We have a very subtle art combined here with apparent artlessness, a design meticulously thought out and matched with improvisation – the secret of more than one kind of great art.

Before Chaucer embarks on the dramatic interchange between the birds and Nature, he gives us a long list of the species that are thronging about her. Catalogues of this sort were a favourite 'topos' in medieval poetry often used by Chaucer himself, as in the 'catalogue of trees' in the *Parliament* (176). Here too, however, this is not merely a list of birds; it plays its own particular artistic part in the poem as a whole. For before the dialogue draws us too into taking sides, we find as it were a rich tapestry unrolled before our eyes, like those from fourteenth- and fifteenth-century Burgundy or Flanders where a colourful abundance of God's creatures is spread out in individual and minutely detailed little pictures. In this case what we actually see prepares the ground for the interplay of ideas; image and verbal interchange are complementary. Furthermore, human attributes are chosen to describe this world of birds; not merely in his attitude to the other species but in his innate being, every bird is characterized by human virtues – or more usually by human vices and failings.[1] Thieving, jealousy, treachery, hatred, deceit, cowardice, bloodthirstiness, drunkenness, and much else is mentioned in connection with individual birds, while the turtle-dove's 'true heart' and the 'wise' raven are much less in evidence. This is a far from peaceable and harmonious company that we meet with here; it is a world of creatures full of antagonism and rivalry.[2] These five stanzas containing the catalogue of birds, then, prepare our minds in divers ways for the drama that is to follow.

### THE BIRDS' DEBATE

In the birds' debate about love at which Nature presides we have another instance of an extremely subtle combination of several genres and specific formal types. In each case certain important characteristics of these traditional genres are *not* taken over; and the formal pattern selected is either expanded and altered in some

[1] Cf. Bennett, *passim*.
[2] The birds which the poet had heard singing 'with voys of aungel in here armonye' (191) have of course nothing in common with *these* birds.

significant respect, or else amalgamated with another basic scheme. We shall be better able to appreciate this art of easy handling, of light and subtle transition, of formal types selected and then intermingled and superimposed, if we glance at the relevant models and conventions.

It was soon recognized[1] that the birds' debate in Chaucer resembled the 'demande d'amour', a special form of the medieval disputation in verse which French literature in particular had developed.[2] Comparison here however, at once brings out marked differences. It was typical of the 'demande d'amour' that a definite alternative between clearly defined objects was stated. The lovers between whom a choice had to be made usually stood for some quality or rank, but the differences had to be so balanced that there was the same measure of good and bad to be argued for each in turn. In the course of the debate, too, this balance had to be sustained, so that the chooser was confronted with a dilemma; and in general no definite choice was in fact arrived at. This kind of 'dilemma' situation, indeed, has affinities with Chaucer's basic intention.

The indecisive result of the eagles' wooing in the *Parliament*, however, bears only a superficial resemblance to that of the *demande*, for it springs from a different root. In the first place Chaucer has disturbed the traditional balance between diverse and clear-cut alternatives; for although his three eagles differ somewhat in the length of their wooing, their conduct of it is more or less the same.[3] Besides, he shows the first eagle in a more advantageous light than the other two and makes it probable that the formel too will prefer him (392, 394 ff., 442 ff., 632 ff.). Chaucer is not in the least interested in nice distinctions on the question of love, but in something simpler, something indeed much nearer to human experience than the artificial casuistry of these 'questions of love'. There are other deviations from the usual pattern, too; the eagles present their suits quite

[1] Cf. Manly, *Studien zur Engl. Philologie* 30 (1913); Farnham, *PMLA* 32 (1917).

[2] Evro Ilvonen, 'Les demandes d'amours dans la littérature français du moyen âge', *Neuphilolog. Mitteilungen* 14 (1912).

[3] Cf. Brewer, *PF*, pp. 10 ff. Bronson is right in calling Chaucer's treatment of the 'demande d'amour' 'a delicious *reductio ad absurdum* of the type' (*Univ. of Calif. Publ. in Engl.* 3, 1935, p. 213).

briefly, and as each of them speaks once only, there is no chance for any controversy between them to develop.

Above all, however, the eagles' wooing is merely the frame-work, the starting-point for something different and much closer to Chaucer's heart. For it would be superficial to consider the discussion among the other birds as simply a debate on the question 'Whom ought the formel to mate with?' It really serves to bring out the differences in the attitudes to the whole problem of love – and in particular of courtly love – shown by the individual birds as representatives of their class. The same is true, too, of each bird's choice of a mate; this is cited at the beginning as the object of the assembly (310, 369, 386); but it takes place at the very end and is disposed of in a few lines. As so often in Chaucer, the opening situation simply provides the opportunity for leading on to something else.

The typical theme, too, of the 'Contending Lovers'[1] – so familiar from fairy- and folk-tales and from shorter romances – is no more than superficially connected with the *Parliament*. True, we have the judge who shall decide which of the suitors has deserved the girl's hand and the general public joining in the argument; furthermore we have the postponement of the decision, which the judge eventually leaves to the girl herself. These items blended with the convention of the birds' 'court of love' bring us somewhere near the design of the *Parliament*; but there are certain important elements in Chaucer's poem which cannot at all be derived from these sources. They cannot have inspired either Chaucer's satirical, comic treatment, the full exposition of courtly love, or the distinctions drawn between the 'estates' as social categories.

Similar reservations must be made, too, with reference to the parliaments or 'parleys' of birds which seem to have been a recurring literary genre during the Middle Ages.[2] For they were without any picturesque detail or action, and are mostly no more than a didactic peg on which to hang a string of maxims. Their abstract design contrasts, once again, with Chaucer's

---

[1] Farnham in *PMLA* 32 (1917), *PMLA* 35 (1920); also in *Wisconsin Studies in Lang. and Lit.* 2 (1918).

[2] Cf. W. Seelmann, 'Die Vogelsprachen (Vogelparlamente) der mittelalterlichen Literatur', *Jahrb. d. Vereins für niederdeutsche Sprachforschung* 14 (1888).

brisk and well-knit dramatic action. Besides, it would be a mistake to take this classification of the birds as being a faithful picture of the parliaments and 'estates' of those days[1] – although it is possible to draw some comparisons here (see below p. 241 f.).

When we consider all the types and individual works which served as a model or a stimulus for Chaucer's *Parliament* – the poems of the 'court of love' tradition, for instance, and such debates as the *Owl and the Nightingale* or the *Thrush and the Nightingale* – we realize the range of his sources, for the *Parliament* took over aspects of the 'folk-tale' tradition and the sophisticated dialectic of the French school, of popular poetry and the didactic and artificial variants of the 'demande d'amour'. The result is that the design of the *Parliament*, drawn from such divers sources, represents a unique synthesis of then prevailing stylistic currents which normally run counter to one another and are rarely mingled. In the *Parliament* we have in fact a microcosm of that process of fusion between heterogeneous stylistic worlds which is obvious on a larger scale in Chaucer's poetry as a whole.

This blending of forms demonstrates once again clearly that we are not dealing here with 'derivation' of any kind; what we have in this case is a kind of novel creation in which the poet is completely free in his approach to the source from which he took his material. This is not an instance of 'influence', but of the artist's conscious choosing and re-shaping, discarding what is useless. Chaucer only hints at the literary conventions handed down by literary tradition and familiar to his public. He raises certain expectations only to disappoint them again as he leads on to some other theme. He avoids whatever is stiff and dogmatic about any convention of which he makes use. Formal stereotyped features fade and dwindle, leaving room for something nearer to real experience and for truer characterization. We saw how Chaucer rejected the balanced alternatives and lengthy reasoning of the strictly correct 'demande d'amour', and gave us a greatly shortened version of the 'Contending Lovers' theme. There is barely a hint, too, of the archetype of the 'débat' so familiar to the Middle Ages; for in place of the regular alternation of two or three contestants piling argument on argument,

[1] Cf. Brewer, *PF*, p. 35; M. Emslie, *EC 5* (1955).

we have a lively discussion carried on by quite a number of speakers, in the course of which the original inquiry is carried much further. Instead of the random catalogue of birds that appeared in the Old French poems we have an assembly of real types whose gestures, speech and behaviour contrast very sharply with one another.

### THE ART OF CONTRAST
### AND VERBAL CHARACTERIZATION

In the past, 'interpretation' of the *Parliament* and in particular of the birds' debate was too often considered without reference to artistic effect and the poet's method of presentation. Building up an abstract frame of reference and remote analogies in regard to concepts and ideas – supported by textual evidence so slight as to amount to no more than suggestion – can easily involve ignoring what was then and still is of vital importance for the reader of Chaucer. In the birds' dispute this vital aspect is displayed in the superb manner in which the types of birds, each tellingly delineated and all subtly distinguished, engage in a lively, dramatic discussion. Their standpoints, views and temperaments are contrasted and the whole is seasoned with humour and satire. With the ease and objectivity that are the mark of a really great dramatist, each one of them is given his due in the end; any 'taking of sides' is unobtrusively done and by no means implies any relative assessment. The way in which this little drama is sustained and expressed quite rightly strikes the reader as being quite incomparable; and we shall now turn to it more closely.

The narrator's unambiguous 'But to the poynt' (372) carries us forward from the description of the 'background' to the main scene; and we see Nature depicted, holding the formel on her wrist and turning to her in delighted affection. In typically Chaucerian manner this little miniature is closely linked with words of comment and praise, with lines that bring the world of courtly chivalry and its standards before us:

> But to the poynt: Nature held on hire hond
> A formel egle, of shap the gentilleste
> That evere she among hire werkes fond,

> The moste benygne and the goodlieste.
> In hire was everi vertu at his reste,
> So ferforth that Nature hireself hadde blysse
> To loke on hire, and ofte hire bek to kysse. (372)

The formel's praise is matched by that of the royal eagle:

> The foul royal, above yow in degre,
> The wyse and worthi, secre, trewe as stel, (394)

and these epithets once again evoke the ethos of courtly chivalry. After such introductory companion passages, the speech in which the tercel woos the formel – its vocabulary, thought, and the gestures that accompany it – quite naturally keeps within the sphere of 'courtoisie', of 'courtly love'. He speaks 'with hed enclyned and with ful humble cheere' (414), choosing his words with care and deliberation; and he expresses his meaning aptly, with conscious dignity and grave urgency. Chaucer brings into this speech a considerable number of the basic terms and conceptions of chivalry, and these four stanzas read almost like an abstract of 'fine amour'.[1] There is no 'gross exaggeration' and yet the ironic tones in the royal tercel's lofty protestations are unmistakable. His utter abasement before the sovereign lady of his choice, his readiness to die on the spot or – if unfaithful – to let himself be torn in pieces, his vow of unwavering service however distant the beloved, and especially his repeated appeals to the lady for 'mercy', for 'grace', as well as his reference to his own 'wo' (416–41) – in all this we hear the language and constantly reiterated clichées of 'fine amour'. But when it is given us in so pointed and concentrated a form, and above all in the context of a parliament of birds, it cannot fail to produce an effect of delicate satire and subtle irony. The opening lines of the stanza that follows is a piece of intentionally 'fine' writing; and the poetic comparison in them, portraying with special care and emphasis the formel's modest blushes at this noble suit,

---

[1] 'Unto my soverayn lady, and not my fere,/I chese, and chese with wil, and herte, and thought' (416) Whos I am al, and evere wol hire serve,/Do what hire lest, to do me lyve or sterve;/Besekynge hire of merci and of grace,/As she that is my lady sovereyne;/Or let me deye present in this place. (419) And cf. the later use of 'untrewe' (428), 'disobeysaunt' (429), 'unkynde' (434) and the subsequent description of the eagle as 'the worthieste/Of knyghthod . . . most of estat, of blod the gentilleste' (548) and 'the gentilleste and most worthi' (635).

serve to throw the tercel's preceding speech into yet sharper relief. Furthermore, Nature's motherly, reassuring words to the formel as the stanza ends, 'Doughter, drede yow nought, I yow assure' (448) round off this noble initial wooing with a subtle, gently-ironic thrust.

The second eagle likewise uses the vocabulary of chivalric love (servyse 459, honour 461), and his wooing speech might include him in the poet's own praise when he says later that never in his life did he hear 'So gentil ple in love or other thyng' (485). And yet, having called him 'of lower kynde', Chaucer does distinguish him clearly from the first eagle. The very first words of his suit, his curt 'That shal nat be' strikes a new note, reinforced by the sturdy tone of his 'do me hangen by the hals' (458) and 'by seint John' (451). Besides, this eagle's over-confident insistence on how worthy and deserving his own love is, and the vow by which he pledges his entire possessions (al the good I have, 462), is quite unlike the royal eagle's 'ful humble cheere' (414). This eagle's speech is in contrast to that of the first; and the same is true of the third eagle's words. For his avowal 'Of long servyse avaunte I me nothing' (470) sounds like a criticism of the whole system of 'long service' due to one's lady. They seem indeed to place the second eagle's protestations in an ironic light. It has been mistakenly supposed that Chaucer intended these three eagles to be faithful representatives of a single ideal and social rank, a similar attitude; he depicts them however with slight differences which set up ironic contrasts between them.

At this point the abuse and impatience of the other birds breaks in upon this atmosphere of courtly wooing which the poet himself had likewise evoked in an admiratory stanza (484). Their impatience had been foreshadowed in almost dramatic fashion by the third eagle's opening lines:

> 'Now, sires, ye seen the lytel leyser heere;
> For every foul cryeth out to ben ago
> Forth with his make, or with his lady deere;
> And ek Nature hireself ne wol not heere,
> For taryinge here, . . . (464)

Chaucer uses this device to remind us from time to time of the many other impatient birds, even while the three eagles are exchanging their stilted speeches. Nature herself is mentioned more than once, and she too has had enough of listening to the eagles's wooing. All this serves to hint that the wooing interests no one but the eagles, and so we are not surprised when with their loud 'Have don, and lat us wende!' (492) (which the poet felt made the whole wood 'shake'), the other birds break out in indignation. This new tone corresponds to a new attitude too; what follows contrasts with the courtly demeanour evident in the style, vocabulary, thought and reactions in what had gone before. The realistic 'Kek kek! Kokkow! quek quek!' (499) of the goose, duck and cuckoo, following on the impatient general cry of 'Com of!' (494), seems to come as an anticlimax to the fine chivalric phraseology.

At the same time, too, the subject is expanded. For it is part of Chaucer's artistry that, as they comment on the eagles's wooing and the choice to be made by the formel, the answers and counsels of the different birds at the same time reveal their attitude to the problem of love. The discussion develops into a subtle and amusing interplay between the different conceptions of love held by the various 'estates'; and the various attitudes serve to throw light on one another.

Furthermore, the verbal characterization of the two opposite parties is stressed and carried forward. The way the lesser birds speak – as in the passages already cited – is curt and direct; and they use proverbial and popular turns of phrase (592, 595, 589); the example provided by the goose's blunt opening 'Al this nys not worth a flye' (501) shows how far removed it is from the courtly and formal phrases used by their counterparts. By contrast, the falcon, spokesman of the nobility, goes out of his way to speak considerately and courteously; this is brought out in his frequent choice of the subjunctive and of certain polite turns of phrase.[1] The syntax, too, as well as the language, serves to differentiate the two social levels; the speeches of the three eagles and of the falcon involve subordinate clauses, are built up logically point by point, and make liberal

[1] Ful hard were it (534) Thanne semeth it there moste be batayle (539) if that I durste it seye (541) Were sittyngest for hire, if that hir leste (551) Me wolde thynke (548) For, sires, ne taketh not agref, I preye, It may not gon . . . (543).

use of conjunctions or adverbs for proving, deducing, or making reservations, whereas the goose for instance seems to favour parataxis.

The two spheres however are in some degree interrelated. The sparrowhawk's speech, for example, as he voices his indignation at the 'parfit resoun of a goose', resembles the colloquial and proverbial phrases used by the 'lesser' birds;[1] and yet he by no means feels himself to be one of them. But the anger he thus vents at the goose's folly is aptly expressed in this kind of everyday language. The dove occupies an intermediate position in regard to the courtly ideal of love, though she is one of the 'sedfowl' listed fourth in the hierarchy of individual groups. She evidently approves of unwavering constancy, using the aristocratic terms 'lady' and 'serve'; and she is horrified at the advice of the goose who says that the suitor whose love is not requited had better choose someone else (567): 'Nay, God forbede a lovere shulde chaunge!' (582). This aristocratic, courtly attitude clearly goes far beyond the prescribed limits of her own 'degre', and her unusual sympathy with the ideals proper to the higher orders provokes the duck's ironical 'Well bourded . . . by myn hat' (589). When the dove first speaks she does so very modestly and cautiously, conscious of her own unworthiness and in particular revealing a sense of her own limitations which escapes both the eagle and the goose and cuckoo. Their confidence and arrogance are thus heightened by contrast with the dove.

## THE 'DUAL ASPECT'

In the course of the birds' discussion, Chaucer makes use of the 'dual aspect' as a dramatic device. What the narrator regards as a 'gentil ple' – so prolonged indeed that it even includes the poet's own 'inexpressibility-topos'[2] – seems like 'cursede pletynge' (495) and a waste of time to the lesser birds. What appears as a mark of distinction and merit from one point of view – perpetual constancy, long service, patient waiting, pangs of

---

[1] Cf. Emslie, *EC* 5 (1955), p. 15.

[2] This is the technical term used in the English translation of Curtius's book for the poet's conventional contention that he is unable to give expression to the subject (Curtius, Ch. 8, § 5).

longing and readiness to die – seems to the goose and the duck
to be unbelievable folly and absurd bombast. Yet the remarks
made by the lesser birds about the ideal of courtly love are so
phrased as to bring home to us not merely their narrow-minded
arrogance but also the grain of truth, the portion of sound
commonsense and unbiased critical judgment that these words
include. Our own sound commonsense tells us, too, that in these
three eagles with the single object of their suit we are confronted
with an insoluble problem implicit in the ideal of courtly love
itself. The formel can choose only one of the eagles, and the
remaining two are thus doomed to pine in unrequited longing
for the rest of their lives. It is in fact this insoluble problem
which excites the lesser birds' criticism.[1] What the duck says
about the senselessness of a love for ever unrequited:

> That men shulde loven alwey causeles,
> Who can a resoun fynde or wit in that?
> Daunseth he murye that is myrtheles?
> Who shulde recche of that is recheles? (590)

justly provokes the 'gentil tercelet' to cry out 'Now fy, cherl! / . . .
Out of the donghil cam that word ful right!' (596). But in the
wider context of the whole discussion the duck's arguments by
no means fall on deaf ears – as is borne out by the cuckoo's
remarks.[2] At the close of the debate, too, Chaucer chooses a
subtle way to make us aware of the somewhat ironical state of
'frustration' into which the eagles have fallen with their wooing.
Not only do we know that only one of these three, who all pro-
test the same undying constancy, can win the formel; they are
moreover bound to remain a whole year in a state of suspense,
while the other birds' desires are at once satisfied. Nature,
who obviously disapproves of the delay pleaded by the formel
(654 ff.), comforts the eagles by saying that a year of waiting
is 'tolerable':

> Beth of good herte, and serveth alle thre.
> A yer is nat so longe to endure, . . . (660)

---

[1] Cf. Brewer, *PF*, p. 22.

[2] On the other hand – as Malone (p. 76 f.) points out – it is the cuckoo who makes
meaningless and ridiculous suggestions.

But there is no mistaking the contrast between the delight of all
the rest as they now depart to choose their mates (And, Lord,
the blisse and joye that they make! 669) and the presumed
'inactivity' of the eagles who have to retire unsatisfied. Yet
Chaucer's delicate irony here is not of such a kind as to justify
drawing any fundamental conclusions about an implied contra-
distinction (already touched upon above) between 'natural' and
'courtly' love.[1] For the essence of the whole poem and the particular artistic effect of the birds' debate lies in the fact that there
is no 'taking of sides' in the matter; no moral is drawn. Chaucer's
aim was to let each point of view throw light on the other.[2]
Each standpoint was both right and wrong, and therefore each
could be shown with subtle irony as both reasonable and at the
same time prejudiced. We had already noted this ambivalent
and finely-graded sort of criticism. These examples of the third
eagle and the turtle-dove now clearly show it as coming 'from
within', not 'from without'. The falcon, the chosen spokesman
of the 'foules of ravyne', for instance, opens his speech with
these lines:

> Ful hard were it to preve by resoun
> Who loveth best this gentil formel heere;
> For everych hath swich replicacioun
> That non by skilles may be brought adoun.
> I can not se that argumentes avayle:
> Thanne semeth it there moste be batayle. (534)

In a wider literary context these lines might sound like a criticism
of the 'jugements', the 'demandes d'amour', the love-disputes in
which questions of love were to be resolved by an interchange of
arguments. But the falcon's words also contain a veiled criticism
of the speeches made by the three eagles, for it was 'by resoun',
that is to say, by means of argument, that they were plead-
ing their suit and their right to be 'heard'. What is now said

---

[1] These observations, based upon the text, accord in part with what is said in a
perceptive and illuminating article by M. Emslie, 'Codes of Love and Class Distinctions', *EC* 5 (1955). The present writer cannot however agree with Emslie's
principal conclusions. Cf. Cecily Clark and Brewer in *EC* 5.

[2] Muscatine (p. 119) speaks of 'a comic reflection of one attitude on the other;
each is partly admirable, partly foolish'.

reiterates[1] what the assembled birds had impatiently exclaimed at the end of the eagle's wooing:

> How sholde a juge eyther parti leve
> For ye or nay, withouten any preve? (496)

The three eagles seem therefore to be paying lip-service only, and their speeches do not advance the present problem in any way. And yet the alternative suggestion made by the falcon 'there moste be batayle' is just as 'typical of his rank'; it obviously provides no useful solution, although – with another ironic touch – the three eagles at once cry 'Al redy!' to a 'batayle'.

The 'verdit' of the goose, too, is in this same comic, ironic vein. For the goose had pushed forward even before it had been decided to choose a representative for 'every folk', a spokesman to give the 'verdit'. In her eagerness she had thus anticipated the general decision (503). But it is just this kind of pushing impudence of hers, 'with here facounde gent', that gets her chosen by the assembly of waterfowl to be their spokeswoman (554 ff.). She goes on, however, to preface her simple single-line verdict ('But she wol love hym, lat hym love another!' 567) with such pompous words and claims ('My wit is sharp' 565) that she makes herself once more ridiculous (575), and the sparrow-hawk's 'Lo, here a parfit resoun of a goos' (568) puts her back in her place again. But the hawk's words recall the falcon's final:

> Thy kynde is of so low a wrechednesse
> That what love is, thow canst nat seen ne gesse. (601)

and here we have a pointer to an understanding of the whole situation. The lower orders are in fact incapable of rightly appreciating the 'gentils' and their code of love. Every social order has been assigned its 'degre'; each has its own ideals, its view of life and sphere of perception. That being so, it is pre-sumptuous, 'meddlesome', as the dove had already called it (515), to attempt to judge the standards of any other social order.

The notions 'degre' and 'order' often occur and remind us of the hierarchical order expressed not only in the disposition and

---

[1] Nature's first words after the end of the general debate (624) also recall the falcon's words.

grouping of the birds round Nature, but also in the long catalogue of their divers species. This 'order' is further brought
home to us by Chaucer's choice of a language reminiscent of
parliamentary procedure in his day. We must bear in mind that
until well into the fourteenth century any writer who spoke of a
'parliament' meant only an 'assembly of nobles'.[1] Chaucer however is the first English poet to portray an assembly of the different 'orders', a parliament of 'gentils' and 'commons' side by side.[2]
Chaucer's *Parliament*, then, has something in it of the criticism
of the social orders that was to be so dominant a feature of the
*Canterbury Tales*. In the present poem the imitation of parliamentary procedure underlines the satire and the comic element.
For the different standpoints are not the outcome of informal
discussion of any kind; they are shown against a contrasting
background of ceremony, of weighty counsel and the formal
choice of representative spokesmen; the contrast is all the more
striking, then, between these 'humanized' birds behaving like
people, and the real feathered kingdom. It is not birds, in fact,
but humans that are made laughable.[3] This *allegoresis* from the
animal world has the effect of stressing mankind's contradictory,
strange and complex ways and conventions more strongly than
any direct portrayal could have done.[4]

Drawing attention to these hints of social satire, however,
and the occasional references to parliamentary procedure, does
not imply that Chaucer has any intention here of giving us yet
another of the many portrayals of the 'three estates'.[5] That would

---

[1] Cf. Willi Pieper, 'Das Parlament in der mittelenglischen Literatur', *Herrigs Archiv* 146 (1923). Certain features in Chaucer recall the parliament of his day: Nature's address (383–404) corresponds to the speech by the Chancellor at the opening of parliament; the distinction between 'statut' and 'ordenaunce' (387, 390); the election of a spokesman. For further critical references see Brewer, *PF*, p. 38: Malone, p. 71.

[2] Cf. the use of the epithets 'gentil' and 'gentilesse', and – for the other party – 'lewed' and 'lewednesse' (616, 520).

[3] 'The central irony: birds, the symbols of fertility, might be expected to go straight to the matter in hand . . . but they become human and complicate the bio-logical demands with elaborate conventions, differences of mores, different attitudes towards the choice . . .' Dorothy Bethurum, 'The Centre of the *PF*', *Essays in Honour of Walter Clyde Curry*, 1955, p. 46.

[4] On its function in this connection, see B. H. Bronson, *In Search of Chaucer*, 1960, p. 43.

[5] Cf. Ruth Mohl, *The Three Estates in Medieval and Renaissance Literature*, 1933.

involve more than one drastic alteration.[1] Chaucer introduced both his social satire and the literary parliament purely for reasons connected with his art – that is to say, to further his essential purpose – and this was to bring different attitudes and types together in genially impartial contrast.

By contrasting the different ideals of love, moreover, he not only achieved an artistic effect whose humour is ageless; he also epitomized a development clearly apparent in literature between the end of the fourteenth and that of the fifteenth century. The pining, ever-hopeful suitor is then being replaced by a different type, a less patient, more level-headed lover. The ideal of 'fine amour' fades and meets with adverse criticism. Chaucer's poem reminds us of the swing from courtly ideals to those of the middle-classes which took place in the fourteenth and fifteenth centuries. Yet it would be an error to read any marked 'tendency' into this delightful poem. Chaucer does nothing to affront the feelings of the courtly audience for whom his poem was composed, an audience in whose eyes 'fine amour' was still a living ideal. He does not criticize, but presents both aspects; he 'dramatises', choosing this indirect way in fact to stimulate a critical appraisal.

### THE FINAL SONG OF THE BIRDS

That Chaucer expressly avoids any 'tendency' one way or the other, any taking of sides, any definite answer to the questions he hints at during the poem is also clear from the final song which the little birds sing together in honour of Nature (To don to Nature honour and plesaunce 676) and in celebration of St Valentine's day. In fact, it is not the 'gentils' with their problems who have the last word, but the hitherto unregarded little birds[2] for whom the festive day brings the fulfilment of their desires (Sith ech of hem recovered hath hys make 688) and so both delight and happiness. We are thus led away from the unsolved problem of the eagles' wooing with its inconclusive result. Our

---

[1] Where would the turtle-dove fit in? Chaucer gives us *four* classes of birds; to which 'order' do the 'water fowl' and the 'worm-fowl' belong? Cf. also Bronson, p. 48.

[2] Cf. Brewer, *PF*, p. 25.

eyes are directed to something else, something at once simpler and wider – though it has little to do with the matters that were under discussion. The poem leaves us, then, with a feeling of relief and happy expectation. Besides, it can hardly be by accident that the most romantic among the major poems of Chaucer's earlier years should end with a jewel of pure lyricism so happily set within the fabric of the poem. This 'roundel' (680 ff.), like the famous opening lines of the Prologue to the *Canterbury Tales*, breathes an indescribable freshness and an unstudied charm. The poem ends by opening a window for the reader on to a bright, gay world full of promise; and it lends a new lustre to the undying theme of glad welcome for warmer days. Quite obviously Chaucer was consciously rounding off his problematic poem in an unproblematic way. Yet the final lines which the dreamer speaks on waking gently hint that life and with it the poet's own search will go on.

### CHAUCER'S POEM AND LITERARY CURRENTS

The *Parliament* as the last of the three longer poems considered here offers a striking example of how certain dominant tendencies in the development of English literature were modified by Chaucer's art. The satire which pervaded a large part of the literature of England and France in the thirteenth and fourteenth centuries appears in the *Parliament* only in a very veiled and qualified form. It is barely hinted at, and is used to serve artistic and didactic ends; it represents a subtle ingredient in a genial and entertaining presentation; but it is no longer the main consideration. What distinguished a great deal of satirical poetry in that century is the didactic, aim, the harsh censure, the strident complaint at deficiencies, the blatant exposure of abuses.[1] A tolerant, genial use of satire, providing entertainment and comedy for their own sake, is rare indeed; it most often appears in such animal satires as the version of the *Roman de Renard* or in animal fable such as *'Wolf and Fox'*.[2] It is therefore of

---

[1] Cf. S. M. Tucker, *Verse Satire in England before the Renaissance*, 1908; L. Levrault, *La Satire (Evolution du genre)*, 1925; J. Peter, *Complaint and Satire in Early English Literature*, 1956.

[2] *Early Middle English Texts* ed. by Dickins and Wilson, 1952.

significance that Chaucer with his talking birds is also offering us an 'animal satire'.

Chaucer's satirical art is not stimulated, however, by the ethics of a moral reformer or the invective of a militant scoffer; it has its roots in the genial delight in observation of one who knows his fellow-men well. The element of satire, like many others in Chaucer, is refined, indirect and restrained. There is no frontal attack, no zest for exposure; instead we have a contrast and the balancing of one type against another, that leads each to reveal its own nature. The germ of such delineation of types may occasionally be found in social satire, animal fables and other works; but this art of making a figure come to life by its own individual way of speaking, thinking and moving, is new in the course of literary development. And it is only possible for a creative writer with a strong dramatic vein. Dramatic qualities predominate, in fact, in this impartial juxtaposition of sharply defined types and in the creation of what is at once a discussion and a vivid scene.

In Chaucer's *Parliament*, then, we hear the first tones of that genial and also dramatic characterization which was to be the keynote of the *Canterbury Tales*. Here, Chaucer is still keeping to the allegorical idiom, and showing us birds which stand for different types of people. Soon it was people themselves, and then later on in the *Nun's Priest's Tale* he gave us birds once more, superbly characterized and acting out a little drama among themselves. When one remembers, too, that the *Parliament* is a work in the allegorical tradition of poetry, one realizes how novel this art of Chaucer's is. He broke down the limitations of allegorical poetry by giving us a vivid realistic scene and entertaining comedy within the framework of an allegory. The *Parliament* thus completes a modification in the form of allegorical poetry[1] which brought it near to disintegration. We have followed this process in the poems already considered.

There is also a further important difference from French courtly poetry of the fourteenth century, likewise bound up with Chaucer's dramatic talent. The works of Machaut, Froissart, Deschamps and other court poets keep rigidly to one key and never abandon the level of polished expression and chivalric

[1] Cf. C. S. Lewis, *The Allegory of Love.*

convention; but Chaucer introduces counterpoint into his poem. Instead of uniformity, his diction and presentation display a varied, richly contrasting gradation. The world of courtly love as presented in the *Parliament* is thrown into sharper relief by being given its contrasting counterpart. What we have here is something more than simply 'continuing to write' in a particular tradition; Chaucer keeps his distance from this tradition, and so he is able to see its features more clearly than someone totally involved in it. He himself was a man of many interests, whose life had brought him into contact with various spheres and who could stand back from what he was studying (his humour is proof incontrovertible of this); and so he succeeds in a greater degree than any other man in the whole of medieval literature in delineating the most diverse and contrasting types, characters and opinions with the same sympathetic and tolerant indulgence. In other words, he captures the whole of life. His superb command of literary genres and styles as well as his gift for dramatic presentation later helped him to achieve a delineation of the most varied characters on the scale of the *Canterbury Tales*. In the *Parliament* we can already see the seeds of this later development.

# 4

# Minor Poems

*An ABC – The Complaint unto Pity – A Complaint to his Lady –
The Complaint of Mars – Anelida and Arcite.*

The *Book of the Duchess* is our best source for discovering to
what degree Chaucer learned from Machaut and introduced
aspects of French poetry into that of England. His chief models
here were Machaut's longer allegorizing narrative poems.
Machaut's French successors on the other hand were influenced
rather more by his *ballades, virelays, roundels, complaintes*, etc.,
for which he also usually composed the music. These, with their
difficult rhythmic patterns, their studied language, and their
frequent changes of stanza-form within the same poem, were
something new in the history of French poetry. The complex
forms he used for his stanzas served as examples some decades
later for the French treatises on rhetoric[1] which dealt for the
most part with the rules for building up intricate stanzas and
lines. Machaut's lyric poems are possibly the most artificial and
conventional products of the whole fourteenth century. With
Machaut all personal and original expression is paralysed by
the exaggeration and over-elaboration of rules and forms. What
mattered in these poems was not what was said but that the
same rhyme should be used fifty or more times on end, with
numerous other artistic devices introduced as well. The technical,
formal element was employed more and more for its own sake;
and this brought with it a considerable weakening in the content
and range of themes. The same thought is stretched out to cover
a lengthy succession of rhymes, there is repetition of the same
themes as well as a lack of organic cohesion, conciseness and
logical construction. Such features are typical of this highly
impersonal and artificial style of poetry.

[1] Cf. Langlois, *Recueil d'Arts de Seconde Rhétorique*, 1902; Langlois, *De Artibus
Rhetoricae Rhythmicae*. Thèse, Paris 1890.

As soon as we turn from the formal French poetry of the fourteenth century to Chaucer, we notice the essential difference. What Chaucer has chosen here as 'models' and patterns ran clean counter to his own nature as a poet. There were two special qualities about this superficial poetry, based on technical tricks and subtleties, from which all real poetic feeling had evaporated. These were pedantry and sameness; and both were completely at variance with Chaucer's poetic temperament. Even in his early works there is little trace of either. What we have constantly seen in various forms in his longer poems has been change, diversity, variety of images, and individual characterization by means of comparison and contrast. Indeed, we often see him tending towards the dramatic dialogue that is so clear a feature of his later work. A dislike of pedantic rigidity and stiff formalism lies moreover so deep in Chaucer's nature and is so obvious throughout his work that it requires no exemplification.

In the history of literature, 'influence' is often used to imply that in the author's eyes the works whose influence he feels had accomplished what he himself was aiming at. This is a definition which can only be applied with many reservations in the case of Chaucer and his French predecessors. When we study his earlier poetry including the minor poems dealt with in this section, we become aware how critical and divided this relationship had been from the beginning. There is undoubtedly a negative side to what we here call 'influence'. On the one hand, it was Chaucer's intention to learn and absorb from formal French poetry much that English poetry did not as yet possess. On the other hand, these very qualities which appealed to Chaucer were linked in the works of the French poets with various features which he was bound to resist from the start. These early, shorter poems, in fact, offer a clear illustration of this dual phenomenon of absorption and repulsion, of imitation and 'resistance'.

It may be assumed that much of what Chaucer wrote in the first decade of his productive period, many conventional love-poems after the Machaut pattern (*ballades*, *roundels*, and *virelays*), have not come down to us.[1] So we can have only an incomplete

[1] Cf. the Prologue to *The Legend of Good Women*, G.411. Brusendorff (*The Chaucer Tradition*, London 1925, especially Chapters IV and VI) refers to lost Chaucer manuscripts. For an appreciation of the relevant passages in the Prologue to the *Legend* cf. Brusendorff, p. 432.

picture of Chaucer's attitude to these genres. But what remains shows us clearly that the poet avoided any extremes of artificiality (as for instance when Machaut uses only one or two rhymes for an entire poem), and that in general he writes more succinctly and with far fewer, wearisome repetitions. Admittedly, in feeling and content his early 'Complaints' (*Complaint unto Pity*, *Complaint to his Lady*), written under French influence, are as impersonal and conventional as their models. Yet why should we expect originality and a personal note from poems which were in no way aiming at being 'original'? Later on, however, Chaucer learned to transmute even this impersonal and conventional formula. In his *Anelida and Arcite,* usually dated after the *House of Fame*, we see him bringing a more personal note into the 'Complaint' than was inherent in that lyric genre; while in the *Complaint of Mars* we have a greatly extended version of it as well as a number of new and independent features.

Obviously, then, we cannot consider Chaucer's 'lyrical output' (if we may give this name to his accurate and methodical composition of love-poems) in the light of an organic artistic development. These poems seem conditioned by technique, by external circumstances, to a greater extent than any other group. Many may have been commissioned and do not aim at being anything but an accurate replica of French models. And we must not hesitate to admit that most of these minor courtly poems are definitely inferior in quality compared with the achievement of the three longer works which we have discussed. But this should not cause us to overlook the importance these poems have for Chaucer's linguistic and poetic development. He is rightly regarded as the first great versifier in English literature.[1] Not only was he the first to introduce certain stanzas and metres into English poetry; he also handled his metrical line with admirable delicacy and with a technical mastery scarcely equalled by any successor or imitator. In this respect it was a great benefit to him to have learned from Machaut, who had laid over-much emphasis on ingenious verse-construction. For the great variety

[1] Miss Hammond stresses this point in *English Verse between Chaucer and Surrey,* 1927. On Chaucer as versifier, cf. Ten Brink, *Chaucers Sprache und Verskunst,* 1920 (3rd ed.). Paull F. Baum, *Chaucer's Verse,* 1961; James G. Southworth, *Verses of Cadence. An Introduction to the Prosody of Chaucer and his followers,* 1954.

of his metrical patterns provided any keen student with abundant material to work upon.

Another advantage gained from Chaucer's study of the formal lyric poetry of France was an enrichment of his own linguistic expression. In order to move at all within the strait and comfortless trappings of these complicated lines and stanzas, one had to possess a rich vocabulary and much resource in the matter of synonyms, assonance, expletives and epithets. Such rigid formal constraint imposed a constant demand on the linguistic material. That the result was frequently forced and artificial is of less importance than that it inevitably stimulated the ability to find suitable wording and to manipulate the language with skill. In the case of the *Book of the Duchess* Chaucer chose out turns and phrases from Machaut's longer poems; while some awkward and some superfluous elements in his formal lyric poetry show that here he was more constrained in his selection of linguistic material.

We may assume that many of the poems now lost to us were translations, free versions such as the *Complaint of Venus* which derives from three 'Balades' by Otes de Granson, or the *ABC* which is based on an episode in Deguilleville's *Pélerinage*. The value for Chaucer's development of this kind of translation can hardly be exaggerated; for here we often have a creative type of translation that leads on to something new. In these works the original text sometimes seems no more than a threshold which Chaucer steps across to find his own language. The words of the 'author' only seldom appear to be an irksome restriction; more often they are felt to be a stimulus and an inspiration to the poet to continue along his own line of writing and thinking.

The work of translation could have this fruitful effect only because the medieval poet drew no sharp line of distinction between original and borrowed material. In past centuries the poet has had certain reservations about taking over another writer's expressions and stock phrases word for word. If this is done at all, it is usually a case of a conscious 'Imitatio', an intentional echoing of another's diction and wording. The modern poet (excepting contemporary authors like Pound and Eliot) would have found it harder and not easier to write if he had had to incorporate phrases and lines from the work of another author into his own text. With Chaucer the reverse is true. He succeeds in making the most diverse styles and texts so completely and so unequivocally his own that they melt into one with his own modes of expression. He felt the other writer's idiom as a welcome enrichment, not a restriction. Of all medieval authors Chaucer displays perhaps the greatest skill in the fusion of expressions, phrases, linguistic detail – and also on a larger scale in the blending of themes, basic patterns, literary 'genres'. His translations must have greatly fostered this skill in him.

The five short poems dealt with here all still belong to Chaucer's 'early poetry', i.e. they were not written later than the *Parliament of Fowls* (about 1380[1]). *To Rosemounde* and *Womanly Noblesse* could perhaps have been added to our selection as they also belong to the earlier period and show for the first time Chaucer handling the 'ballade'-form taken over from the French. The interpretation of these poems would not, however, have substantially altered the lines of development described here, unless it be that the humour appearing in *Rosemounde* points to an unmistakably new tone even in this lyrical genre.

The five 'ballades' written after *Rosemounde*, namely *The Former Age*, *Fortune*, *Truth*, *Gentilesse*, *Lak of Stedfastnesse* reveal in various ways the influence of Boethius and are therefore usually printed and discussed together as 'Boethian Group'. They represent original variations of the short lyrical poem, particularly typical of Chaucer. Not only do they appeal to us more vividly than the short courtly love poems of the earlier period, but they also seem to contain more of Chaucer's own poetic temperament and are therefore on the whole perhaps more successful than those courtly complaints. The 'Boethian Group' was, however, probably not written earlier than the eighties, after or in connection with Chaucer's translation of Boethius, and therefore presumably in the same years as *Troilus and Criseyde* and *The Knight's Tale*. For this reason we have not reckoned them among Chaucer's 'early poetry'.

[1] Cf. Robinson, p. xxix, also p. 310, p. 520 seq., p. 854.

# Minor Poems

## An ABC

*An ABC* (in all probability the earliest poem to have come down to us) provides a first example of Chaucer's art of free creative transposition.

If we compare it with its French model, the prayer in Deguilleville's *Pèlerinage de l'Ame*, several characteristic differences clearly emerge that throw light on Chaucer's individuality – a quality evident in this still largely derivative work.[1] In place of Deguilleville's abstract and often over-sophisticated diction, we have Chaucer's vivid, and graphic mode of expression. He breaks up the smooth, monotony of Deguilleville's lines by means of interjections and cries; by dividing up the lengthy periods he infuses them with variety and life. Above all, Chaucer's *ABC* shows a greater wealth of images than Deguilleville's poem, a greater intensity conveyed by heightened expression.

The different stanza-form used contributes to this effect. Chaucer's line has five accents in place of Deguilleville's four; the extra one lends the poem a deeper resonance, a more plangent, note.[2] The different rhyme-scheme, too, operates in the same way. Deguilleville uses only two rhymes in his twelve-line stanzas – a limitation that leads to strained and monotonous rhyming. Chaucer's eight-line stanzas however, with its *ababbcbc* rhyme-scheme, allows him more latitude. In this very first poem, then, where much is imitated and borrowed, Chaucer is tending to resist the subtle artifices of the French poets.

This does not mean, of course, that Chaucer replaces elaborate diction with naïve and simple language. On the contrary, he makes use of all his linguistic resources to intensify and adorn this prayer to the Virgin Mary, to lend it dignity, beauty and power. To that end he outdoes his model in titles and images in honour of the Madonna; he chooses his expressions most carefully, and expands the French poet's bald statements into rich, sweeping phrases. Almost every stanza includes many abstract nouns of romance origin (more frequent in this than in his other

---

[1] Robinson's verdict 'The *ABC* being only a translation reveals very little about Chaucer' (Robinson, p. 520) therefore requires some revision.

[2] As Chesterton put it, 'Chaucer is not expanding his metre; he is expanding himself' (*Chaucer*, 1959, p. 120).

early poems) which serve to 'heighten' the language. The *ABC*
is an early and striking example of Chaucer's art of enhancing
the expressive power and resonance of the English language by
a varied and lavish use of words of romance origin.

The opening of the poem clearly shows the keener tension
and urgency with which Chaucer invests his verse. Whereas
Deguilleville writes:

> A toy du monde le refui,
> Vierge glorieuse, m'en fui
> Tout confus, ne puis miex faire;
> A toy me tien, a toy m'apuy.
> Relieve moy, abatu suy:[1]

Chaucer gives us:

> Almighty and al merciable queene,
> To whom that al this world fleeth for socour,
> To have relees of sinne, of sorwe, and teene,
> Glorious virgine, of alle floures flour,
> To thee I flee, confounded in errour.

Here, and as the poem proceeds, Chaucer frequently adds descriptive phrases in honour of the Virgin. These correspond as
e.g. 'of alle floures flour' (4) to traditional epithets recurring in
English and Latin prayers to the Virgin Mary; or they may take
the form of some particularly chosen phrase such as 'Thou art
largesse of pleyn felicitee' (13), or 'thou ground of oure sub-
staunce' (87). Compared to Deguilleville, Chaucer gives us
far more epithets describing the Virgin as the great queen of
Heaven.[2] This is in line with the general conception of the Virgin
in the fourteenth century. In his very first address however,
'Almighty and al merciable queene' Chaucer goes far beyond

---

[1] For a synoptic survey of Deguilleville's French text with Chaucer's, see
Skeat I, 1894 p. 261.

[2] Besides what the two have in common (137 ff. and 205 ff.), Deguilleville's
only contribution is 'dame de misericorde' (37), and 'noble princesse du monde'
(145); whereas Chaucer has 'almighty and al merciable queene' (1), 'blisful
hevene queene' (24), 'queen of misericorde' (25), 'queen of comfort' (77, 121),
'noble princesse' (97), and 'hevene queen' (149). In this connection Th. Wolpers
('Geschichte der englischen Marienlyrik im Mittelalter', *Anglia* 69, 1950) draws
attention to the then increasing importance of the Feast of the Assumption.

doctrinal limits, ascribing to the Virgin the epithet 'Almighty' which is rightly applicable to none but God alone.[1]

The many exquisite words of praise which Chaucer finds for the Virgin makes her seem more present and alive in our minds than in Deguilleville's poem; and this is true even if one thinks of these abundant epithets or praise as no more than an attempt at eloquent and heightened language. The effect of vividness is enhanced, too, by Chaucer's more graphic expression. We have a general, vaguely-outlined image in Deguilleville:

> Un bysson contre nature
> Vit qui ardoit sans arsure. (136)

But Chaucer adds touches that give us a definite picture:

> saugh the bush with flawmes rede
> Brenninge, of which ther never a stikke brende, (89).

Deguilleville chooses abstract and paradoxical terms to describe the mystery by which Christ takes upon Him human form:

> Pour savoir que Diex vint querre
> Quant en toy se vint enserrer; (170)

Chaucer, however, evokes the familiar imagery of the Annunciation:

> Wherfore and whi the Holi Gost thee soughte,
> Whan Gabrielles vois cam to thin ere. (114)

The Angel Gabriel is brought in here to give more life to an image which was very well known; and at a later stage Longinus is similarly introduced[2] (163; cf. Deguilleville 243). Concrete, tangible details are frequently woven in, their clear images appeal to the eye, the ear and the imagination; and they contribute to a transformation of Deguilleville's abstract, intellectual and sometimes sophisticated mode of expression.

But it is when we read Chaucer's *ABC* aloud that its resonance, and intensity of feeling come home to us. The words and prayers which he addresses to the Virgin Mary have a greater

[1] Cf. Wolpers, p. 29.
[2] He, too, is introduced to bring before us the vividly imagined incident of the spear-thrust: 'And made his herte blood to renne adoun' (164).

177

range and a wider sweep; they are more plangent than those in
the French poem. Whether Chaucer is expanding or compres-
sing in relation to the Deguilleville version, the difference is
striking. One has only to compare:

> A toy dont soit le jugement,
> Car de pitié as l'oingnement,
> Mès que merci l'en te prie. (202)

with:

> Mooder, of whom oure merci gan to springe,
> Beth ye my juge and eek my soules leche;
> For evere is you in pitee haboundinge
> To ech that wole of pitee you biseeche. (133)

Or, again:

> Reçoif moy par ta merite
> Quar de toy n'ay point hesité. (221)

with:

> Receyve me – I can no ferther fleen! (148)

Like Chaucer's *ABC* Deguilleville's prayer, too, is always
addressed to the Virgin; yet Chaucer's more urgent pleas,
sometimes expressed in the 'natural idiom', seem to bring the
suppliant and the Virgin closer to one another. In some passages
we seem actually to hear him 'speaking'.[1]

One may interpret the warmth of feeling in Chaucer's poem
either as an expression of genuine religious conviction or merely
as a sign of his eagerness, eloquence and artistry. This is not a
purely scholarly question but one of personal opinion.[2] It ought
however to be borne in mind that, as Huizinga has already
pointed out,[3] the later Middle Ages tended to equate the
beautiful with the sacred, and that in consequence the aesthetic

---

[1] Cf., for instance: 'O help yit at this neede!' (44). 'Spek thou, for I ne dar not
him y-see' (53).

[2] Cf. Th. Wolpers (*Anglia* 69, 1950) (p. 32) who suspects the religious
sincerity of the *ABC*, whereas G. K. Chesterton (*Chaucer*, 1959, pp. 121 ff.) sees
this poem as a particularly impressive example of Chaucer's religious conviction.

[3] Huizinga, *Waning of the Middle Ages*, Ch. 19 and Ch. 12.

**pres**entation had to play a considerable role in the portrayal of religious subjects in literature or art.

Compared with English religious lyric poetry of the fourteenth century, Chaucer's language in this prayer to the Virgin is richer and more skilful, and his syntax more elaborate. Pre-Chaucerian English poems to the Virgin Mary had generally been simpler in expression.[1] Late fourteenth and early fifteenth century poems, however, show English religious hymnody deriving inspiration from the more elaborate verse of the French poets and from Latin liturgical poetry of the later Middle Ages.[2] Chaucer's *ABC* occupies an important place in the growth of this new style of English hymnody. In this as in other developments, we see him acting as an intermediary and contributing to modify the style of this particular genre.

### The Complaint unto Pity

In this early work, the *Complaint unto Pity*,[3] Chaucer displays little originality; he is still held fast by the conventional language of love employed in French formal lyric verse. This 'Complaint' is perhaps the only truly allegorical of Chaucer's poems. An inner experience has been completely rendered by means of personification. There is no attempt to link up with the world of reality such as we find over and over again in the dream-poems. To portray emotional values, indeed, by a co-ordinate system of allegorical personifications, is to use allegory in its most abstract form. This was the pattern that had dominated the Middle Ages and it had been the favourite form for allegorical poetry during the century that followed the *Roman de la Rose*. The subdivision of an emotional content or a psychological action into separate personifications of love, which are then contrasted or compared, is one of the chief characteristics of the

[1] Cf. Carleton Brown, *Religious Lyrics of the Fourteenth Century*, 1924; *Hymns to the Virgin and Christ*, ed. Furnivall, *EETS OS* 24 (1867); F. A. Patterson, *The Middle English Penitential Lyric*, 1911.

[2] For detailed treatment of this development cf. Th. Wolpers, 'Geschichte der englischen Marienlyrik im Mittelalter', *Anglia* 69 (1950).

[3] The title 'Complaint of Pitee' (as Shirley calls this poem; Harl. 78 and Ad. 34360), would be more apt, for it is a complaint 'concerning Pity'. Cf. Brusendorff, p. 272. Furnivall (*Trial-Forewords*, 1871, p. 31) regarded this poem as 'the earliest original work of Chaucer'.

courtly formal verse of the fourteenth century. The *Roman de la Rose* had used this basis to build up an entire love-story with abundance of incident and circumstance; but there are not many later instances of such consistent and elaborate allegorical treatment in the case of longer tales. Though personifications were still introduced, the whole poem was no longer based upon an allegory.[1] At the same time however it is clear that the individual personifications from the *Roman de la Rose* had now grown so familiar as to have shrunk to no more than a passing figure of speech, a 'façon de parler'. When speaking of love-conflicts, longings and the like, writers now dispensed with the whole machinery of the *Roman de la Rose* and simply used figures entitled *Désirs, Dangier, Pitez* etc.[2] A century had passed; and what had been comparatively new in the *Roman de la Rose* was now a commonplace, a natural everyday mode of expression.

In his later poems Chaucer too makes only this abbreviated, figurative use of personifications from the *Roman de la Rose*.[3] In the *Parliament of Fowls*, for example, the traditional personifications of love enumerated in Cupid's train have no real life about them; they are simply a piece of decorative ornament.

We have already noted that none of the traditional personifications of love in Chaucer's allegorical dream-poems is depicted as active or as actually speaking – though this was a feature of every French allegorizing love-poem. Yet after having translated the *Roman de la Rose* Chaucer was of course thoroughly conversant with such figures. One may safely conclude, then, that Chaucer himself considered the personification of feelings and qualities to be too abstract and unnatural a mode of expression. Fame, the golden eagle, the talking birds, were all figures which he could make alive, 'human' and real. But this is a much harder task in the case of an abstract figure personifying a human attribute. Even Jean de Meun was no more than partly successful in endowing his abstractions with realistic traits.

This early poem, the *Complaint unto Pity*, is the only one of

[1] For a general treatment of the love-allegory, see C. S. Lewis, *The Allegory of Love*, 1936.

[2] Machaut's lyrical poetry contains many examples; cf. Complainte II, Complainte VI (*Poésies Lyriques*, ed. Chichmaref, Vol. I, p. 249, 256.

[3] The Prologue to the *Legend of Good Women* contains an instance of this 'figurative' use of personification.

Chaucer's that is based on the design of the *Roman de la Rose*.
No source has yet been traced for it; but the themes are so
conventional and the whole is composed so completely in the
stylised French idiom that it is quite unnecessary to point to any
specific model.[1] *Pite* frequently appears as *Pitiez* (*Pité*) in the
*Roman de la Rose*, usually joining with *Fraunchise* to resist
*Dangier*.[2] Chaucer's *Cruelte* more or less corresponds to the
*Dangier* of the *Roman*. The rest of the personifications he mentions in connection with *Pite* are also drawn for the most part
from the same work; *Jolietez, Beautez, Jeunece* (10456), the
'barons' attendant upon the love-god have their counterparts in
Chaucer's *Jolyte, Beaute* and *Youthe* (39 f.); while Chaucer's
*Lust* (39) corresponds to *Leece* or *Deduit*, and his *Drede* to *Peur*
etc. Many names in Chaucer's list also echo the personifications
of love found in Machaut and Froissart.[3] But surely he could
hardly be expected to keep pedantically to the order and itemi-
zation of such lists.

The lament for a dead and vanished *Pite* was a theme that
had occurred in Machaut and Deschamps;[4] and one of Petrarch's
sonnets contains the image of Pite buried in the heart.[5]

[1] Lowes (*MP* 14, 1917) described Skeat's assumption that 'Chaucer took his
notion of personifying Pity from Statius' as superfluous. Cf. Robinson, p. 855.

[2] *RR* 3249, 3337, 10737, 21281, 21314. 'Pitiez's' fight with 'Dangier' and
'Honte' is more fully described at *V.* 15388–15459.

[3] Cf. Froissart, *Le Joli Buisson de Jonece* (ed. Scheler, II, 1870), V. 2405,
3012, 3911; Machaut, *Dit dou Vergier* (ed. Hoepffner, *SATF* I), V. 612; *Jugement
dou Roy de Navarre* (*SATF* I), V. 1152. Machaut also contrasts 'Pité' with 'Cruauté',
which does not appear in the *Roman de la Rose*; cf. *Dit dou Vergier* (*SATF* I).
945 f. or V. 1009. A personified 'Pitez' often appears in Deschamps's *Balades,
Virelays* and *Rondeaux*, likewise in opposition to the 'Dangier' and 'Honte' etc. Cf.
Balade no. 804 (ed. Saint-Hilaire, *SATF*, III), p. 372; Virelay no. 567, 568, 727
(*SATF*, IV), pp. 26, 27, 198; Balade no. 842, 947 (*SATF*, V), pp. 13, 164.
And see E. Flügel in *Anglia* 23 (1901).

[4] E. Flügel, *Anglia* 23 (1901).

[5] Brusendorff (p. 270) compares Chaucer's 'I fond hir ded, and buried in an herte'
(14) with

> Ite, caldi sospiri, al freddo core;
> Rompete il ghiaccio che pietà contende; . . .
>
> (*Son*. CXX)

Since he regards the whole poem as coloured by 'il dolce stile nuovo' Brusendorff
thinks it should be dated somewhat later (after Chaucer's first journey to Italy).
This dating is not impossible, as the stanza-form, the 'rime royal', might have been
taken from the Italian 'ottava rima'. Yet it is difficult to agree that the 'dolce
stile nuovo' influenced this poem. There is nothing in the least 'dolce' about it.

Chaucer's *Complaint unto Pity* shows the transformation which the old genre of the 'Love Complaint' underwent through the influence of the artificial and stereotyped French poetry of the fourteenth century. Feelings are no longer portrayed directly. An elaborate screen of rules and forms seems to shut off any immediate expression of feeling, a scaffolding of abstraction is erected; and a process of analysis into conventional patterns brings to an end any personal emotion.[1] The artificial and 'indirect' method, however, is not confined to the general scheme: every gesture and movement in the poem appears to be regulated by convention. Chaucer's poem reflects the tendency of his age towards ceremony, towards investing every action with formality. The special 'Bill of Complaint' addressed by the poet to *Pite*, the diffuse and pompous manner in which this address is framed, and the pedantic quality of the whole procedure – all these show us court etiquette and court ceremonial translated into the sphere of poetry. Contemporary life, too, afforded an illustration of this formalization of feelings, namely in the courts of love,[2] a part-social, part-literary fashion revived at the end of the fourteenth century in the 'Cour Amoureuse' of Charles d'Orléans.[3] In the present poem even Chaucer's terminology seems to be determined by the conventional figures of the allied or rival 'barons' of the love-god – those metaphorical characters so often occurring in poems belonging to the 'court of love' tradition.[4]

The artificial treatment of the 'Complaint' is evident, too, in the manner in which the 'Love lament' repeatedly takes on the tone of an elegy and makes use of its 'topoi' and terminology. The clearest instance is at lines 22–5 which might come straight out of an elegy; and elegiac words like 'dead', 'buried', 'mortal', 'sleyn', 'corps', 'herse', recur throughout the poem. The combination of elegy and love-lament is met with in later *Complaints*;

[1] The relation of the 'courtly lyric' to life or to a fictional 'game of love' is treated from a new angle by John Stevens in his recent book *Music and Poetry in the Early Tudor Court*, 1961, Part II.

[2] Cf. A. Piaget 'La Cour Amoureuse dite de Charles VI', *Romania* 20 (1891) and 31 (1907).

[3] On this point see especially Huizinga, *Waning of the Middle Ages*, 1955, p. 111 ff.

[4] Cf. v. 65, 71, 83, 89. On the frequency of such concepts, cf. W. A. Neilson, 'The Origins and Sources of the Court of Love', *Studies and Notes in Philology and Literature* 6 (1899).

and here of course it is only natural, for the poet has framed his love-lament as a lament for *dead Pite*, 'buried in an herte' (14). Then the original image of pity buried in the heart is abandoned and at line 36 we hear of *Pite*'s bier round which the contrary attributes stand in triumph. His artificial treatment involves the poet in logical contradictions; it is never explained whether the *Complaint unto Pite* is addressed to *Pite* or to the loved one herself. This however is a question which bears less on the sense of the whole than on whether the promise in the title has been strictly fulfilled. Indeed, Chaucer may well have introduced this ambiguity on purpose. Besides, it springs naturally from the dual character of his lament. For we hear the poet grieving at the same time over the death of *Pite* and over his own rejection and grievous sorrow. Both themes deal with one and the same thing.

The artificiality in the treatment, the abstract *allegoresis*, the conventional phrases, repetitions and expressions, the absence of a logical sequence of thought – all these features in the poem point both to the influence of the French school and to a lack of originality on Chaucer's part. Even in this early poem however we can see some indication of his own individual intention. To begin with, there is the metrical scheme. This poem makes it clear that Chaucer is not prepared to adopt Machaut's metrical subtleties or his purely technical devices (in particular the endless repetition of the same rhyme). French poets had already made use of the 'rime royal' stanza which Chaucer chooses here; it allows of a more pronounced subdivision into individual and independent stanzas than do their lengthy declamations. At the same time it involves achieving a continuity that spans and links the stanzas; and in this task Chaucer was not yet fully successful. But he does soften the outlines of Machaut's rigid pattern of successive and self-contained lines. In order to do so, he frequently uses *enjambement*; and this in turn was mainly a result of his use of something approaching colloquial language. There are passages indeed which could be written out as prose (e.g. 71 ff.) – a procedure quite unthinkable with most of the poems belonging to the Machaut school. Not only do we find here the interpolations so typical of Chaucer's later style, such as 'yf I shal not feyne' (4), 'as thoughte me' (37), 'sothly for to seyne'

(96), 'allas, that hyt is soo' (117); there are also instances of
the individual way in which Chaucer uses pronouns and adver-
bial clauses to insert explanations, reasons, reservations, and
arguments.[1] The result is something like a piece of reasoned
prose that at times might actually be 'the language of speech',
for instance at lines such as:

> And further over, yf ye suffre this,
> Youre renoun ys fordoo than in a throwe;
> Ther shal no man wite well what Pite is. (85)

Yet these are more or less incidental and unconscious stylistic
effects. For Chaucer's real aim in this early poem was to make
use of the English idiom to render the polished, sonorous, elegant
and yet dignified language of the court as reproduced in French
poetry; in the lines that begin 'The Bille' this is precisely what
he does:

> Humblest of herte, highest of reverence,
> Benygne flour, coroune of vertues alle,
> Sheweth unto youre rial excellence
> Youre servaunt, yf I durste me so calle, (57).

Today we find it hard to understand the position that *Pite*, the
object and theme of our *Complaint*, occupied in the medieval
hierarchy of virtues connected with love. The modern conception of love no longer recognizes 'compassion' as one of its main
motive forces; but this feeling played a most vital role in medieval wooing and relationships.[2] The classical Christian virtue
of *caritas*, which survived in the 'compassion' of chivalry, lent
a particular dignity to this ideal. But 'compassion', like so many
of the chivalric virtues, underwent a change in the fourteenth
century. In French formal poetry it came to represent the sentimental mood of the languishing lover; this noble virtue, which
had called for action, had now become merely a stereotyped
gesture. We can trace this sentimentalizing of *pite* in Chaucer

[1] Cf. 29, 32, 33, 71, 76, 99, 109, 111.
[2] Cf. the chapter on 'Pitié' in J. W. Kleinstück, *Chaucers Stellung in der Mittelalterlichen Literatur*, 1956. For numerous instances of Chaucer's use of *pite*, see G. H.
Gerould, *Chaucerian Essays*, 1952, Ch. V.

too; but he invests it with a new significance and makes it one of the central conceptions in his range of values. *Pite* is one of the ways by which the narrator seeks contact with his reader or hearer, by either arousing or showing sympathy or by portraying it convincingly in the story he tells. *Troilus and Criseyde*, however, shows us *Pite* once again becoming a noble virtue, a sign of true affection, an aspect of that sympathy which a man feels for his fellows. *Pite* had degenerated into no more than an empty, stereotyped and sentimental gesture; with Chaucer it became human again. This early poem betrays little of the future role of compassion in Chaucer's world; and yet it seems fitting that he should have chosen *Pite* as the theme of one of his *Complaints*.

## A Complaint to His Lady

In its structure and in the treatment of its theme, *A Complaint to His Lady* is possibly even closer to the French school than the *Complaint unto Pite* is. This latter work attempts at sketching in some 'background' to the actual complaint – an attempt repeated with success in the *Complaint to Mars*; but here there is nothing of that kind. The love-lament is quite baldly presented; and furthermore, it is addressed to the lady herself with no figure acting as intermediary. The lover's attitude, too, the contrast between his own unworthiness and the exaggerated praise of his lady, and also his own self-pity, are in the true tradition of the court.[1] Only the two introductory stanzas are in any way remarkable as to their content; for here, as at the beginning of the *Book of the Duchess*, Chaucer portrays the poet's wakefulness, despair and helplessness in a typically indefinite fashion. We do not know what the poet is really aiming at. One might think it was all leading up to some vision seen in a dream; but what follows is something quite different – namely, a succession of loosely-knit stanzas of love-lament after the customary pattern.

There is indeed so frail a connection between these stanzas,

---

[1] On the conventional nature of these poses see John Stevens, *Music and Poetry in the Early Tudor Court*, 1961 Part II. 'The Courtly Makers from Chaucer to Wyatt'.

and so little trace of any general continuity of thought, that some have taken the line that the *Complaint to his Lady* consists of three distinct poems which ought therefore to be printed separately.[1] But surely 'continuity of thought' is an idea derived from comparatively modern poetry. French formal poetry of the fourteenth century includes a large number of poems composed as variations on a theme, with no attempt at continuous development or logical connections. The *Complaint to his Lady* represents a series of this sort, like 'Exercises' in different keys on a conventional theme. This is brought out still more clearly by the contrast achieved by using a different metre for each section. In this poem Chaucer is experimenting and practising; we must not regard it as a finished and final expression of his art.

In this case too it is the diction and the versification, not the theme, that are typically Chaucerian. His method of expression is simpler, more artless and everyday, than that of French lyric poetry of the period. There is no sign of the rhetorical figures which determine the style of the French *Complaintes*. Whereas Machaut and his contemporaries tend to point and exaggerate every phrase, Chaucer seems at pains to reproduce the accents of natural speech; and he aims less at 'brilliance' than at simple sincerity. One could very easily recast this poem in prose – an attempt that would be far more difficult in the case of the French *Complaintes*. This fluent and natural diction that comes near to prose, also involves a different treatment of the line; there is no break or pause at the end of each, as we find in Machaut. Chaucer so constructs his sentences that they do not run counter to the metre; yet at the same time we are not made conscious of the individual line as the unit. For Machaut on the other hand the chief thing was not the sentence but the line. The new stanza-forms which Chaucer uses here and which bear witness to Italian influence, favoured these tendencies. For the cross-rhyming in both the 'terza rima' – here used for the first time in English poetry – and the ten-line stanza in the fourth Part (from line 40) – likewise an innovation – enabled Chaucer to achieve an impression of steady continuous movement and an interweaving pattern within the stanza. The French poets too made

[1] Cf. Brusendorff, p. 273, Robinson, p. 856.

use of *enjambement*; but the passage now quoted shows how incomparably stronger the impression is in Chaucer's verse that the sentence is flowing on and bridging the hiatus of each line:

> But nevertheles, my righte lady swete,
> Thogh that I be unconnyng and unmete
> To serve, as I coude best, ay your hynesse;
> Yit is ther fayner noon, that wolde I hete,
> Than I, to do yow ese, or elles bete
> What so I wiste that were to you [distresse]; (68)

These lines also show Chaucer's characteristic technique; he takes conjunctions whose function is to limit, support or contradict, and uses them in order to bring out a connection or a contrast, or else to pass from one idea to the next. In this poem (especially in the fourth Part) we are more conscious than we were in the *Complaint unto Pite* of a style that puts both points of view at the same time, in the manner of a dialogue. 'For', 'And therfor?' 'And yit', 'Thogh' etc. bring in explanations and excuses, to suggest arguments for and against. The result is a movement in which the argument dips and rises in a curve. In the fourth Part of the poem, indeed, we seem to have a kind of dialogue; although no protagonist is present, he is always presumed to be there and is as it were taken for granted.

In the *Complaint unto Pite* it was clear that Chaucer's main object was to take the sonorous terminology of the French courtly love-lyric and bring it to new life in the English tongue; in the *Complaint to his Lady* he seems to be doing the opposite; for he shuns any lofty elaborate style and aims at a simple almost naïve utterance, full of sincerity and employing the rhythm of the 'spoken word'. What we are hearing is in fact the first faint tentative tones of the poet's 'speaking voice', the unmistakable note later to be heard in all Chaucer's major works:

> My dere herte and best beloved fo,
> Why lyketh yow to do me al this wo,
> What have I doon that greveth yow, or sayd,
> But for I serve and love yow and no mo? (58)

But leveth wel, and be not wrooth therfore,
And lat me serve yow forth; lo, this is al!
For I am not so hardy, ne so wood,
For to desire that ye shulde love me;
For wel I wot, allas! that may nat be;
I am so litel worthy, and ye so good. (82)

## The Complaint of Mars

It was inevitable that Chaucer should find the traditional 'complainte d'amour' too narrow and too rigid a form. This is also shown in the *Complaint of Mars* which probably belongs to the early period of Chaucer's writing.[1] The conventional elements in this genre are presented here in a different context and fulfil a new function. Furthermore, this work displays fresh aspects of style, construction and presentation quite unsuited to the *Complainte* as a genre but in line with Chaucer's poetic intention and characteristic of his later development. For instance, the *Story* stresses the element of narration at the expense of the lyrical aspect. Chaucer was no lyrical poet by nature; so when he takes over such a largely lyrical form as the *Complainte* from the French, he uses it in his own way, bringing in his own reflective or epic elements to mingle with the lyrical ingredients. A purely abstract analysis of sentiments such as was usual in the formal French poetry of the period was just as foreign to him. So we find him transforming what was in essence a purely psychological action, into a series of images, episodes and dramatic scenes which serve to illustrate it. Furthermore, he revises and amplifies what had been the lover's typical attitude in the French *Complaintes* and *Regrets*. For we now hear another strain besides the hopeless lamentation and monotonous repetition of clichés telling of absolute submission, adoration and praise; within the conventional form of the *Complainte* indeed, we find Chaucer posing the basic question of the sense or senselessness of love itself.

The *Complaint of Mars*, like the *Parliament of Fowls*, is another example from his early poetry that shows us Chaucer introducing other poetic forms and conventions into an existing

[1] Cf. Robinson, p. 856 f.

basic genre. At the same time he treats this same dominant genre in an unexpected and striking manner, repeatedly bringing in a note of irony.[1] This is what makes the *Complaint of Mars* more complex, richer in contrasts and in surprises than the proceding minor poems. Chaucer's easy adroitness not only in weaving in the conventional themes but also in touching here and there on more serious questions is as obvious as is his ability to unite charm, wit and poetic variety with a suitably diversified style and diction.

As in the longer poems, an ingenious erection leads our steps on to the main body of the poem, the *Complaint*. Again we have to pass through a whole series of rooms before reaching what the title had promised. The *Proem* and *Story* together are longer than the *Complaint* itself. The latter forms a skilfully constructed unit in its own right, consisting of five 'sets' of these stanzas. Each of these parts deals with a separate theme, but all are essentially interconnected, so that here Chaucer was able (as in the *Complaint to his Lady* he was not) to prevent his poem from falling into separate sections. The whole construction betrays the 'goût de complication' which is further evidenced by the somewhat confusing sequence of speakers. The first two stanzas are spoken by a bird – though we do not learn this until the last lines of the second stanza (13–14) where the poet himself is speaking. It is he who turns to 'Seynt Valentyne' and tells of the bird-song he had heard on the saint's nameday. In the third and fourth stanzas we then have the birds' exhortations in connection with St Valentine's day and after this the *Story* which the bird explains he is about to relate. At the end of the *Story* there follows the 'compleynt' of Mars – in his words but still spoken by the bird – at the close of which he turns to 'ye lovers' (290) to whom the bird had already addressed himself in the *Proem* (5). Thus the first and last stanzas of the poem are joined and the circle is complete. However, when reading the poem one tends to become confused among the different 'speakers'; for the final stanzas grouped under Part V of the *Complaint* and addressed to the courtly audience are unmistakably spoken by the poet

[1] See especially the article by G. Stillwell (*PQ* 35, 1956, pp. 69–89) which places this poem in a new light and to which the writer of the present chapter is glad to acknowledge his debt.

himself. The diction, moreover, is not yet varied enough to match this ingenious complexity.

The *Complaint of Mars* begins in a mood that is far from suggesting lamentation. The gay, charming opening lines in which the poet calls the birds to rejoice and herald the day, evoke a tranquil rural scene from which graphic details emerge (Lo! Venus, rysen among yon rowes rede! 2). With its repeated imperatives and its twice-uttered 'Lo!' (2, 7) this opening breaks upon us and we are present at what is a precise and definite occasion.

These first stanzas with their mention of love's cares, of 'sorowes smerte' (10) also suggest the main themes. Yet such cares do not go very deep at this stage; one day, we are told, they will vanish completely (11). The lovers' parting sorrow and the 'hevy morowe' seem a natural price to pay for the 'glade nyght' (12). In the middle of the stanza, however, the poet changes his theme and appears in his own person. By a typically Chaucerian transition he is now made to address St Valentine whose festival is being kept that day. As in the first stanza, we are reminded once more of the dawn. We have already remarked on the immediacy of the opening lines; and now the poet's own testimony is brought in to emphasize and reinforce this, and the mention of a special date confirms it – a date, moreover, which is bound to awake new associations in every hearer or reader. For whereas the first two stanzas are in the tradition of the morning-song, and 'aubade',[1] the next two follow the conventions and rites of St Valentine's day, when the lovers choose their partners for the coming year.[2]

The *Proem* occupies only twenty-eight lines; but it is full of allusion and provides a skilful introduction to prepare us for the whole poem. By recalling first the 'aubade' and then St Valentine's day, Chaucer had set his poem in a framework perfectly familiar to a courtly reader and had linked it directly up with the tradition of *amour courtois*. But the situations established in this way are not merely rich in allusions; they also lead on to ironic and subtle contrasts to what is to follow. The opening situation

---

[1] C. R. Baskervill (*PMLA* 36, 1921) first drew attention to this. Unlike Stillwell (*PQ* 35, 1956) he makes no references however to points of divergence.

[2] H. Braddy in *PMLA* 54 (1939), pp. 359–68.

of the *Complaint of Mars* is at the same time a 'farewell' from
his lady – a farewell, too, it must be added, quite out of keeping
with the usual morning-song. Not only is the placid and hopeful
tone of the *proem*'s 'farewell' quite unsuited to the abrupt and
almost grotesque departure and flight of Mars as the *Story*
relates them; the lady he leaves behind him has meanwhile
accepted another's friendly protection.[1] In the bird's exhortation
to patient service in the *Proem*:

> Confermeth hyt perpetuely to dure,
> And paciently taketh your aventure. (20)

we have a similar contrast to the impatient, intransigent attitude
of Mars who not merely laments but also accuses:

> Alas! that ever lovers mote endure,
> For love, so many a perilous aventure! (198).

There are of course precedents for this kind of accusation; indeed,
it might almost be called a 'topos'. But there is conscious irony
in the contrast between this 'topos' and the lines in the *Proem*.

The image of the rising sun, too, mentioned more than once
in this serene natural opening (4, 7, 14) links up with what
follows. For it is Phoebus whose jealousy later makes him
break in on Mars and Venus together; the very first stanza
indeed, calls the sun 'the candel of jelosye' (7). These connections however are all wholly unobtrusive; the freshness in the
tone of this poem serves to disguise the conventions and allusions.

The *Story* which now follows recounts the stages in the love-
story of Venus and Mars, their meeting and mutual attraction,
their union, their farewell and separation. All this is told in such
a manner that although every movement, every step can be
traced to the prescribed courses of the respective planets, yet
every incident in the story is based on spontaneous human
motives – desire and the lust for power, longing, fear and
jealousy, resistance to jealous malice, the need for security and
the anguish of separation. Chaucer's contemporaries must have
greatly admired the art with which at each stage astronomical
conceptions (houses, aspects, ascendancies, zodiacal signs,
degrees etc.) woven subtly and aptly in, were used to establish

[1] Cf. G. Stillwell, *PQ* 35 (1956).

the parallels. His artistry reveals the consummate knowledge of astronomy and astrology possessed by the author of the *Treatise on the Astrolabe*, a knowledge which enabled him to manipulate his material with such ease and skill. Medieval poets were fond of 'humanizing' astronomical occurrences in this way by relating them to classical mythology,[1] and there are other instances in Chaucer. But here Chaucer intends an even more complex relationship. In this *Story* a love, whose course appears to be determined by spontaneous feeling, is constantly being related to a second plane on which nothing whatever happens by choice and everything is bound by immutable laws. At first this appears to amount to a complete paradox; but in fact it illustrates the relationship between free-will and determinism, option and compulsion. The bird's exhortation to 'perpetual service' (20), the behaviour and words of Mars and Venus, and especially the lament that rounds off the whole poem must be seen against this background; and then they acquire a different aspect. Chaucer has taken a problem that engaged him again and again, and has here touched upon it in a charming way in a 'courtly love' story that is a blend of myth and astronomy.

This introductory story is furthermore of importance in relation to the *Complaint* which Mars now utters. For here Chaucer gives us a new version of the problem whether the lover's fate and sorrow are inevitable and divinely ordained – a question to which the *Story* had already given an answer.[2]

The *Story* also throws light on Chaucer's technique of presentation. It shows how even in the course of such a comparatively short tale he varies his method, here and there building up separate little scenes out of the continuous narrative. The love of Venus and Mars is told in a mere couple of stanzas, and this largely abstract description, couched in terms of courtly love,

---

[1] Cf. J. Seznec, *The Survival of the Pagan Gods. The Mythological Tradition and Its Place in Renaissance Humanism and Art* (translated from the French), 1953. On the allegorizing of astrological situations as part of the 'Game of Love' see John Stevens, *Music and Poetry in the Early Tudor Court*, 1961, p. 175 f.

[2] Whether the story of Mars and Venus refers to any particular court scandals and whom these characters represent, is a question which the present author does not propose to treat. Theories advanced in this connection are based purely on supposition and can do nothing to further real understanding of the poem. Cf. what Robinson, p. 857, and Cowling, *RES* 2 (1926), have to say on the subject.

works to a climax in the last lines which proclaim the 'sove-reignty' of Venus in subtly ironical terms:

> And thus she brydeleth him in her manere,
> With nothing but with scourging of her chere.(41).

After this the narrative is interrupted. The relationship of 'lord-ship and service' now established between Mars and Venus is viewed from a fresh angle and a new perspective is brought in by the narrator's pairs of questions which seem to epitomize the two preceding stanzas (43–6).

The 'til hyt fil, oň a tyde' (51) brings us back to the events of the story. This is then interrupted by direct speech; both Mars and Venus speak (57, 90, 136), but there are also characteris-tically Chaucerian interruptions by the narrator[1] such as:

> Ther is no more, but unto bed thei go;
> And thus in joy and blysse I lete hem duelle. (73)

These lines with which Chaucer steps down from the pedestal of 'amour courtois' as idealistically presented, bring in a tone of gentle irony which also pervades the ensuing tale of the two lovers' misfortune. The hostile figure of Phoebus enters; dra-matic tension is sharpened, the tempo quickens, the narrative grows more objective and the tone harsher. The two stanzas after Phoebus's appearance which describe the departure of the wrathful, bellicose Mars, are an example of the consummate artistry with which Chaucer presents movement and action briskly, forcefully and vividly. His use of words is as noteworthy here as is the inversion that lends them emphasis (92–8). And it should be remarked how not only within the stanza but throughout the whole *Story* Chaucer sustains the 'flow of the narrative', fitting the individual moving parts syntactically together with 'And, For, But, And yet, Sith, Wherfore' etc. The device of referring back to former passages (at 78, for instance), and that of stressing the passage from one theme to another (as at 123), also forge links and further the reader's or hearer's understanding. As the poem proceeds, in fact, the unaffected, natural mode of expression, sometimes coming near a 'speaking voice', grows stronger. This effect is brought about

[1] Cf. also 106, 115, 122, 141.

not merely by such asides as 'for sikerly' (59), 'as I best can' (152), 'nay, certes' (194), 'as I gesse' (195), but by many colloquial and often casual turns of phrase which pervade and serve to lighten the conventional lines[1] with their lofty rhetoric and occasional bombast.

It has rightly been stressed[2] that the *Story* of Mars and Venus is neither what the bird had promised nor indeed what might have been expected of a 'St Valentine's gift'. Chaucer uses the same method here as in his version of classical tales; he 'disillusions' us, setting the sober disenchantment of reality side by side, with what corresponds to an idealized view of things. He brings both Mars and Venus into situations quite alien to the conceptions of 'amour courtois' and so creates an ironic or paradoxical contrast. Of course, Ovid (*Met.* IV, 171–89) had told the story of how the amused Gods had burst out laughing when they heard how the lovers Venus and Mars were unluckily caught *in flagranti delictu,* and all heaven had continued to enjoy this 'notorious tale' for some time.[3] But Chaucer's opening is different; his story is to be an example of 'noble love' and he begins it with a mutual oath of undying constancy. The transition from these lines:

> He bynt him to perpetuall obeisaunce,
> And she bynt her to loven him for evere, (47)

to the description of the somewhat undignified role of all-powerful Mars if already a 'falling-off'. And then the contrast grows sharper when we hear that apparently someone else (Mercury) has meanwhile offered the kindest of welcomes to the distant beloved of Mars:

> And Venus he salueth and doth chere,
> And her receyveth as his frend ful dere. (146)

What lends the poem its charm, however, is the way it swings to and fro between the poles of the ideal and its disillusionment, between convention and the break-through of the unconventional touches that shatter its dignity. At the end of the story, for in-

---

[1] Cf. 155, 212, 290.
[2] For this and the following cf. G. Stillwell, *PQ* 35 (1956).
[3] '. . . superi risere diuque/Haec fuit in toto notissima fabula caelo.'

stance, we are reminded again of the solemn occasion and conventional framework of the poem. We now hear no more of the
'hevy morowe' (12) but of 'this lusty morwenynge' (151). The
bird reappears as the narrator of the *Story* and announces the
*Compleynt* which follows; and he rounds off his stanza with the
pious wish 'And God yeve every wyght joy of his make!' (154).[1]
This wish is perfectly suited to the meaning and conventions of
St Valentine's day, but in view of what had gone before and what
is to follow, it is tinged with irony.

There is irony too – as has been noted[2] – in the pedantically
fulsome and verbose way in which the war-god (unused to such
literary exercises) announces his *Complaint* in a *Proem*. This
draws particular attention, moreover, to the rules governing the
composition of a Proem; and we might therefore expect a correct
and conventional *Complainte* to follow. The exaggerated praise
of the lady and the vow of absolute devotion (which make up
part I) are indeed in the customary vein – although the parenthetical sigh 'how dere I have hit boght!' (168) strikes a rather
odd note in this context. In part II, however, we are struck by
the impatience in his questions. The questions, answers and
arguments exchanged in them make these stanzas read almost
like someone talking to himself. The usual attitude in the *Complainte* was one of sentimental lamentation, but here we have a
frame of mind of one who means to get to the heart of the matter.
At the same time however Chaucer shows a certain sly humour
when he makes Mars curtly break off his general observations
on the fickleness of love; for they are diverting him from his own
case:

> But what availeth such a long sermoun
> Of aventures of love, up and doun?
> I wol returne and speken of my peyne. (209)

In part III the *Complaint* quite ceases to follow the customary
pattern. For one thing it is unusual in this type of poem for the
poet as it were to challenge God Himself; he asks why God allows
all this to happen, since it is both unjust and meaningless. The

---

[1] Here Stillwell draws attention to the irregularity in the metre which makes
this line stand out from the rest (p. 84).

[2] Stillwell, *PQ* 35 (1956), p. 85.

paradoxical nature of love is brought out, too, in a striking way; it is revealed as senseless, incalculable and yet inevitable. At this point Chaucer breaks down the limitations of what has been a rigid and stereotyped convention; and he now questions its very premises:[1]

> To what fyn made the God that sit so hye,
> Benethen him, love other companye,
> And streyneth folk to love, malgre her hed?
> And then her joy, for oght I can espye,
> Ne lasteth not the twynkelyng of an ye,
> And somme han never joy til they be ded.
> What meneth this? What is this mystihed?
> Wherto constreyneth he his folk so faste
> Thing to desyre, but hit shulde laste? (218)

It would be vain to look for a stanza like this in any comparable French poem. The lament is obviously moving away from the sphere of the French *Complainte* and approaching that of the middle-Latin *planctus*. Instead of rhetorical questions flung into the void and reiterating what had been said countless times already, we now have an urgent questioning that appears to pose a fundamental problem for discussion.

These three stanzas comprising the third Part of the *Complaint* are unusual in content; and so too is the realistic picture in the third stanza which likens God to a cunning fisher and the lovers to fish; they are madly eager for the bait and yet they die as they bite at the hook or else are sorely wounded by it.

This simile of the fisher is continued in the fourth group of stanzas which brings us the *exemplum* of the Brooch of Thebes and also goes back to the basic problem of part III. Here God as the lady's creator is made responsible for the misfortune of love, though the lover too shares in the 'guilt' in this matter:

> For thogh my lady have so gret beaute
> That I was mad til I had gete her grace,
> She was not cause of myn adversite,
> But he that wroghte her, . . . (264)

[1] Stillwell's assessment (*PQ* 35, 1956, pp. 86–88) of the thought in the *Complaint* is mainly based on the character of Mars. But surely Chaucer's conception and treatment of the whole genre is a totally different one.

Finally, in part V, these thoughts which recall *Troilus and Criseyde* to mind, give place to stanzas addressed directly to the courtly company, to all who also suffer and therefore lament. What this represents however is something more than a return to the social setting and convention which the urgency in the verses of the last two Parts had overstepped. For what we have here is the generalization of an individual case. *All* who love, not merely the 'knyghtes of renoun' and 'my ladyes', are now repeatedly called upon to join in lamentation. All love and loving is precarious, uncertain and indeed 'misguided'; and this contention adds point to the reverence shown in the concluding lines to the lofty ideal of courtly virtue:

> Compleyneth thilke ensample of al honour,
> That never dide but al gentilesse;
> Kytheth therfore on her sum kyndenesse. (296)

The *Complaint of Mars*, then, represents a significant expansion of the genre and a skilful blend of contrasting attitudes and features; it also points to a trend which, as *The Complaint of Chaucer to his Purse* shows, led to an ironical treatment and with it the disintegration of the genre as such. But what makes the *Complaint of Mars* stand out among Chaucer's early works is not so much the interesting formal and stylistic features or this expansion, as the fact that it poses the question of whether love is by nature constant or variable – a question that reappears, in an expanded form in *Troilus and Cryseyde*. Love is an emotion which dwells with inconstant men in a transient world and so is itself subject to change; can it then claim to be eternal and immutable, can it make permanence and steadfastness an article of its faith? This is the question which Chaucer asks in the third Part of his poem; and by doing so he brings the *Complaint of Mars* to the very threshold of the profoundly moving analysis which was to make *Troilus* one of the most serious medieval poems in English.

## Anelida and Arcite

*Anelida and Arcite* was probably written in the same year as the *House of Fame*, and it bears the same experimental, tentative and unequal stamp. The poem shows us Chaucer seeking but not yet finding new modes of expression. Perhaps that is why both the *House of Fame* and *Anelida and Arcite* have remained fragments.[1] Here Chaucer is feeling his way – still in a somewhat spasmodic manner – towards something that he was to express in the *Knight's Tale* with a greater degree of both conviction and precision. In the present poem problems are still being treated inconclusively and at surface level.

This poem is thus a typical transitional work. There are some very beautiful and impressive passages in the *Complaint*, unsurpassed indeed anywhere in Chaucer's work.[2] But these lyrical passages stand almost isolated in the poem, and are not convincingly brought within the framework of the 'Story'. The epic and lyric elements do not harmonize, although Chaucer's addition of narrative elements to the *Complaint* show that he was aiming at a harmony of this kind. In the *Complaint* he reveals himself to be a master of rhyme; and he almost outdoes French courtly poetry in the complexity of his metrical design.[3] But the more personal, human note which Chaucer lends to this poetic lament, as well as its wealth of narrative detail, show that he wanted to get away from the abstract and consciously impersonal French love-lyric.[4]

The strange, round-about way in which the introduction is given strikes one still more forcibly here than in the three longer poems. One wonders what lies behind it. Is it a wish to mystify the reader, a change of plan with the poem, delight in experimenting with epic forms and themes, or skilful 'postponement' of the real beginning of the story? For the episode of Anelida and Arcite does not begin till line 71; and any connection it may have with what goes before is at best loose and at times almost imperceptible. It is indeed doubtful if any logically consistent

---

[1] Cf. Shelly, p. 89.

[2] W. P. Ker speaks of 'the finest work of Chaucer in the more abstract and delicate kind of poetry' (*Essays on Medieval Literature*, 1905, p. 82).

[3] W. P. Ker, indeed, sees the 'Complaint' as the culmination of the whole French school. 'The lyrical complaint of Anelida is the perfection of everything that had been tried in the French school.' (*Medieval English Literature*, repr. 1955, p. 175.)

[4] This view is however not shared by H. A. Mason, who in his recent book *Humanism and Poetry in the Early Tudor Period*, 1959, stresses the artificiality of 'The compleynt of Anelida' which he takes to be Chaucer's 'most formal piece' (p. 160).

solution will ever be found to the unsolved problems posed by this long introduction.

The first three stanzas, called the 'Invocatio', are full of promises that are not kept and statements that are not true. The fulsome invocation to Mars and Bellona would be suitable for some longer poem, an epic tale, perhaps, telling of wars. In[1] Boccaccio's *Teseida*, on whose first three stanzas (in inverted order) Chaucer bases his own first three, this kind of invocation was appropriate. Even Boccaccio however made no appeal to both Mars *and* Bellona as deities of war; he addressed Mars alone. As in the *House of Fame*, we see Chaucer setting a massive apparatus in motion to serve a very minor cause. For only seven at most of the ensuing stanzas deal with war, while the narrative and indeed the whole poem treat quite a different theme.

When we examine Chaucer's own putative sources we become aware of other similar discrepancies calculated to mystify the reader. In the first stanza, for instance, of the 'storia antica' that he is about to relate, Boccaccio writes 'che latino autor non par ne dica'; but Chaucer asserts the opposite: 'This olde storie, in Latin which I fynde'; and at the end of the third stanza he plainly cites his sources: 'First folowe I Stace, and after him Corynne.'[2] In reality however only the first three stanzas of his story recall the *Thebaide*; his main source is the *Teseida*, and indeed it is his only one for the stanzas covering lines 50–70. Moreover, the episode of Anelida, the main content of Chaucer's poem, occurs neither in Statius nor in Boccaccio. Only inconclusive suggestions have been put forward on the subject of 'Corynne', whom Chaucer himself cites as a source.

Chaucer quite obviously feels the need to emphasize his indebtedness to some source, however indirect or indeed fictitious. Other fourteenth-century authors were much readier to assert the originality of their works – although there are examples in contemporary French poetry where the author names

---

[1] On this unmotivated invocation, cf. J. S. P. Tatlock, *The Mind and Art of Chaucer*, 1950, p. 54.

[2] Skeat made this comment: 'Thus it appears that, when speaking of his finding an old story in Latin, he is actually translating from an Italian poem which treats of a story not found in Latin. That is, his words give no indication whatever of the source of his poem; but are merely used in a purely conventional manner.' (*The Works of G. Chaucer*, ed. Skeat I, p. 530.)

a putative, classical source without in fact having made use of it.[1] Fictitious sources are of course cited by many medieval authors; it was considered to enhance the credibility and importance of one's own work if one referred it to some source or 'authority', whether this was actually in evidence or not.[2] In particular works with a 'learned' background required reference to some 'learned' source. In Chaucer's case we may presume that irony and mystification of the reader were among his motives in keeping to this customary practice.[3] He may indeed be poking fun at the insistance of other authors on their putative or fictitious sources; and in the present instance he is certainly also directing his irony against himself.

Chaucer's reference to classical sources, however, also had its serious side – a side perhaps not consciously intended by the poet. To a greater degree than any other medieval writer, Chaucer acts as an intermediary between the literatures of different languages and his debt to sources in the language and literature of other countries is unusually large. Besides this, however, Chaucer is more of a 'humanist' than his contemporaries; he had read more and absorbed more of Ovid, Virgil and Statius than had either Gower, Machaut or Froissart.

Although Chaucer cites Statius as his source, the influence of Ovid was the more varied and the more profound. Yet Chaucer had a good knowledge of the *Thebaide*, one of the most popular classical epics of the Middle Ages; and many of his poems contains echoes and borrowings from it (most of them in *Troilus and Criseyde*). But whereas Ovid influenced Chaucer in certain fundamental matters (by his themes, his sentimentality, his psychology), the influence of Statius is confined to enriching Chaucer's diction by picturesque or mellifluous turns of phrase. The *Thebaide*'s flowery, exuberant style and its tale of knightly valour were no doubt one of the chief reasons why the Middle Ages thought so highly of Statius.

In the first three stanzas of the 'Story' (22 ff.) Chaucer is

[1] Deschamps, for instance, cites a putative Latin or Greek source but makes no use of it (cf. E. Hoepffner, *Deschamps*, 1904, p. 147).
[2] Cf. Friedrich Panzer, 'Vom mittelalterlichen Zitieren', *Sitzungsberichte der Heidelberger Akademie der Wissensch.* Philos. Hist. Kl., 1950. Johannes Spörl, 'Das Alte und das Neue im Mittelalter', *Hist. Jbch*, 50 (1930).
[3] Cf. H. L. Levy, 'As myn auctour seyth,' *Medium Aevum* 12 (1943).

seeking briefly to evoke the setting and atmosphere of an epic tale. The first stanza sets out the circumstances, and marshals the facts, while in the second a few sure strokes give us the pomp and order of the triumphal procession. The third picks out one item from this pageant, the chariot in which Theseus is riding with Hyppolita and Emely. One particularly admires the technique displayed in this introduction – the swift compression from the general to the particular, the conciseness and the abundance of pregnant detail. In three stanzas Chaucer has succeeded in reproducing the characteristic tone of this kind of martial procession. He follows the *Thebaide* and the *Teseida* in his general outline and much of his detail; but the *brevity* of the whole,[1] and the rapid pace at which the narrative proceeds, are Chaucer's own; and in exposition and introduction especially they were to become more and more a feature of his art.

In lines such as:

> That al the ground about her char she spradde
> With brightnesse of the beaute in her face,
> Fulfilled of largesse and of alle grace. (40)

Chaucer created a poetic diction as yet non-existent in English – at least in the verse romances of the fourteenth century. Guillaume de Lorris's descriptive style, to which Chaucer owes much, is vital and sensuous, but it limits itself – as befits the *Roman de la Rose* manner – to only a few subjects. In Boccaccio's poems however Chaucer met with a natural poetic mode of expression that was at once rich and clear, and its influence was to remain with him. It is met with again and again as one compares the *Knight's Tale* with the *Teseida*, or *Filostrato* with *Troilus and Criseyde*.[2]

The first Invocation gives us a clear instance of how the impact of Boccaccio led Chaucer to enrich his diction. Here (as

[1] If we study Chaucer's version of individual stanzas in Boccaccio, we realize that his detail is fuller; he adds more frequent explanatory phrases, asides etc. Yet his narrative flows on more rapidly, passing more quickly from one object to the next.

[2] Robert A. Pratt ('Chaucer's Use of the *Teseida*', *PMLA* 62, 1947), who has made a study of the influence of the *Teseida* on Chaucer, considers that the unique combination in *Anelida and Arcite* derives from the influence of that work: 'he approved of and tried to imitate Boccaccio's incongruous juxtaposition of epic solemnity and medieval love complaint' (p. 605).

in the Invocation to Morpheus in the *House of Fame*) Chaucer amplifies the detail, adding pairs of matching epithets.[1] But it is in the *Knight's Tale* that Chaucer fully utilized Boccaccio's *Teseida*. The stanzas taken over from it in the *Anelida* are like a tapestry backcloth, a stage set from which the story of Arcite and Anelida soon detaches itself and stands free. The *Knight's Tale* however first shows us Chaucer succeeding in weaving the story and the background into a unity. In *Anelida* the atmosphere is only just suggested, and fades again; but in the *Tale* it is sustained, and it influences the characterization, the flow of the action, and the motivation. As Skeat has pointed out, there are many threads running between the *Anelida* and the *Knight's Tale*.

In dealing with a fragment one's duty is always to assess what has been attempted rather than what has been achieved. Here the attempt has been only partially successful; it consisted in combining a *Complaint* with a love-story to which an epic background had been added. There was seldom any specific 'occasion' to prompt the writing of a French love-poem. For the most part they are conventional exercises; nothing connects them with either their author or any definite circumstances or persons. This contributes to making the expression of grief and emotion in these pieces so unconvincing and pedantic. There is no background or occasion for the lament; what is felt and said during the course of such poems seems to lack contact with reality. But Chaucer takes what had been an abstraction and brings it down to time and place. By making the *Complaint* spring from a love-story that leads up to it, he turns something general into a specific case. Yet the lament of Anelida fails to blend into a unity with the narrative in which it is set; and this is also due to the collision of two fundamentally different styles. For the transition from the epic narrative style modelled on Boccaccio to the rigid

[1] Compare Boccaccio's

> Siate presenti, o Marte rubicondo
> Nelle tue armi rigido e feroce.          I, 3

with

> Thou ferse god of armes, Mars the rede,
> That in the frosty contre called Trace,
> Within thy grisly temple ful of drede
> Honoured art, as patroun of that place; (1 ff.)

formalism of French poetry is too abrupt for a hiatus to be avoided.[1]

The story of Arcite who deceives the utterly devoted Anelida after he has won her love, by acting in a false and feigned manner, is an instance of a theme very often treated by Chaucer. Indeed, when he is using material (the Dido-Aeneas episode, for instance) that did not originally stress this particular aspect of unfaithfulness and deceit, he sometimes gives it a new twist in this direction; almost all the legends in the *Legend of Good Women* are coloured after this fashion. The same tendency, too, affects minor episodes like the allegorical tale of the female 'faucoun', deceived by the 'tercelet', which is incorporated into the *Squire's Tale*. Even in the manner of motivation, the details of narrative, and the conclusions drawn, these stories offer many parallels. Correspondence between *Anelida* and the episode in the *Squire's Tale* has already been noted.[2] But there are also similar links with the Dido-episode in the *House of Fame* and with various 'legends'.[3] These parallels bear witness to a common mental attitude expressed in all these tales. From this point of view indeed they seem almost like different versions of the same theme.

We have here a similar technique to that in evidence in the Dido-episode from the *House of Fame* (and again in those of the *Legend of Good Women*); the episode of Anelida and Arcite is interpreted in a certain specific way, and that interpretation is then stressed and put forward with the greatest urgency. In the Invocation, when Arcite is first mentioned, he is called 'fals Arcite' (11); and hardly has he entered the story when we read, after only two lines:

> But he was double in love and no thing pleyn,
> And subtil in that craft over any wyght,
> And with his kunnyng wan this lady bryght; (87)

Chaucer cannot wait for the 'course of events', the gradual

---

[1] Cf. also W. P. Ker, *Medieval English Literature*, repr. 1955, p. 180 ff.
[2] Cf. *The Works of G. Chaucer*, ed. Skeat I, p. 534 ff.; Tupper, *PMLA* 36 (1924).
[3] Cf. for instance *Anel.* 103 with *HF* 332, *Lgd.* 799; *Anel.* 141 with *HF* 302; *Anel.* 162 with *Lgd.* 1311, 1345; *Anel.* 175 with *HF* 316, *Lgd.* 1316, 1324; *Anel* 197 with *Lgd.* 1254, 2559; *Anel.* 162 with *HF* 383, 395.

account of his behaviour, to reveal Arcite as 'false'[1] and deceitful. He breaks in with his own judgments and anticipates what comes later to be quite sure the reader grasps this main point from the very start. That is why, after telling (in the lines just quoted) how Arcite's suit was successful, the narrator goes back, in the next stanza but one, to the earlier stage again which the opening lines had already covered:

> But nevertheles, ful mykel besynesse
> Had he, er that he myghte his lady wynne, (99)

Just as in the Dido-episode, the poet is always breaking in to judge, comment and warn; he steps up to his own story to point out Arcite's baseness and at the same time to show the piteous fate of Anelida: 'But he was fals; hit nas but feyned chere:' (97); 'But al this nas but sleght and flaterie;' (125). The warning sounds clearly again and again. Just as in the Dido-episode, too, wise saws are used to reinforce the story (105), and here also Arcite's treachery is seen as simply an instance of man's perfidious nature:

> But neverthelesse, gret wonder was hit noon
> Thogh he were fals, for hit is kynde of man, (148)

This intention to offer the Anelida-Arcite episode as an 'exemplum', a warning and a lesson to all, is very strongly brought out in the address to the women of the audience, interpolated before the 'Complaint':

> Ensample of this, ye thrifty wymmen alle,
> Take her of Anelida and Arcite, (197)

In exemplifying man's *untrouthe* in this way, to bring out Anelida's *trouthe* more strongly, Chaucer had a further motive which recurs in his works; this was to state his belief in the value of *trouthe*. In Chaucer's eyes the 'false' lover was also sinning against the idea of love, against *trouthe* and so against virtue itself. Anelida's *Complaint*, where her despair at Arcite's *untrouthe* is couched in more sincere and convincing terms

---

[1] The word *fals* or its derivatives appears no fewer than twelve times during the Anelida-Arcite episode!

Minor Poems

than are used for the story that forms its setting, these lines
occur:

> Almyghty God, of trouthe sovereyn,
> Wher is the trouthe of man? Who hath hit slayn?
>
> (311)

This is not the conventional kind of expression to be found in the
French poems. 'Trouthe is the hyeste thyng that man may kepe,'
as Chaucer later expressed it in the *Franklin's Tale*; and in that
great poem, *Troilus and Criseyde*, the question of *trouthe* is made
the central problem.

Chaucer does not merely wish to 'make his point' in the story
in which this problem is set; he wishes to touch us, to move his
public to 'sympathize'. The poet wishes to bring the reader to
share not only his 'own view', but also the concern he so often
and so forcefully asserts. The invocation, indeed, already reveals
this emotional aspect of the story; Chaucer himself says that he
means

> With pitous hert in Englyssh to endyte
> This olde storie, . . . (9)

And for this reason this tale (like the Dido-episode) is punctuated by the narrator's sighs and ejaculations, 'Alas, the while!'
(103); we even have a whole stanza where, before he describes
Anelida's unspeakable sufferings, the poet expresses these
'inexpressible' torments – thereby anticipating his hearer's possible reaction. Here, then, a new turn has been given to the
traditional 'convention of inexpressibility':

> Alas! what herte myght enduren hit,
> For routhe or wo, her sorwe for to telle?
> Or what man hath the cunnyng or the wit?
> Or what man mighte within the chambre dwelle,
> Yf I to him rehersen sholde the helle
> That suffreth fair Anelida . . . (162)

After this preparation, the description of the despairing and
afflicted Anelida can follow on in just that highly melodramatic
and yet terse tone which today seems to verge on exaggerated

205

sentimentality but in those days was accepted as the essence of a 'pitous tale':

> She wepith, waileth, swowneth pitously;
> To grounde ded she falleth as a ston;
> Craumpyssheth her lymes crokedly;
> She speketh as her wit were al agon;
> Other colour then asshen hath she noon; (169)

In Chaucer's version of the Anelida-Arcite episode we again see him boldly taking sides, in this case using exaggeration in both directions (to evoke pity for Anelida and horror for Arcite), presenting a 'touching tale' as an *exemplum* and at the same time, as he tells it, making all the facts and detail serve his own chief intention.[1] When he relates episodes like these, Chaucer is anything but an 'objective narrator'. His objectivity, for which he has been praised in connection with his gift for dramatic presentation, belongs to an entirely different and higher plane; there is no evidence of it in the individual episodes.

The story in which it is set leads up to the 'Compleynt of Anelida the quene upon fals Arcite'; and here, despite all the artificial features it owes to the French school, her suffering and sorrow are expressed more eloquently and sincerely than in the account that had gone before. For what strikes us about this 'Complaint' is not so much the great technical skill that sustains and varies the complex metrical pattern of the verse; it is the voice of genuine human suffering which we hear behind the veil of Chaucer's artistry. His ability to come near to the 'speaking voice' while employing a stanza so rigidly and intricately constructed is astonishing. So, too, is the way in which he has here transmuted the argumentation of the French *Complaintes* into a real live monologue. The French *Complaintes* had offered polished discussion of one theme after another; Chaucer gives us the ebb and flow of moods, a movement of unconscious feeling that obeys some inner urge as it leads on from one thought to the next. When we come to the end of Anelida's lament we know that we

[1] For instance, all Anelida's actions and behaviour serve to bring out Arcite's shameful treatment of her. There are also negative statements, and others that express reservations, besides general remarks about what she does or does not do; and all these too are made with the sole object of showing up Arcite (e.g. 107, 110, 113, 117, 127, etc.).

have taken part in a personal story and at moments have heard a real person in her distress – a very different impression from that made by the French laments.

When we analyse the 'Complaint' we find much that bears out and exemplifies this general impression. In the first place the speech is a striking mixture of artificially-conventional expressions and perfectly simple and natural turns of phrase. The 'Proem' of the 'Complaint' begins with the elaborate lines:

> So thirleth with the poynt of remembraunce
> The swerd of sorowe, ywhet with fals plesaunce,
> Myn herte, bare of blis and blak of hewe, (211)

but the 'Strophe' opens with the artless admission:

> I wot myself as wel as any wight;
> For I loved oon with al myn herte and myght, (220)

This kind of direct, unaffected expression occurs frequently in the 'Complaint'; and it is reinforced at times by cries, protestations, and questions thrown in (e.g. 238, 256, 274, 277, 301, 338), and often by a break in the syntax within the line. This device also retards or modifies the tempo (e.g. 229, 277, 297–8, 301, 312, 341) and lends variety to the rhythm.

There is a further difference, too, which makes this lament seem more personal and convincing than the French examples of the genre. Compared to the *Complaintes* of Machaut, Froissart and Deschamps, Chaucer's 'Complaint' changes both thought and theme more rapidly and abruptly. The French poets liked to draw out a theme, to take a thought and spin it out in a succession of varying phrases. But with Chaucer the thought is richer and also it flows on more consistently.

Chaucer achieves a particularly lively effect, too, by stressing the point that his poem takes the form of a letter. The French poets had not insisted upon this. Again and again, however, Anelida addresses herself eagerly and directly to her lover. This partner who is adjured, questioned, accused and whose pardon is then implored, is thus constantly kept before us as the 'Thou' who is being spoken to; and at times the 'Complaint' resembles a genuine conversation. Here and there this conversation with the lover as the 'Thou' skilfully and yet plausibly merges into a monologue (e.g. 238 ff., 299 ff.). The particular blending of dialogue and monologue, an evidence of Chaucer's dramatic gift, keeps the 'Complaint' from developing into an abstract exposition (after the French fashion) of arguments for and against; and it restores the direct relationship between partners which the French had often failed to keep alive.

Chaucer achieves an immediacy of direct personal expression, then, by using the form of the letter; and he may well have been influenced here by Ovid's *Heroides*. Not that he took over any actual individual themes;[1] but the *Heroides* are less abstract and artificial than the French *Complaintes*, and each is the outcome of a definite and particular case.

The chief reason why Anelida's expression of her grief is so convincing is that she is not content simply to lament and to describe her woe – as is the case in some of the French poems. She considers every possibility arising out of her situation and searches for some way out; but she finds none. Her complaint has a wide emotional span; we seem to be following someone on the road of despair that leads her from one mood to the next without her finding the solution she is so desperately seeking. We hear her deep grief alternating with indignant accusations; and then these give way to fresh avowals of love; and helpless describe her woe – as is the case in some of the French poems. distracted note (as each idea is considered and abandoned), of this frustration and despair, is that this poem carries far more conviction than its French counterparts do; for they are built up according to a clear and conscious plan, leaving room in most cases for a gleam of hope. The last lines of Chaucer's lament sound this same distracted note, however:

> But me to rede out of this drede, or guye,
> Ne may my wit, so weyk is hit, not streche.

[1] E. F. Shannon (*Chaucer and the Roman Poets*, 1929) has surely stressed Ovid's influence unduly. He cites individual themes as showing the influence of the *Heroides*: namely, separation from the lover amounting to death for the beloved; the beloved too ready to trust the lover's words, etc. But these are all to be found in the French writers also. Besides, these themes are not expressed in anything like the same way by Chaucer. The comparison of her own lament with the swan's song, however, which is common to both the *Heroides* and *Anelida*, is worth noting (p. 35 ff.).

Then ende I thus, sith I may do no more, –
I yeve hit up for now and evermore; (340)

And as the 'Story continued' breaks off after a single stanza, the whole poem may be said to end without solution or reconciliation.

If we look at *Troilus and Criseyde*, however, we see that a new mood has replaced this attitude of hopelessness. Anelida's helpless despair has become the self-knowledge of a Troilus schooled by grief; placed in a like situation to Anelida's he calls to mind the power of fate. There is much in Chaucer's early poems, in fact, which reaches fulfilment and a new depth in his later work.

Chaucer's later poetry, however, is much more than a continuation and expansion of what his earlier poems had begun. For it presents entirely new themes, new forms, and new problems demanding their own poetic treatment. Many earlier features are retained and further developed; but at the same time new aspects emerge which lead us far away from the sphere of Chaucer's early poetry.

# Index

# Index

# Index

213